image COMICS PRESENTS

INVINCIBLE

REBOOT?

CREATED BY
ROBERT KIRKMAN
& CORY WALKER

image

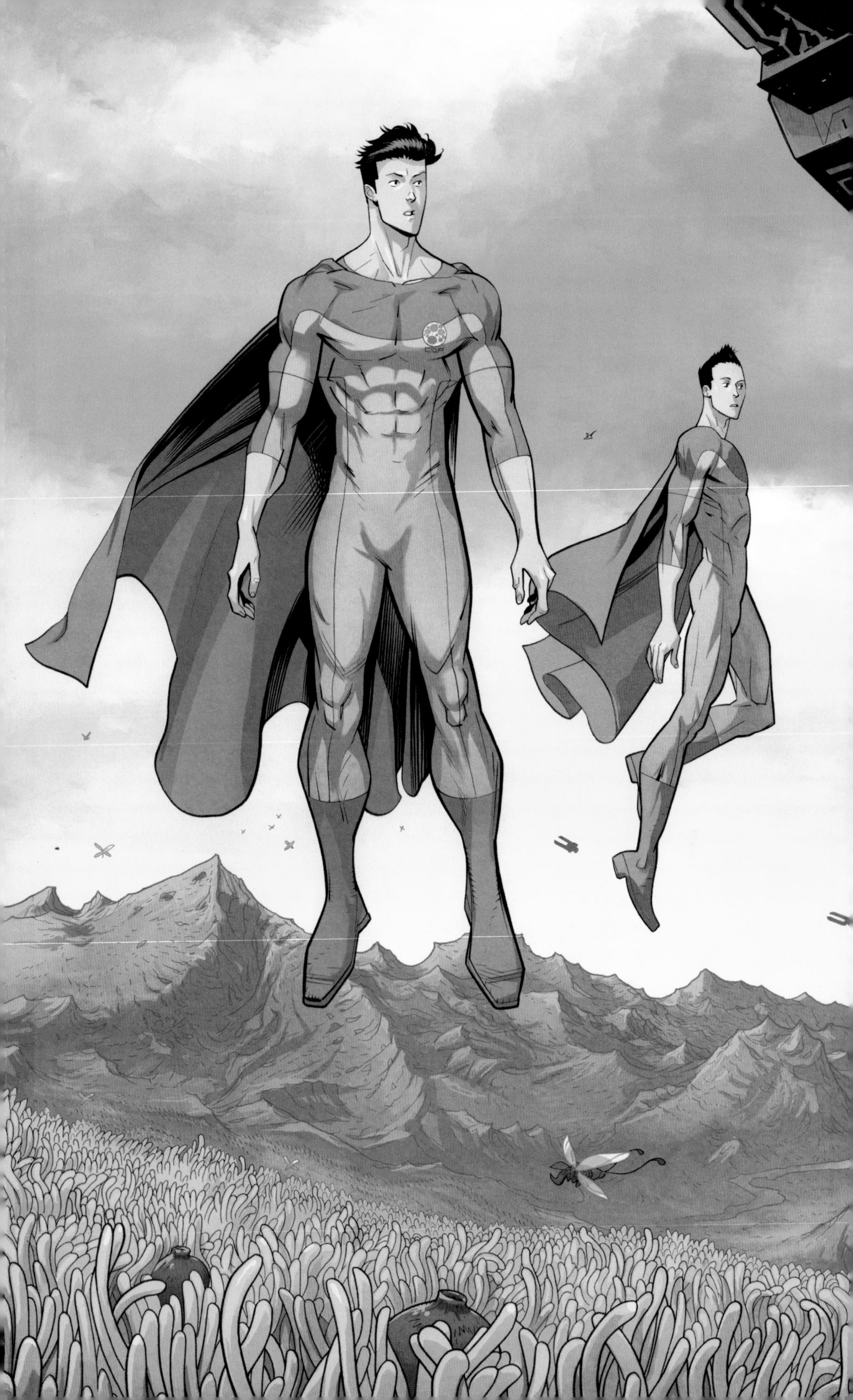

writer
ROBERT KIRKMAN

penciler
RYAN OTTLEY

inker
CLIFF RATHBURN
(chapters 1-3, chapter 4, pgs 1-13)
RYAN OTTLEY
(chapter 4, pgs 14-20, chapters 5-6)

colorist
JEAN-FRANCOIS BEAULIEU

letterer
RUS WOOTON

editor
SEAN MACKIEWICZ

cover
RYAN OTTLEY
& JEAN-FRANCOIS BEAULIEU

INVINCIBLE, VOL. 22: REBOOT?
ISBN: 978-1-63215-626-6
First Printing

Published by Image Comics, Inc. Office of publication: 2001 Center Street, 6th Floor, Berkeley, California 94704. Image and its logos are ® and © 2016 Image Comics Inc. All rights reserved. Originally published in single magazine form as INVINCIBLE #121-126. INVINCIBLE and all character likenesses are ™ and © 2016, Robert Kirkman, LLC and Cory Walker. All rights reserved. All names, characters, events and locales in this publication are entirely fictional. Any resemblance to actual persons (living or dead), events or places, without satiric intent, is coincidental. No part of this publication may be reproduced or transmitted, in any form or by any means (except for short excerpts for review purposes) without the express written permission of the copyright holder. Printed in the USA. For information regarding the CPSIA on this printed material call: 203-595-3636 and provide reference # RICH – 664063

SKYBOUND ENTERTAINMENT
www.skybound.com

Robert Kirkman - CEO
David Alpert - President
Sean Mackiewicz - Editorial Director
Shawn Kirkham - Director of Business Development
Brian Huntington - Online Editorial Director
June Alian - Publicity Director
Rachel Skidmore - Director of Media Development
Jon Moisan - Editor
Arielle Basich - Assistant Editor
Dan Petersen - Operations Manager
Sarah Effinger - Office Manager
Nick Palmer - Operations Coordinator
Genevieve Jones - Production Coordinator
Andres Juarez - Graphic Designer
Stephan Murillo - Business Development Coordinator

International inquiries: foreign@skybound.com
Licensing inquiries: contact@skybound.com

IMAGE COMICS, INC.
www.imagecomics.com

Robert Kirkman - Chief Operating Officer
Erik Larsen - Chief Financial Officer
Todd McFarlane - President
Marc Silvestri - CEO
Jim Valentino - Vice-President

Eric Stephenson - Publisher
Corey Murphy - Director of Sales
Jeff Boison - Director of Publishing Planning & Book Trade Sales
Jeremy Sullivan - Director of Digital Sales
Kat Salazar - Director of PR & Marketing
Emily Miller - Director of Operations
Branwyn Bigglestone - Senior Accounts Manager
Sarah Mello - Accounts Manager
Drew Gill - Art Director
Jonathan Chan - Production Manager
Meredith Wallace - Print Manager
Briah Skelly - Publicity Assistant
Randy Okamura - Marketing Production Designer
David Brothers - Branding Manager
Ally Power - Content Manager
Addison Duke - Production Artist
Vincent Kukua - Production Artist
Sasha Head - Production Artist
Tricia Ramos - Production Artist
Jeff Stang - Direct Market Sales Representative
Emilio Bautista - Digital Sales Associate
Chloe Ramos-Peterson - Administrative Assistant

CHAPTER ONE

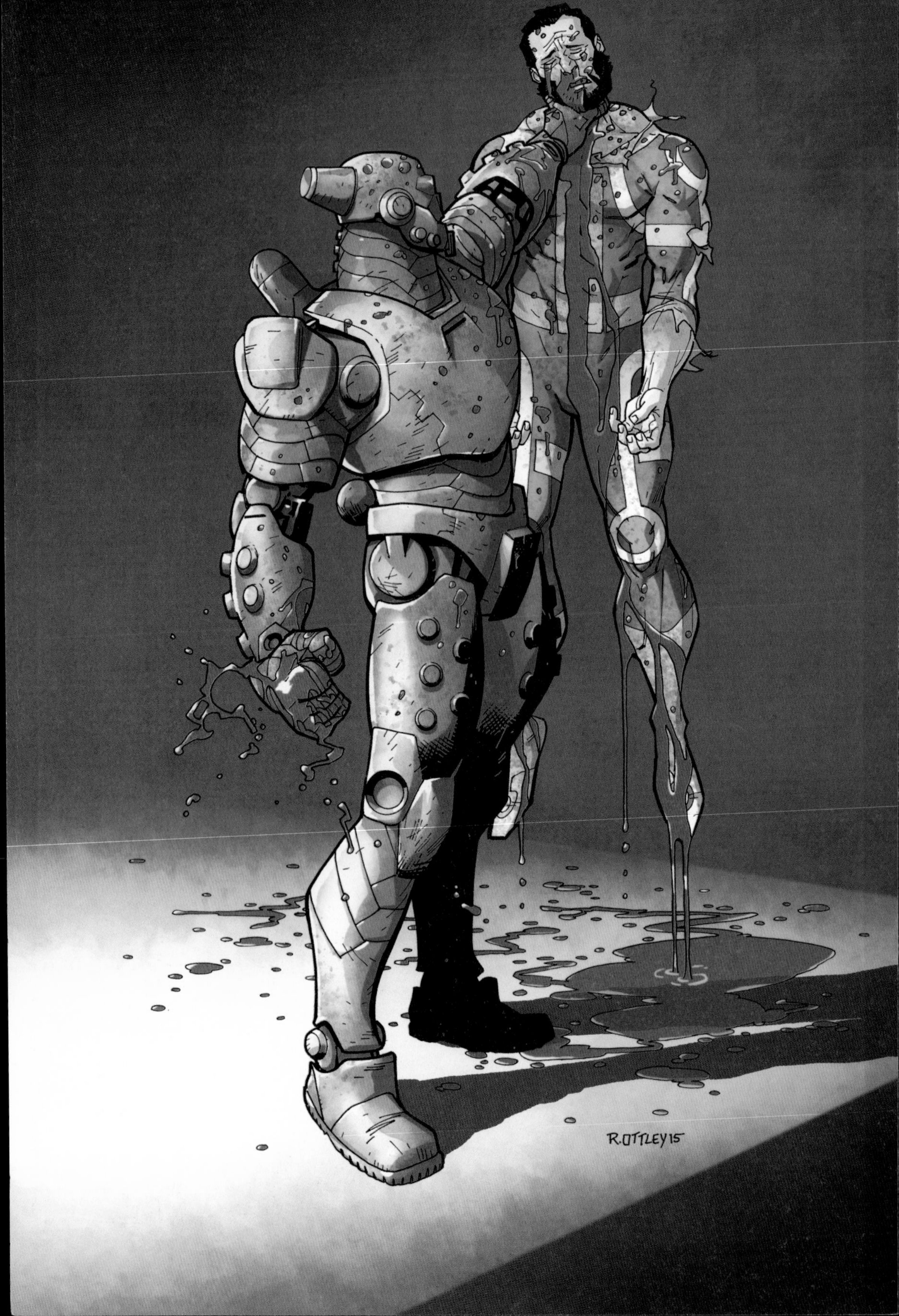
R.OTTLEY15

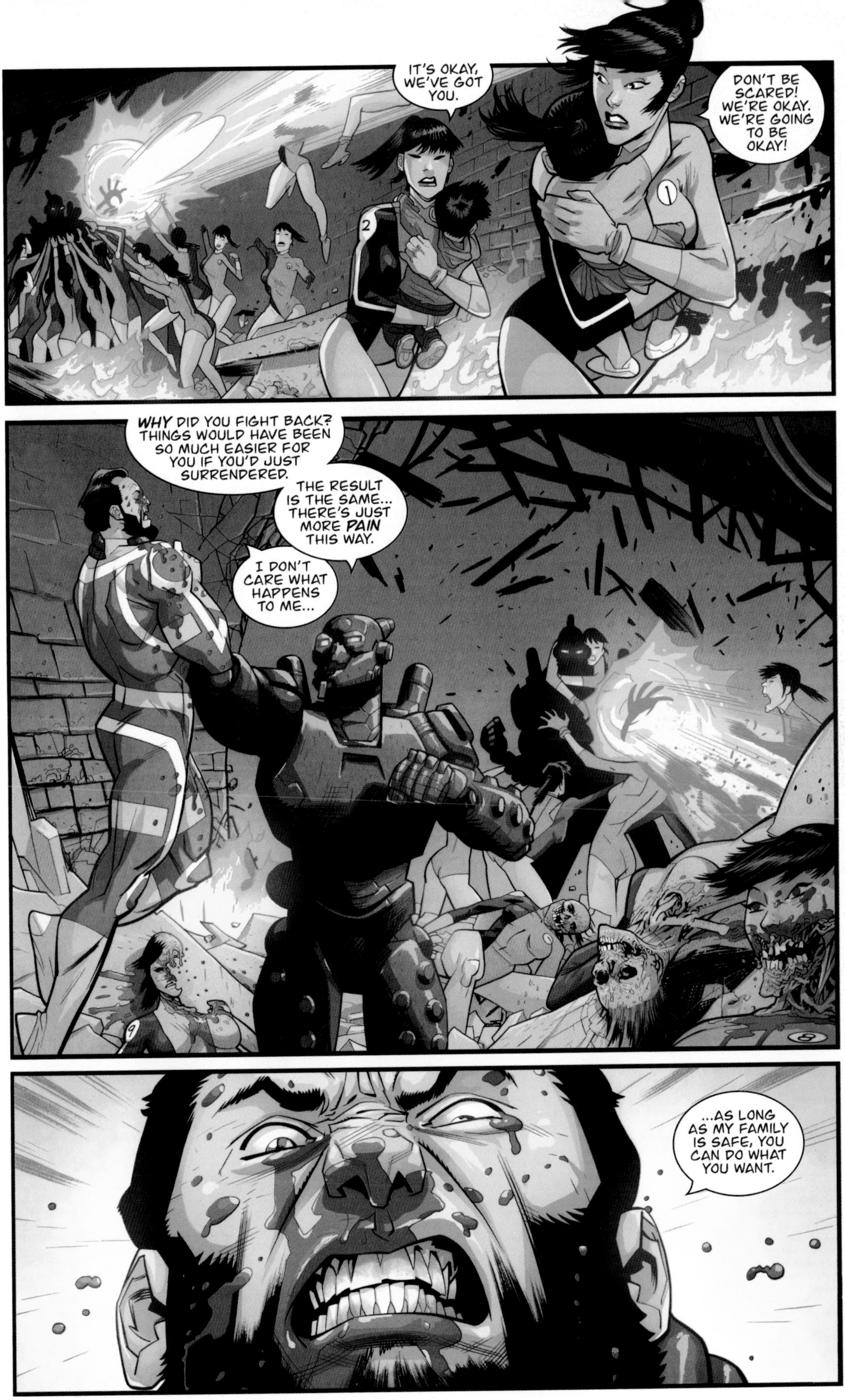
IT'S OKAY, WE'VE GOT YOU.
DON'T BE SCARED! WE'RE OKAY. WE'RE GOING TO BE OKAY!
WHY DID YOU FIGHT BACK? THINGS WOULD HAVE BEEN SO MUCH EASIER FOR YOU IF YOU'D JUST SURRENDERED.
THE RESULT IS THE SAME... THERE'S JUST MORE *PAIN* THIS WAY.
I DON'T CARE WHAT HAPPENS TO ME...
...AS LONG AS MY FAMILY IS SAFE, YOU CAN DO WHAT YOU WANT.

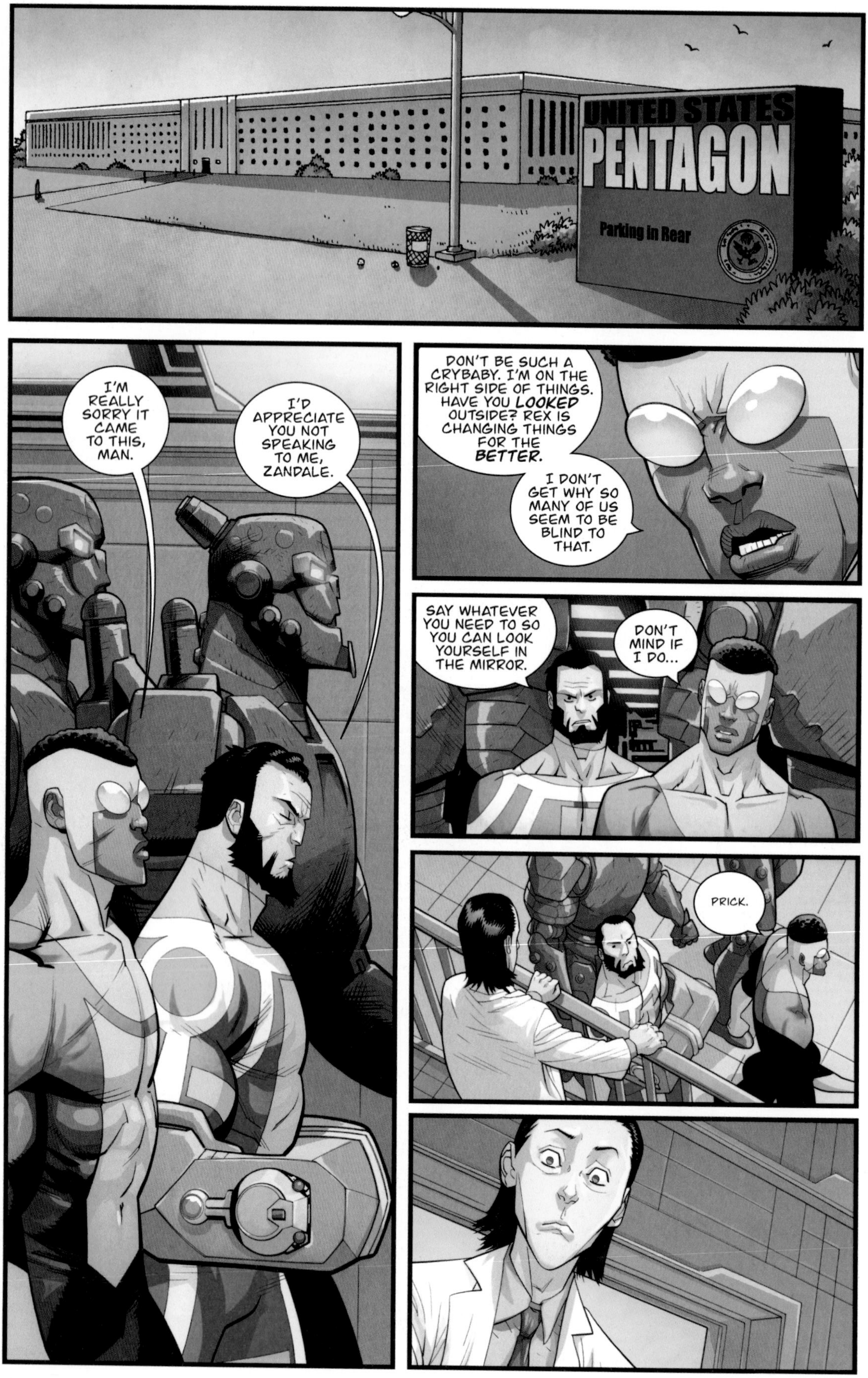
UNITED STATES
PENTAGON
Parking in Rear
I'M REALLY SORRY IT CAME TO THIS, MAN.
I'D APPRECIATE YOU NOT SPEAKING TO ME, ZANDALE.
DON'T BE SUCH A CRYBABY. I'M ON THE RIGHT SIDE OF THINGS. HAVE YOU LOOKED OUTSIDE? REX IS CHANGING THINGS FOR THE BETTER.
I DON'T GET WHY SO MANY OF US SEEM TO BE BLIND TO THAT.
SAY WHATEVER YOU NEED TO SO YOU CAN LOOK YOURSELF IN THE MIRROR.
DON'T MIND IF I DO...
PRICK.

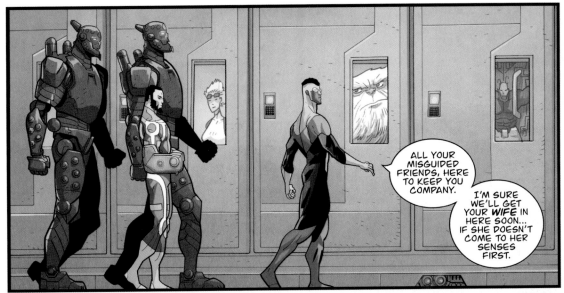

ALL YOUR MISGUIDED FRIENDS, HERE TO KEEP YOU COMPANY.

I'M SURE WE'LL GET YOUR *WIFE* IN HERE SOON... IF SHE DOESN'T COME TO HER SENSES FIRST.

OKAY-- IT'S TIME.

EVERYONE TO THE BACK OF YOUR CELLS!

WHAT?!

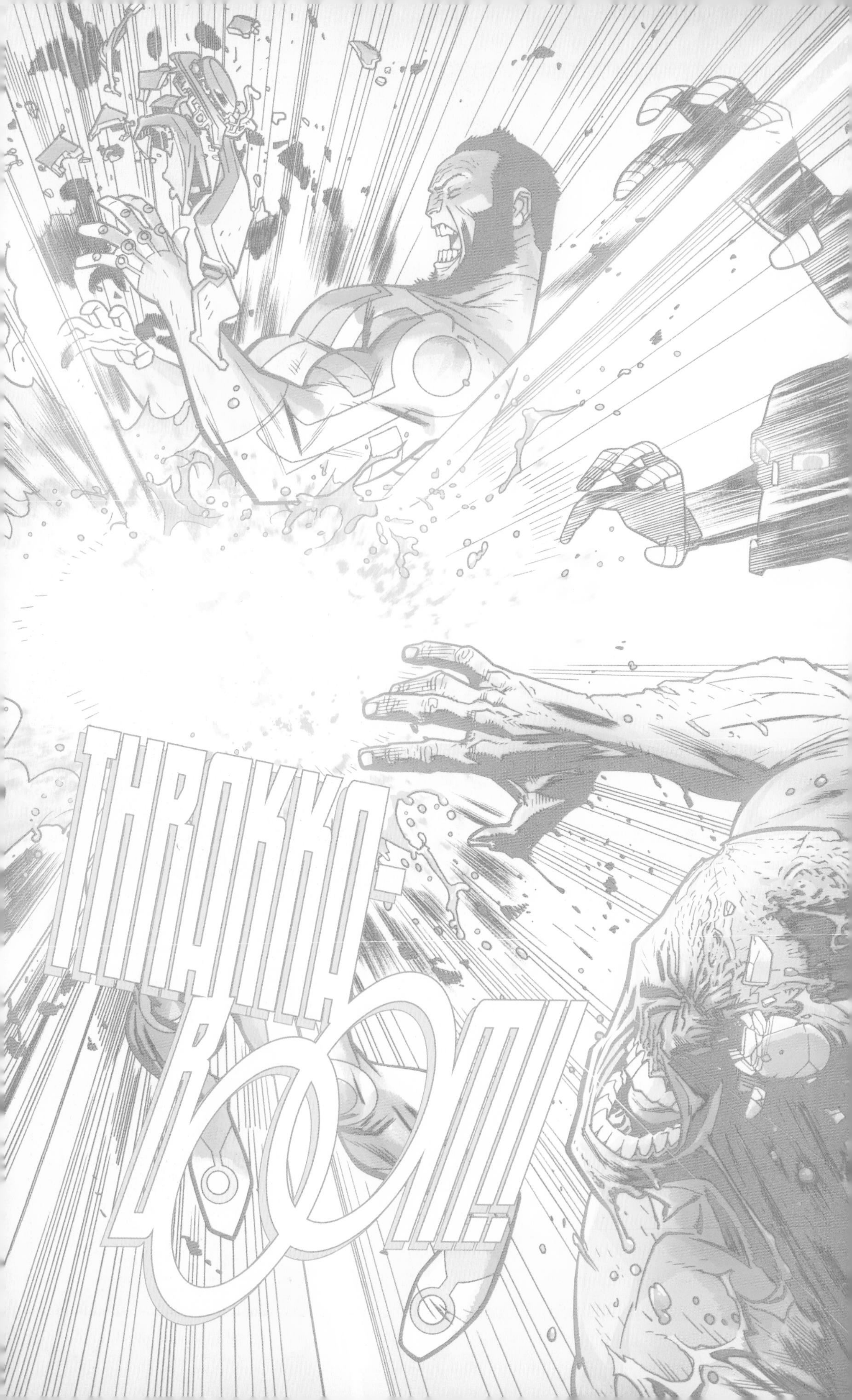
THROKKA-BOOM!!

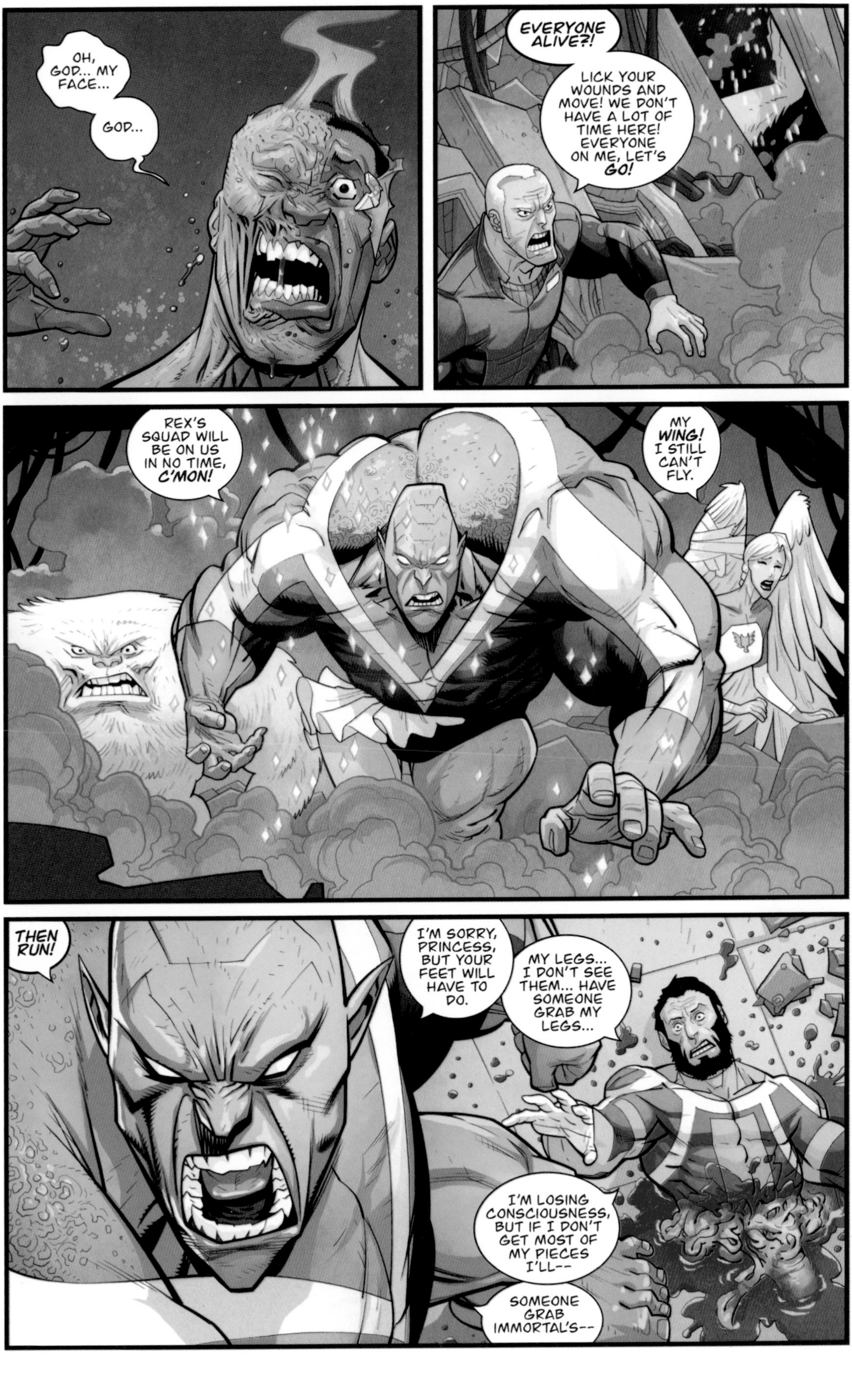
OH, GOD... MY FACE...
GOD...
EVERYONE ALIVE?!
LICK YOUR WOUNDS AND MOVE! WE DON'T HAVE A LOT OF TIME HERE! EVERYONE ON ME, LET'S GO!
REX'S SQUAD WILL BE ON US IN NO TIME, C'MON!
MY WING! I STILL CAN'T FLY.
THEN RUN!
I'M SORRY, PRINCESS, BUT YOUR FEET WILL HAVE TO DO.
MY LEGS... I DON'T SEE THEM... HAVE SOMEONE GRAB MY LEGS...
I'M LOSING CONSCIOUSNESS, BUT IF I DON'T GET MOST OF MY PIECES I'LL--
SOMEONE GRAB IMMORTAL'S--

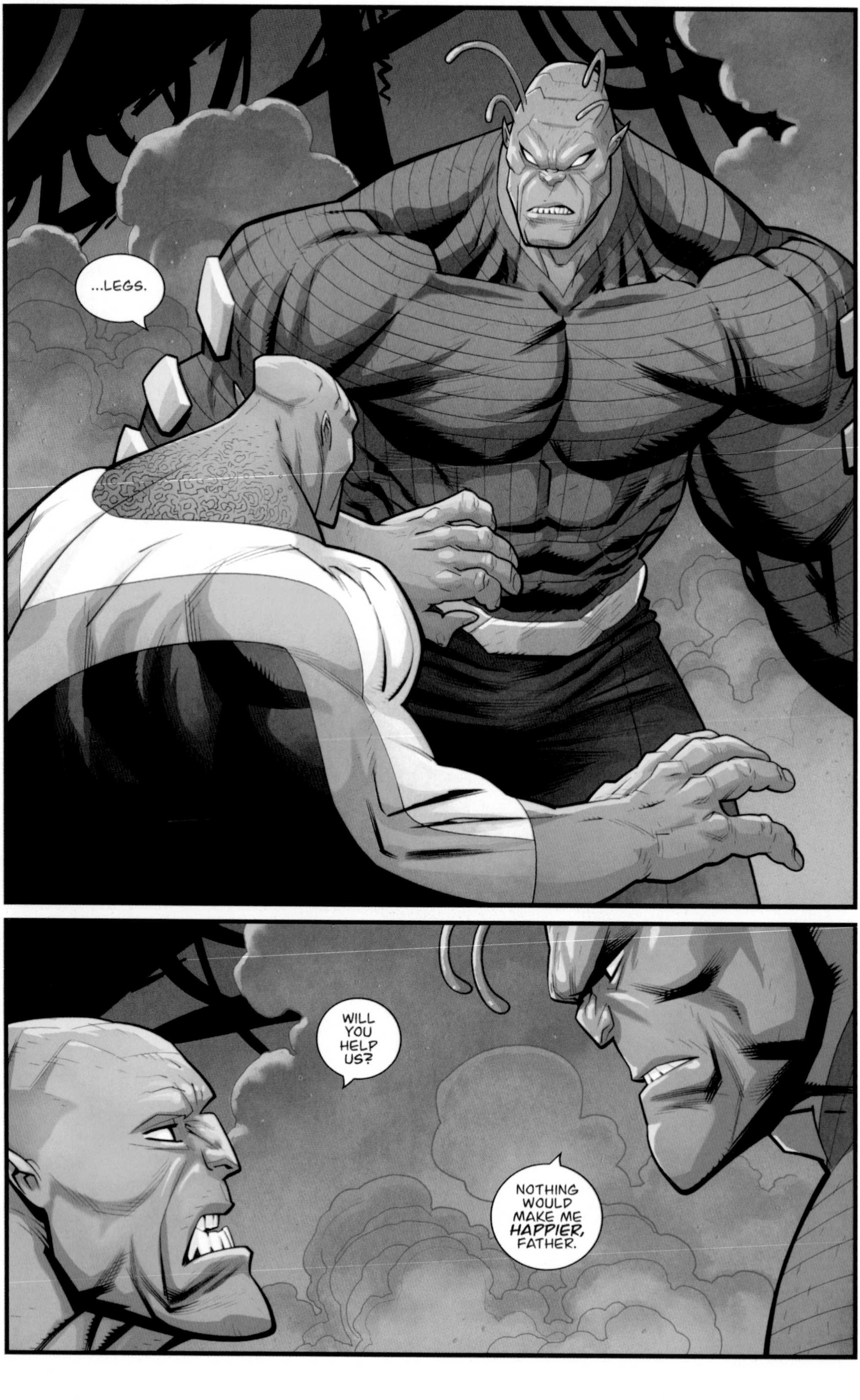
...LEGS.
WILL YOU HELP US?
NOTHING WOULD MAKE ME HAPPIER, FATHER.

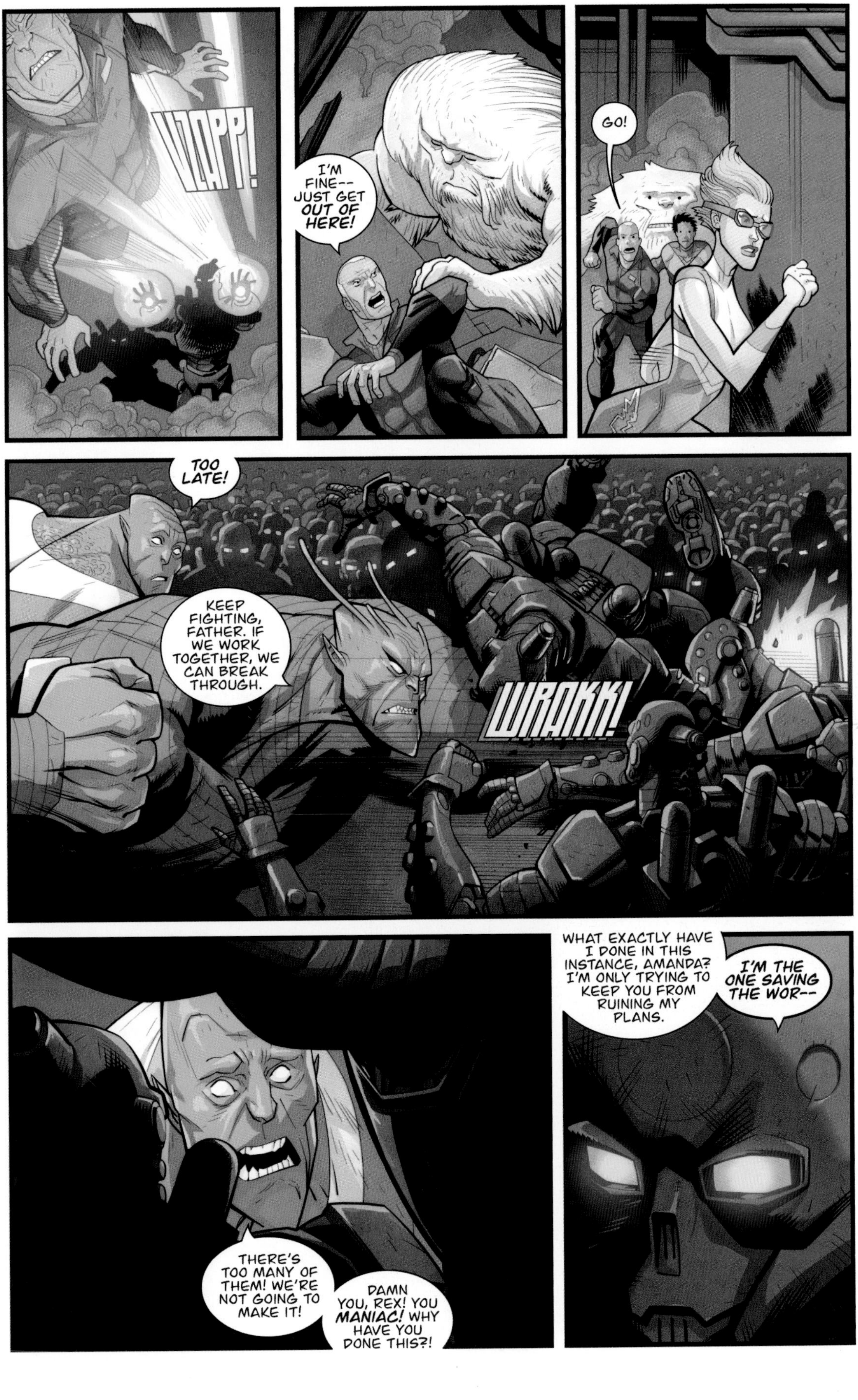

VZOPP!
I'M FINE-- JUST GET OUT OF HERE!
GO!
TOO LATE!
KEEP FIGHTING, FATHER. IF WE WORK TOGETHER, WE CAN BREAK THROUGH.
WRAKK!
THERE'S TOO MANY OF THEM! WE'RE NOT GOING TO MAKE IT!
DAMN YOU, REX! YOU MANIAC! WHY HAVE YOU DONE THIS?!
WHAT EXACTLY HAVE I DONE IN THIS INSTANCE, AMANDA? I'M ONLY TRYING TO KEEP YOU FROM RUINING MY PLANS.
I'M THE ONE SAVING THE WOR--

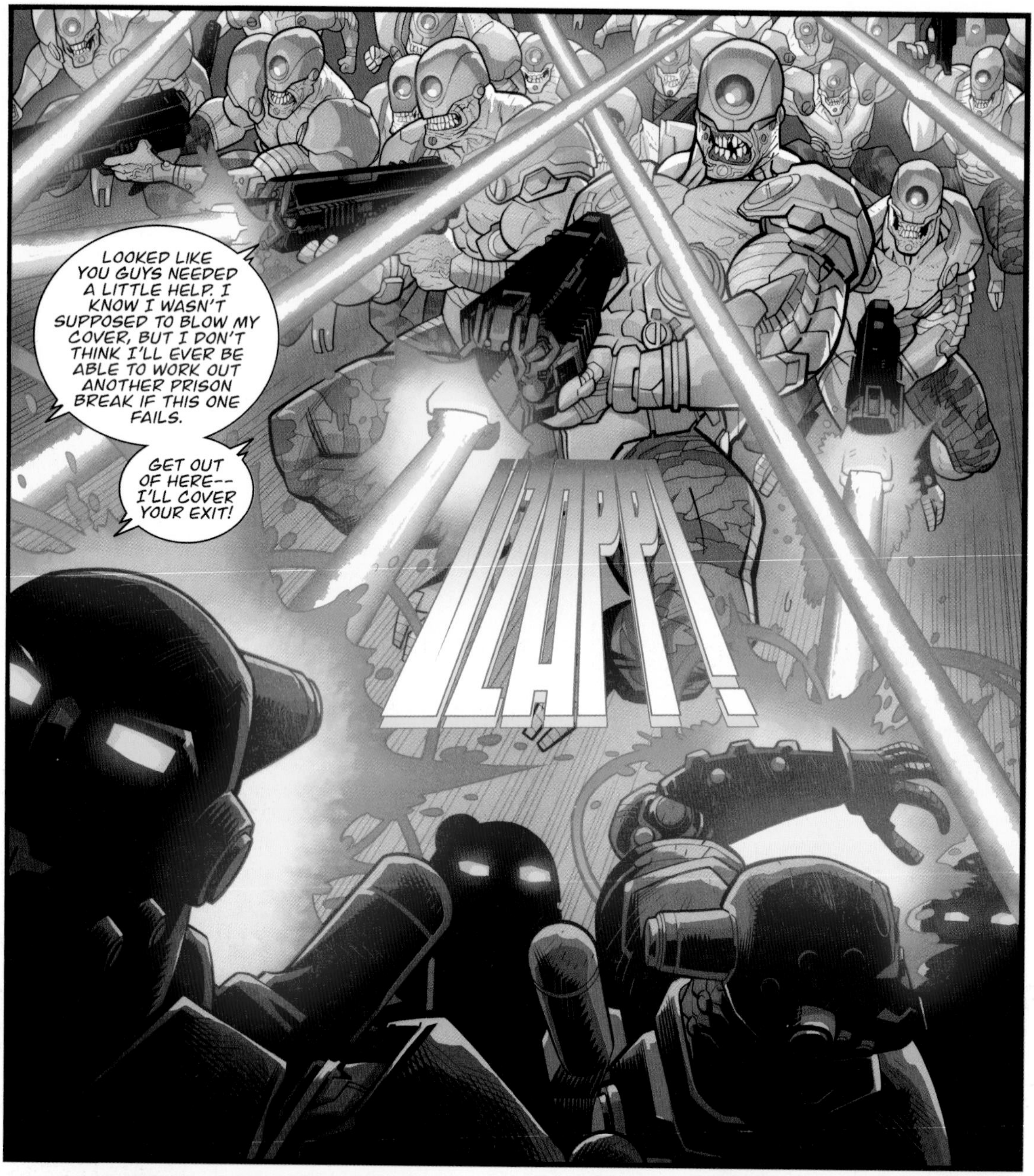
LOOKED LIKE YOU GUYS NEEDED A LITTLE HELP. I KNOW I WASN'T SUPPOSED TO BLOW MY COVER, BUT I DON'T THINK I'LL EVER BE ABLE TO WORK OUT ANOTHER PRISON BREAK IF THIS ONE FAILS.
GET OUT OF HERE-- I'LL COVER YOUR EXIT!
VZAPP!!

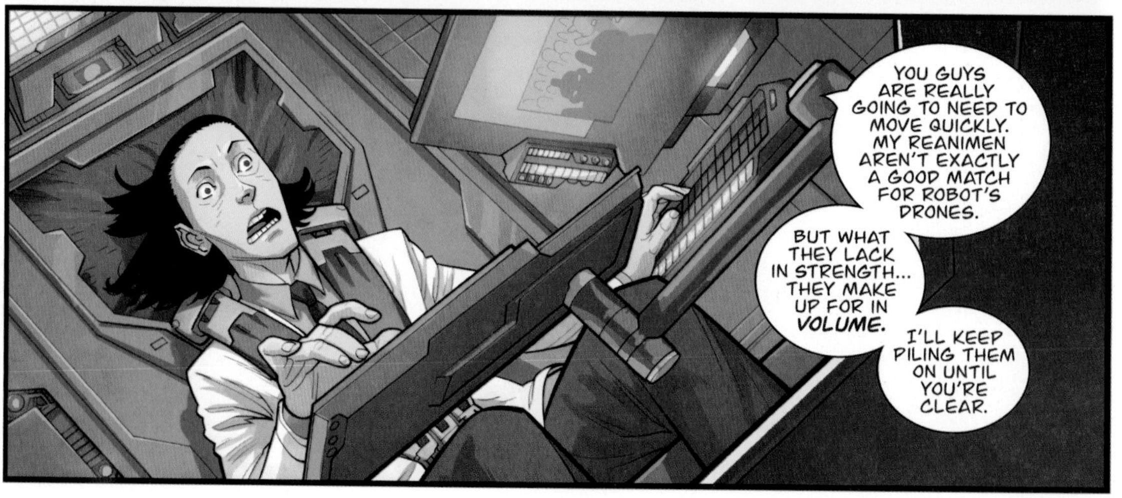
YOU GUYS ARE REALLY GOING TO NEED TO MOVE QUICKLY. MY REANIMEN AREN'T EXACTLY A GOOD MATCH FOR ROBOT'S DRONES.
BUT WHAT THEY LACK IN STRENGTH... THEY MAKE UP FOR IN ***VOLUME.***
I'LL KEEP PILING THEM ON UNTIL YOU'RE CLEAR.

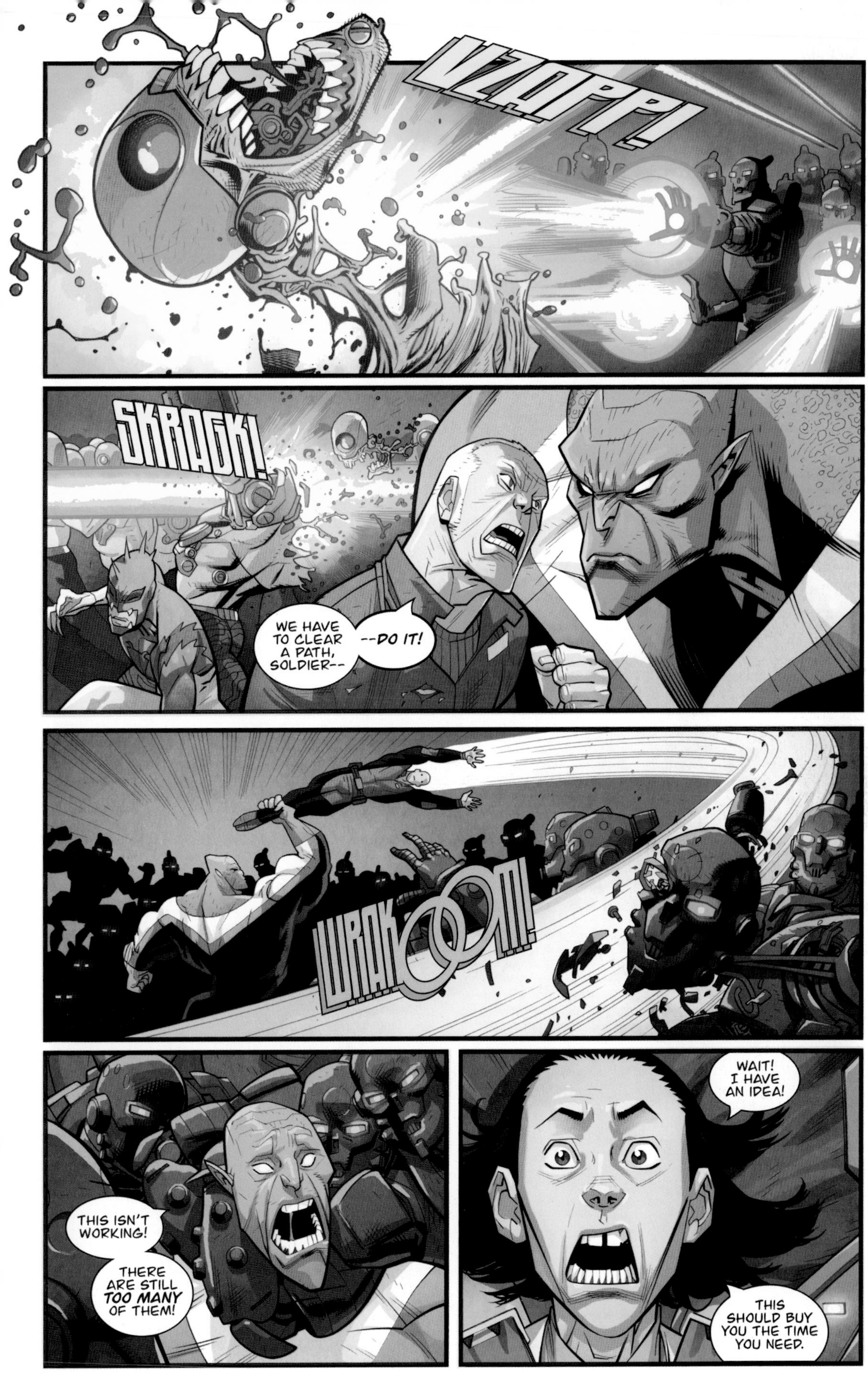
VZAPP!
SKRAGK!
WE HAVE TO CLEAR A PATH, SOLDIER--
--DO IT!
WRAKOOM!
THIS ISN'T WORKING!
THERE ARE STILL *TOO MANY* OF THEM!
WAIT! I HAVE AN IDEA!
THIS SHOULD BUY YOU THE TIME YOU NEED.

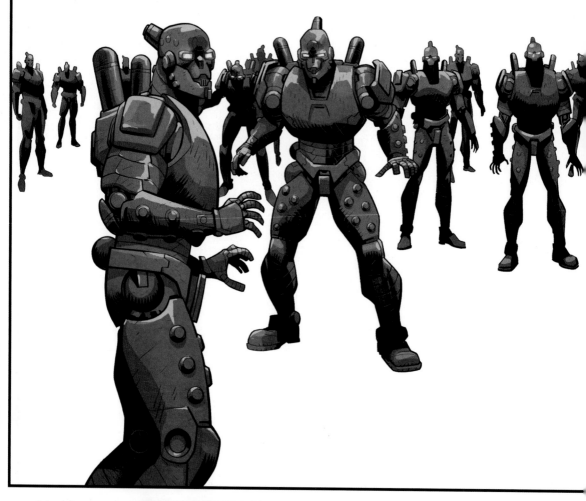

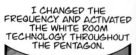
I CHANGED THE FREQUENCY AND ACTIVATED THE WHITE ROOM TECHNOLOGY THROUGHOUT THE PENTAGON.

UNTIL HE FIGURES OUT A WORKAROUND, YOU'RE INVISIBLE TO REX'S DRONES!

SWEET!

SHH!

SINCLAIR!

WHAT ARE YOU DOING?!

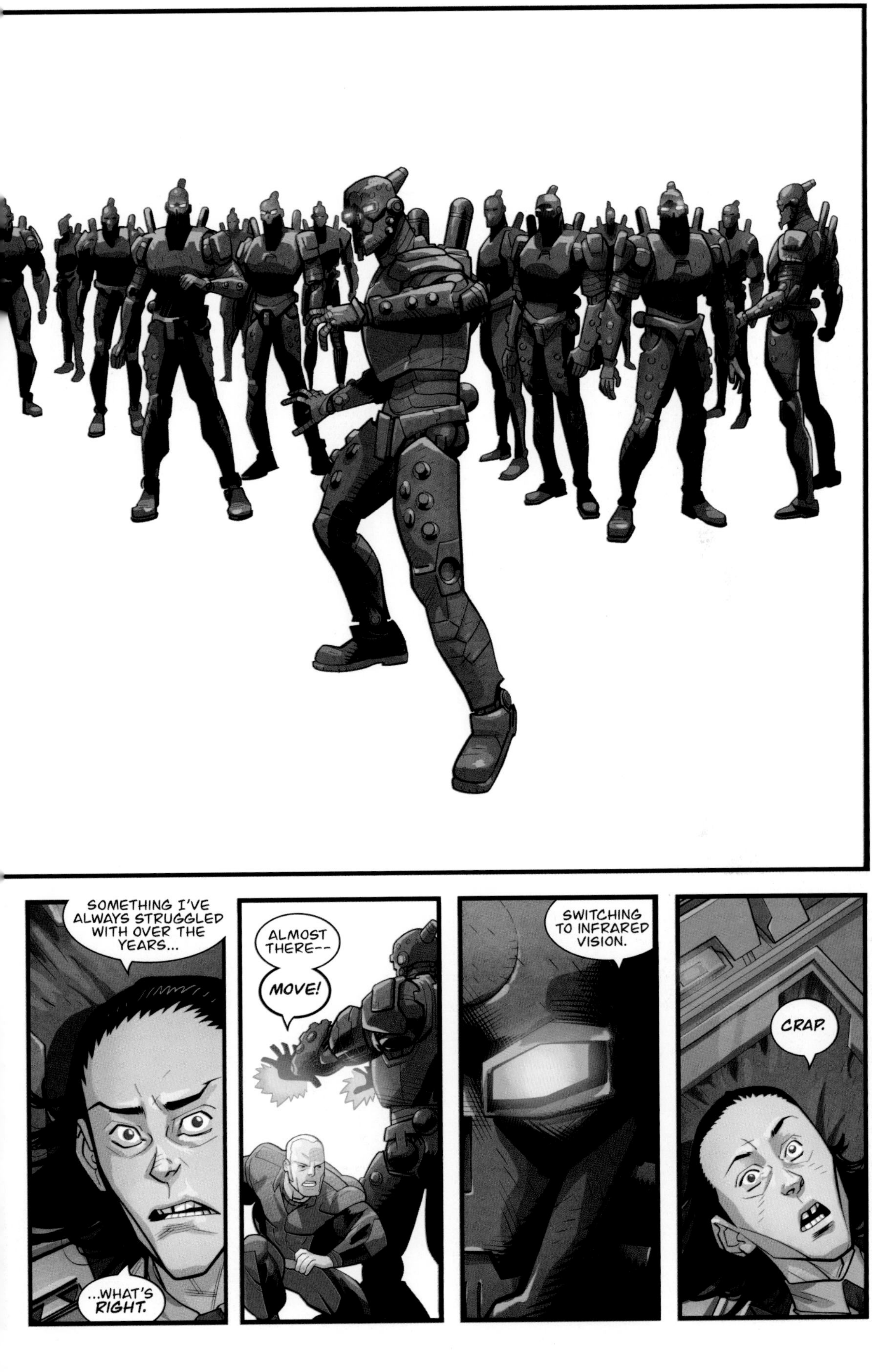
SOMETHING I'VE ALWAYS STRUGGLED WITH OVER THE YEARS...
...WHAT'S RIGHT.
ALMOST THERE--
MOVE!
SWITCHING TO INFRARED VISION.
CRAP.

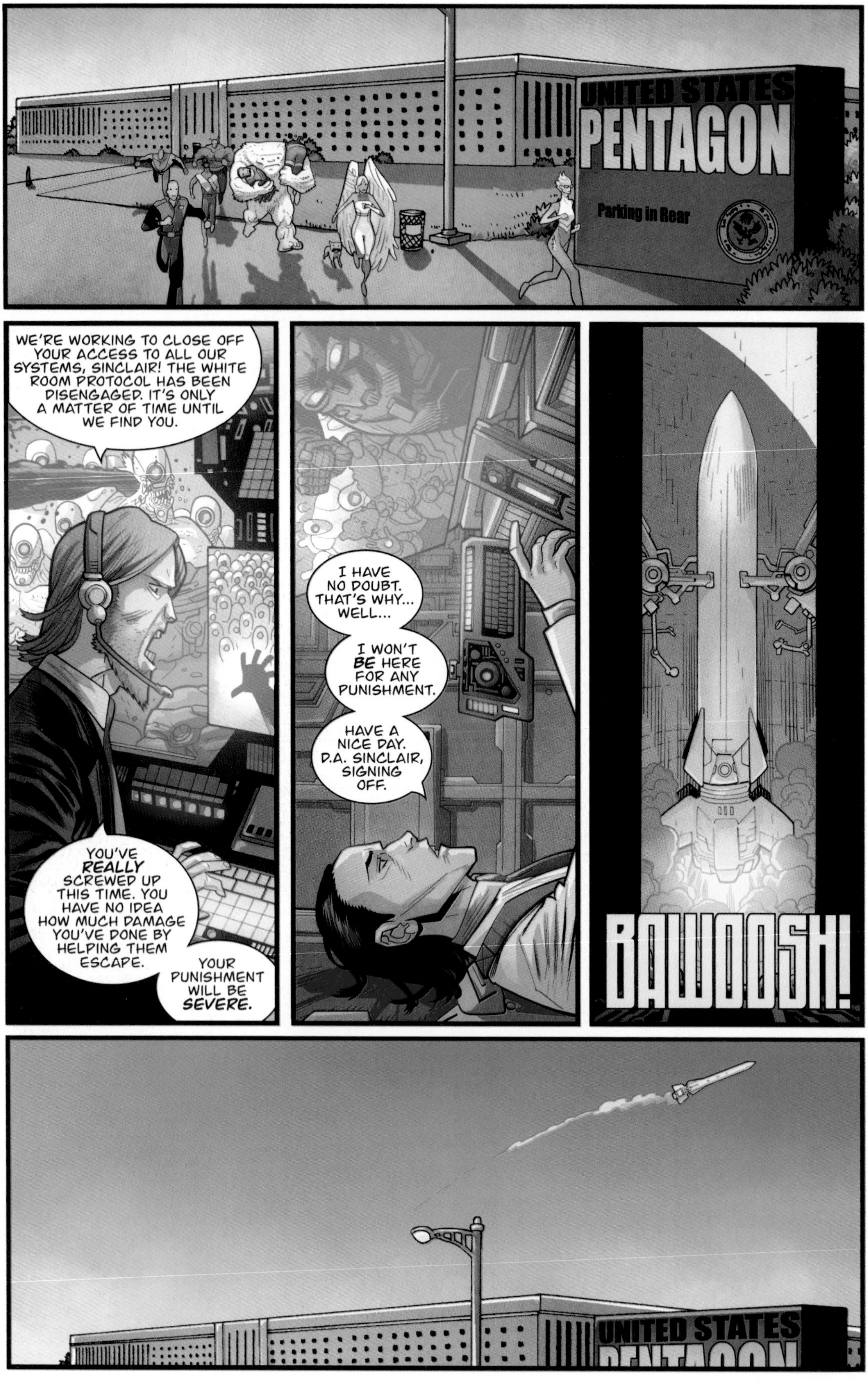
UNITED STATES
PENTAGON
Parking in Rear
WE'RE WORKING TO CLOSE OFF YOUR ACCESS TO ALL OUR SYSTEMS, SINCLAIR! THE WHITE ROOM PROTOCOL HAS BEEN DISENGAGED. IT'S ONLY A MATTER OF TIME UNTIL WE FIND YOU.
YOU'VE **REALLY** SCREWED UP THIS TIME. YOU HAVE NO IDEA HOW MUCH DAMAGE YOU'VE DONE BY HELPING THEM ESCAPE.
YOUR PUNISHMENT WILL BE **SEVERE.**
I HAVE NO DOUBT. THAT'S WHY... WELL...
I WON'T **BE** HERE FOR ANY PUNISHMENT.
HAVE A NICE DAY. D.A. SINCLAIR, SIGNING OFF.
BAWOOSH!
UNITED STATES

MY FACE... MY FACE...

WE CAN FIX IT. CALM DOWN.

NO... I DESERVE THIS.

THIS IS WHO I AM, THE THINGS I'VE DONE... THIS BETTER REFLECTS WHAT'S ON THE *INSIDE*.

WE'RE DOING GOOD HERE, ZANDALE.

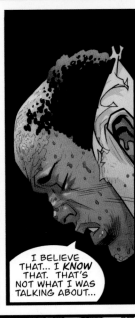

I BELIEVE THAT... I *KNOW* THAT. THAT'S NOT WHAT I WAS TALKING ABOUT...

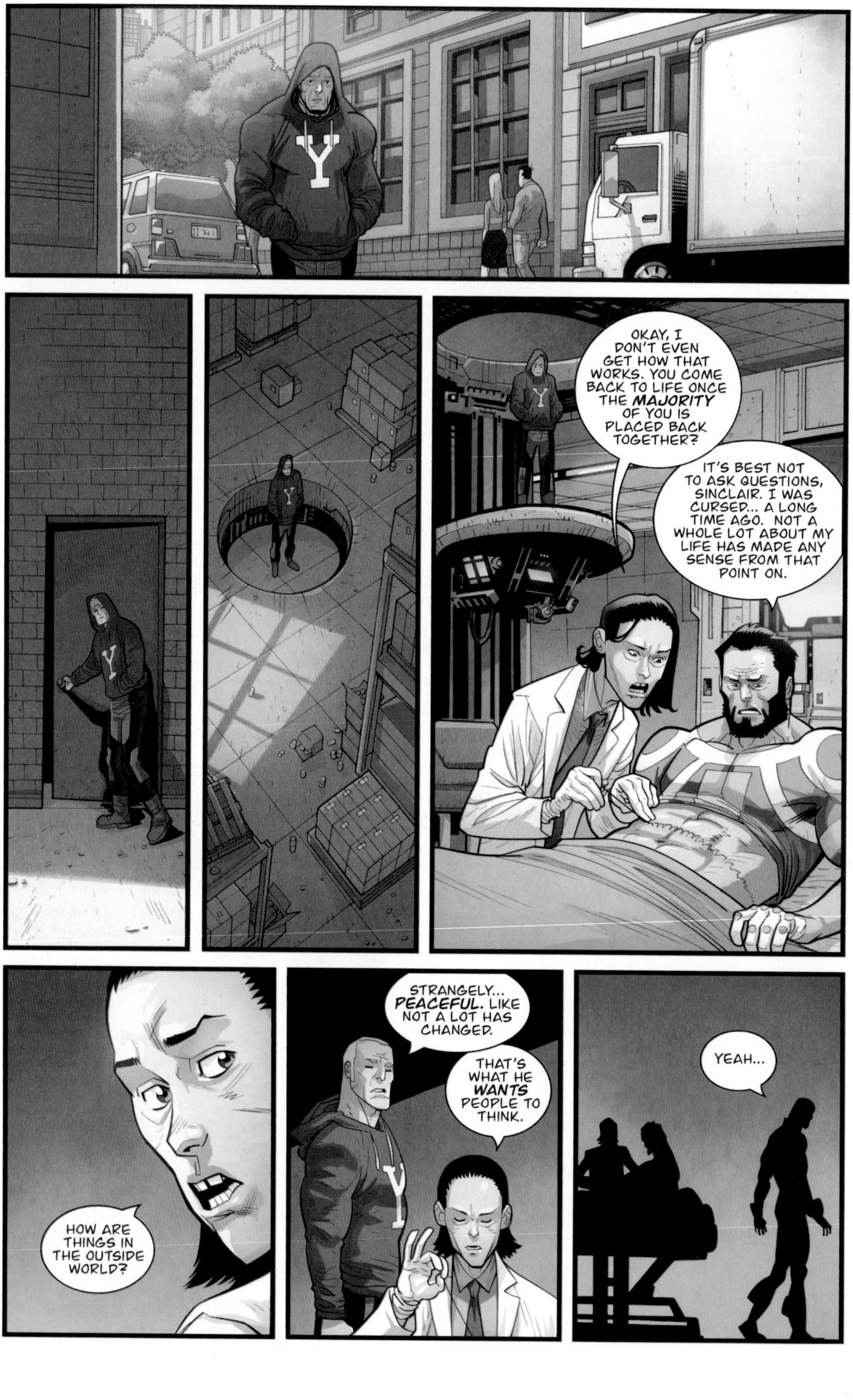
OKAY, I DON'T EVEN GET HOW THAT WORKS. YOU COME BACK TO LIFE ONCE THE MAJORITY OF YOU IS PLACED BACK TOGETHER?
IT'S BEST NOT TO ASK QUESTIONS, SINCLAIR. I WAS CURSED... A LONG TIME AGO. NOT A WHOLE LOT ABOUT MY LIFE HAS MADE ANY SENSE FROM THAT POINT ON.
HOW ARE THINGS IN THE OUTSIDE WORLD?
STRANGELY... PEACEFUL. LIKE NOT A LOT HAS CHANGED.
THAT'S WHAT HE WANTS PEOPLE TO THINK.
YEAH...

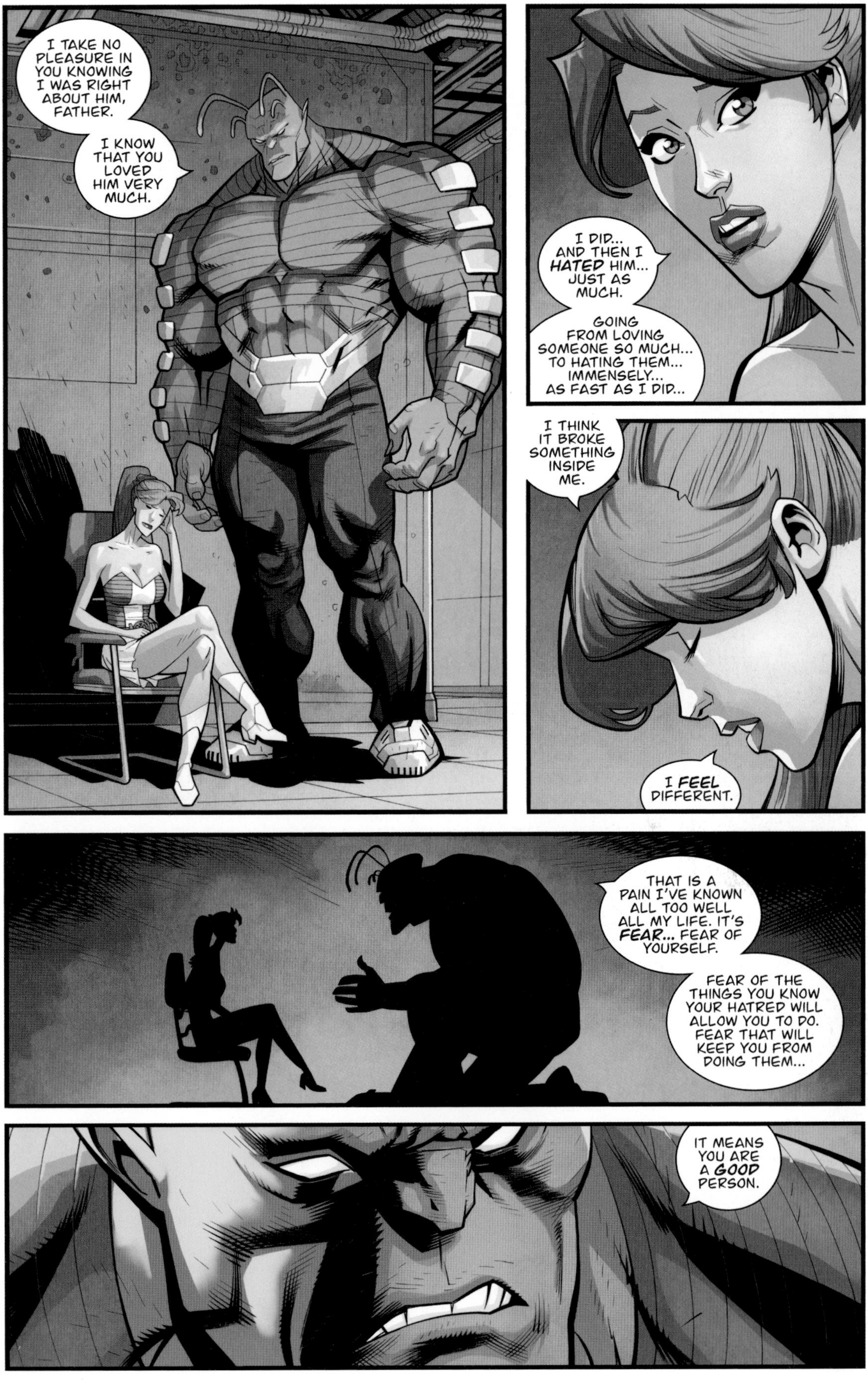
I TAKE NO PLEASURE IN YOU KNOWING I WAS RIGHT ABOUT HIM, FATHER.
I KNOW THAT YOU LOVED HIM VERY MUCH.
I DID... AND THEN I **HATED** HIM... JUST AS MUCH.
GOING FROM LOVING SOMEONE SO MUCH... TO HATING THEM... IMMENSELY... AS FAST AS I DID...
I THINK IT BROKE SOMETHING INSIDE ME.
I **FEEL** DIFFERENT.
THAT IS A PAIN I'VE KNOWN ALL TOO WELL ALL MY LIFE. IT'S **FEAR...** FEAR OF YOURSELF.
FEAR OF THE THINGS YOU KNOW YOUR HATRED WILL ALLOW YOU TO DO. FEAR THAT WILL KEEP YOU FROM DOING THEM...
IT MEANS YOU ARE A **GOOD** PERSON.

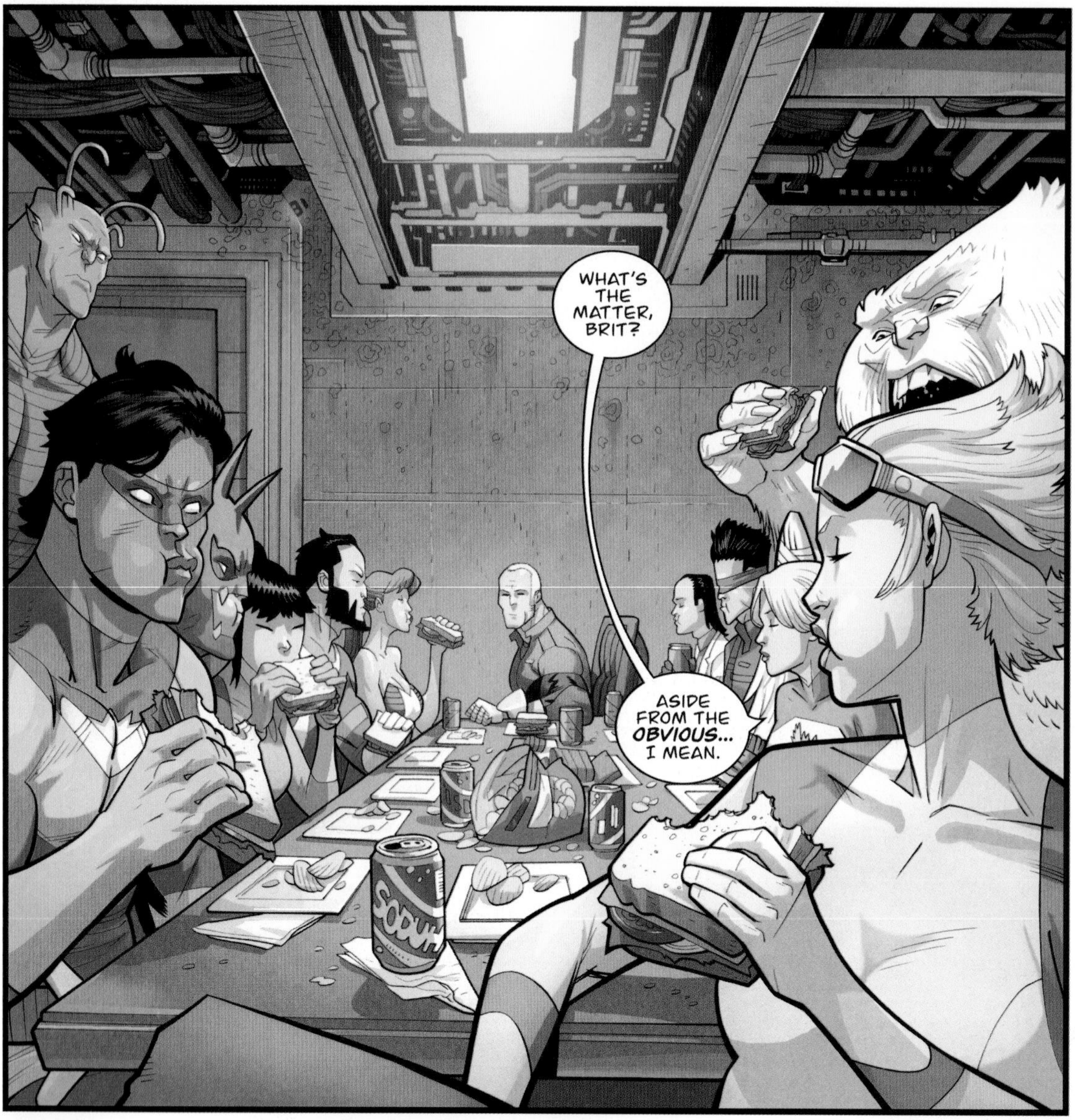
WHAT'S THE MATTER, BRIT?
ASIDE FROM THE OBVIOUS... I MEAN.

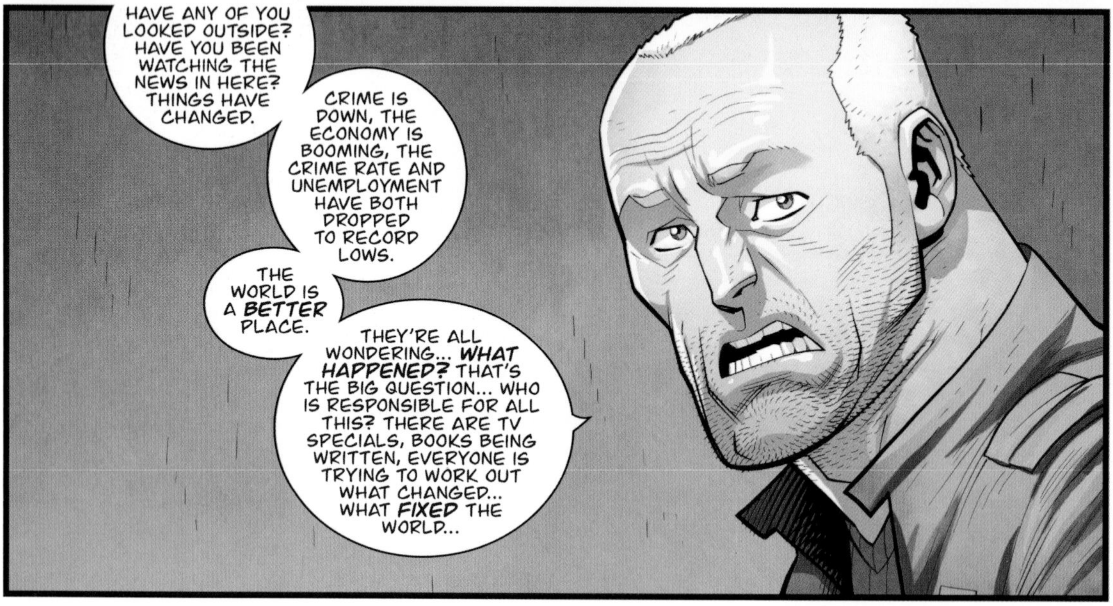
HAVE ANY OF YOU LOOKED OUTSIDE? HAVE YOU BEEN WATCHING THE NEWS IN HERE? THINGS HAVE CHANGED.
CRIME IS DOWN, THE ECONOMY IS BOOMING, THE CRIME RATE AND UNEMPLOYMENT HAVE BOTH DROPPED TO RECORD LOWS.
THE WORLD IS A BETTER PLACE.
THEY'RE ALL WONDERING... WHAT HAPPENED? THAT'S THE BIG QUESTION... WHO IS RESPONSIBLE FOR ALL THIS? THERE ARE TV SPECIALS, BOOKS BEING WRITTEN, EVERYONE IS TRYING TO WORK OUT WHAT CHANGED... WHAT FIXED THE WORLD...

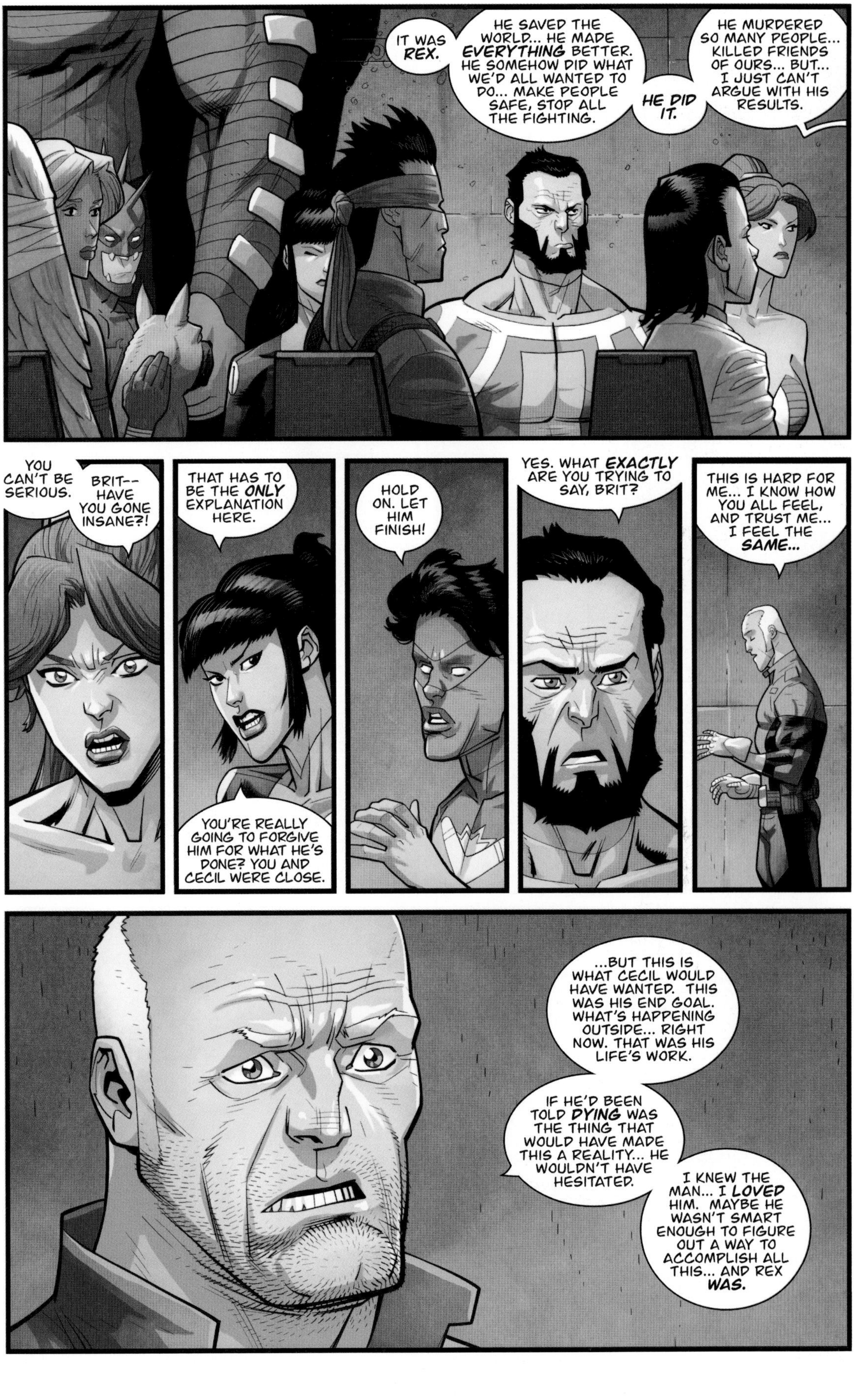
IT WAS REX.
HE SAVED THE WORLD... HE MADE EVERYTHING BETTER. HE SOMEHOW DID WHAT WE'D ALL WANTED TO DO... MAKE PEOPLE SAFE, STOP ALL THE FIGHTING.
HE DID IT.
HE MURDERED SO MANY PEOPLE... KILLED FRIENDS OF OURS... BUT... I JUST CAN'T ARGUE WITH HIS RESULTS.
YOU CAN'T BE SERIOUS.
BRIT-- HAVE YOU GONE INSANE?!
THAT HAS TO BE THE ONLY EXPLANATION HERE.
YOU'RE REALLY GOING TO FORGIVE HIM FOR WHAT HE'S DONE? YOU AND CECIL WERE CLOSE.
HOLD ON. LET HIM FINISH!
YES. WHAT EXACTLY ARE YOU TRYING TO SAY, BRIT?
THIS IS HARD FOR ME... I KNOW HOW YOU ALL FEEL, AND TRUST ME... I FEEL THE SAME...
...BUT THIS IS WHAT CECIL WOULD HAVE WANTED. THIS WAS HIS END GOAL. WHAT'S HAPPENING OUTSIDE... RIGHT NOW. THAT WAS HIS LIFE'S WORK.
IF HE'D BEEN TOLD DYING WAS THE THING THAT WOULD HAVE MADE THIS A REALITY... HE WOULDN'T HAVE HESITATED.
I KNEW THE MAN... I LOVED HIM. MAYBE HE WASN'T SMART ENOUGH TO FIGURE OUT A WAY TO ACCOMPLISH ALL THIS... AND REX WAS.

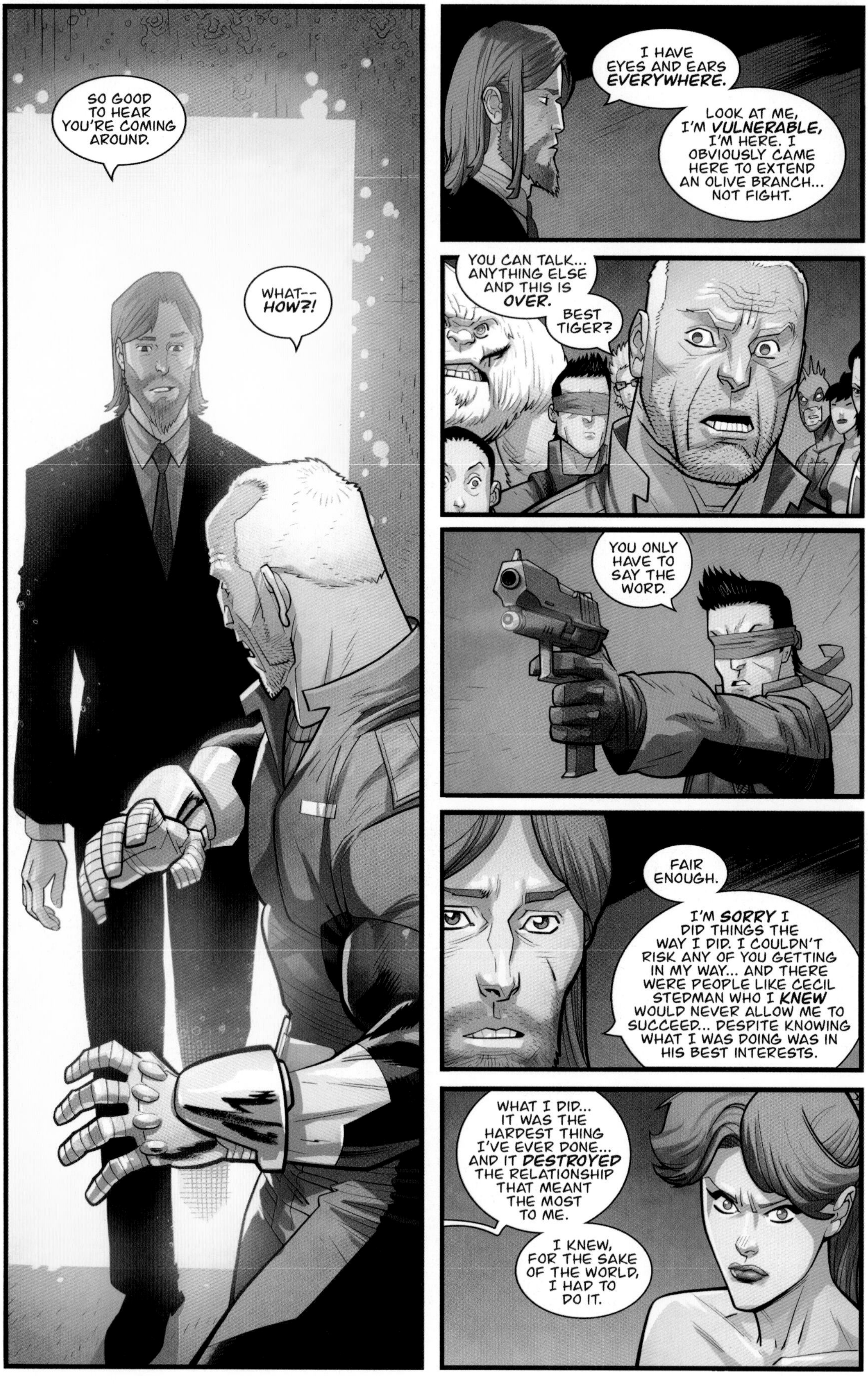

SO GOOD TO HEAR YOU'RE COMING AROUND.
WHAT-- HOW?!
I HAVE EYES AND EARS EVERYWHERE.
LOOK AT ME, I'M VULNERABLE, I'M HERE. I OBVIOUSLY CAME HERE TO EXTEND AN OLIVE BRANCH... NOT FIGHT.
YOU CAN TALK... ANYTHING ELSE AND THIS IS OVER.
BEST TIGER?
YOU ONLY HAVE TO SAY THE WORD.
FAIR ENOUGH.
I'M SORRY I DID THINGS THE WAY I DID. I COULDN'T RISK ANY OF YOU GETTING IN MY WAY... AND THERE WERE PEOPLE LIKE CECIL STEDMAN WHO I KNEW WOULD NEVER ALLOW ME TO SUCCEED... DESPITE KNOWING WHAT I WAS DOING WAS IN HIS BEST INTERESTS.
WHAT I DID... IT WAS THE HARDEST THING I'VE EVER DONE... AND IT DESTROYED THE RELATIONSHIP THAT MEANT THE MOST TO ME.
I KNEW, FOR THE SAKE OF THE WORLD, I HAD TO DO IT.

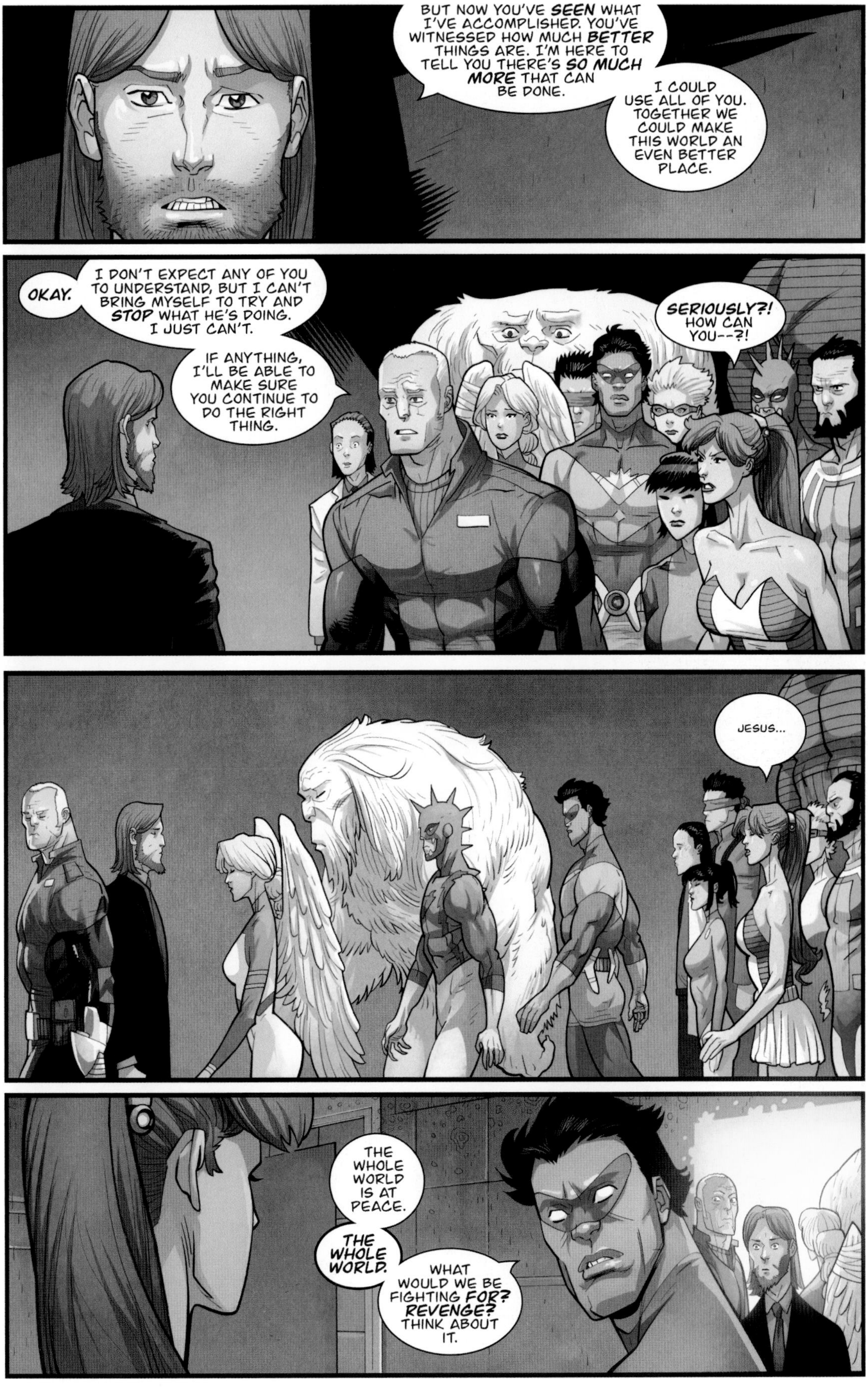
BUT NOW YOU'VE SEEN WHAT I'VE ACCOMPLISHED. YOU'VE WITNESSED HOW MUCH BETTER THINGS ARE. I'M HERE TO TELL YOU THERE'S SO MUCH MORE THAT CAN BE DONE.
I COULD USE ALL OF YOU. TOGETHER WE COULD MAKE THIS WORLD AN EVEN BETTER PLACE.
OKAY.
I DON'T EXPECT ANY OF YOU TO UNDERSTAND, BUT I CAN'T BRING MYSELF TO TRY AND STOP WHAT HE'S DOING. I JUST CAN'T.
IF ANYTHING, I'LL BE ABLE TO MAKE SURE YOU CONTINUE TO DO THE RIGHT THING.
SERIOUSLY?! HOW CAN YOU--?!
JESUS...
THE WHOLE WORLD IS AT PEACE.
THE WHOLE WORLD.
WHAT WOULD WE BE FIGHTING FOR? REVENGE? THINK ABOUT IT.

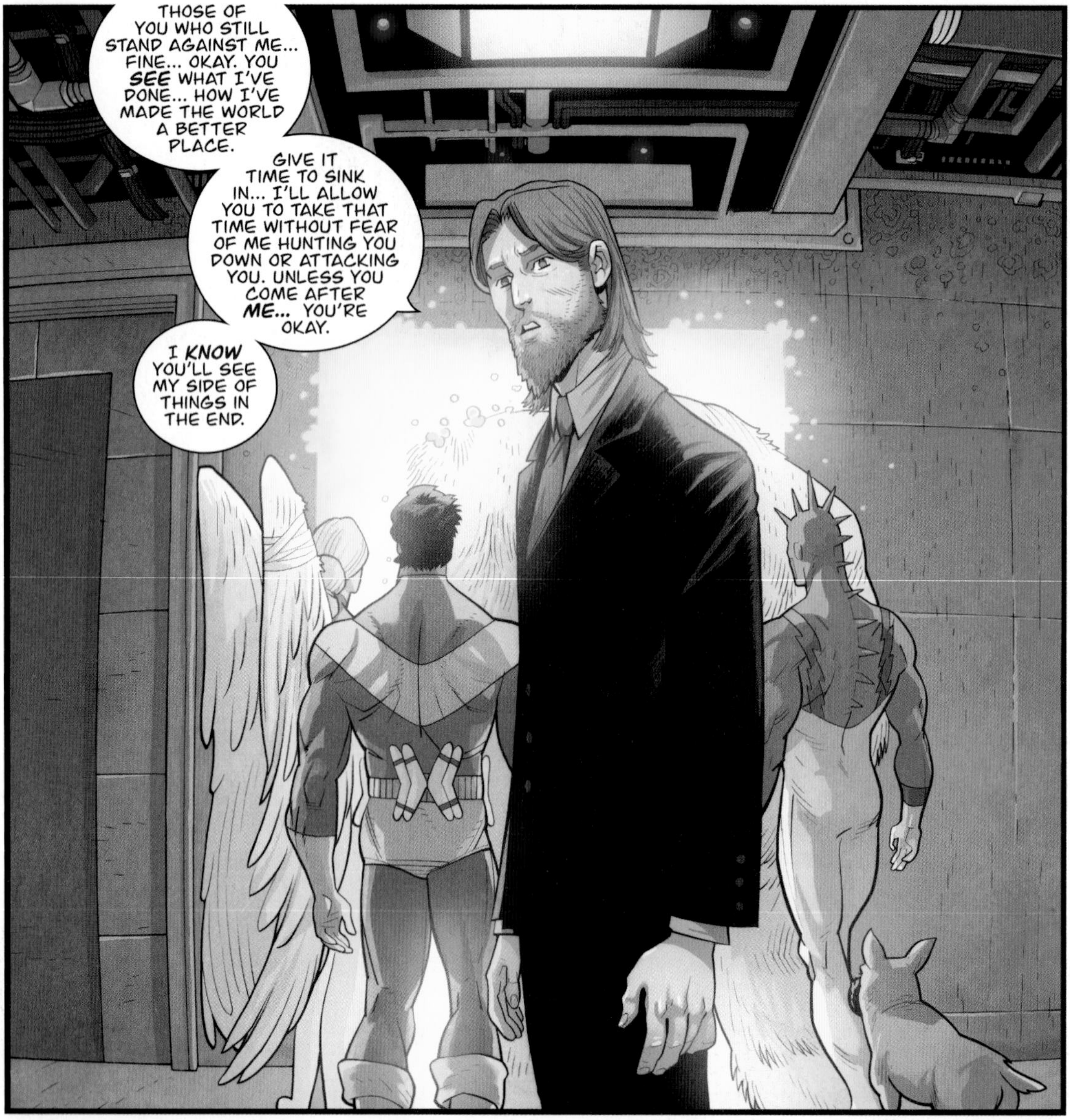
THOSE OF YOU WHO STILL STAND AGAINST ME... FINE... OKAY. YOU **SEE** WHAT I'VE DONE... HOW I'VE MADE THE WORLD A BETTER PLACE.
GIVE IT TIME TO SINK IN... I'LL ALLOW YOU TO TAKE THAT TIME WITHOUT FEAR OF ME HUNTING YOU DOWN OR ATTACKING YOU. UNLESS YOU COME AFTER **ME...** YOU'RE OKAY.
I ***KNOW*** YOU'LL SEE MY SIDE OF THINGS IN THE END.

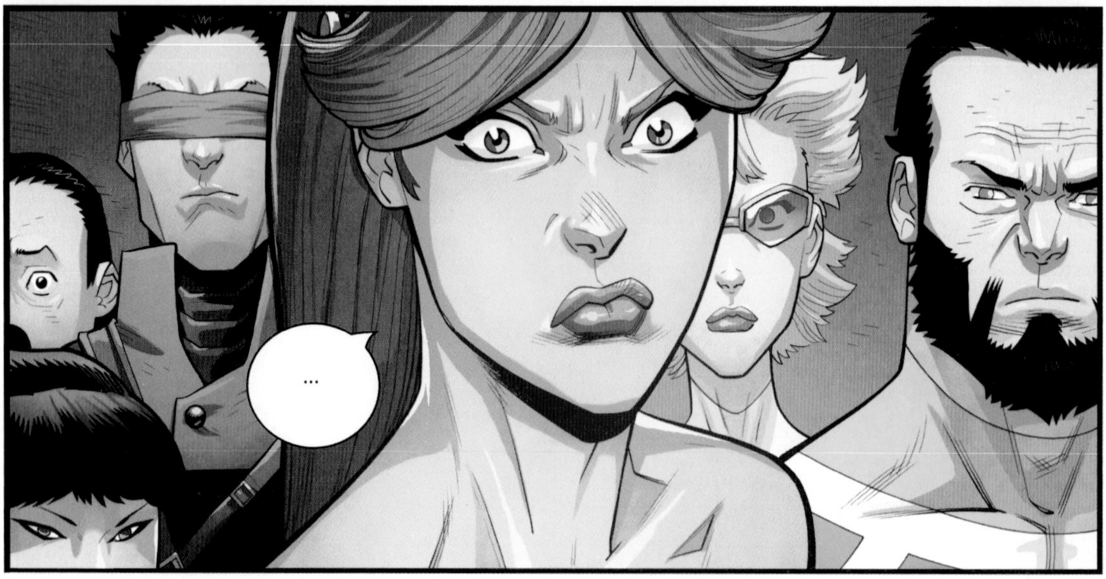
...

CHAPTER TWO

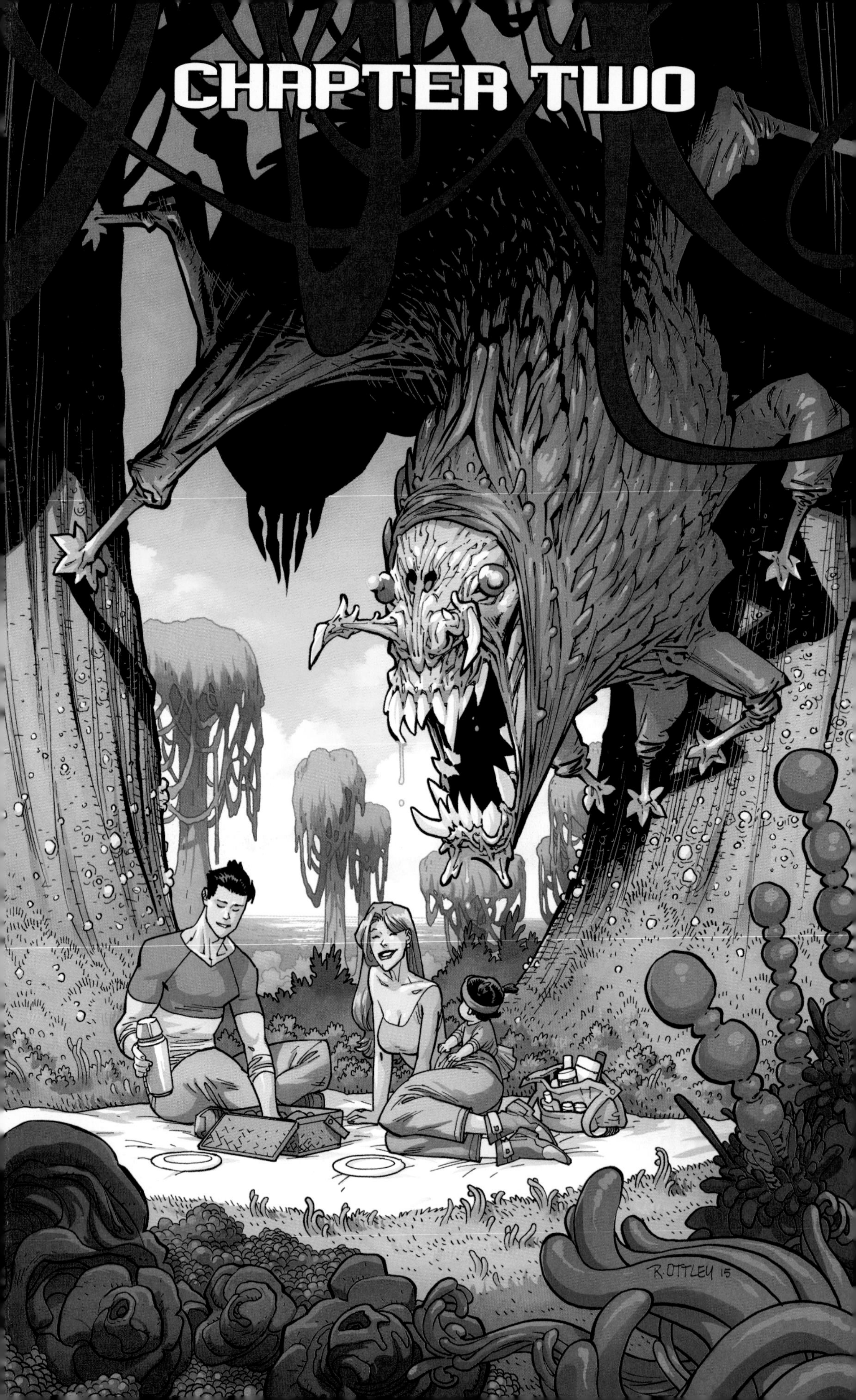
R. OTTLEY 15

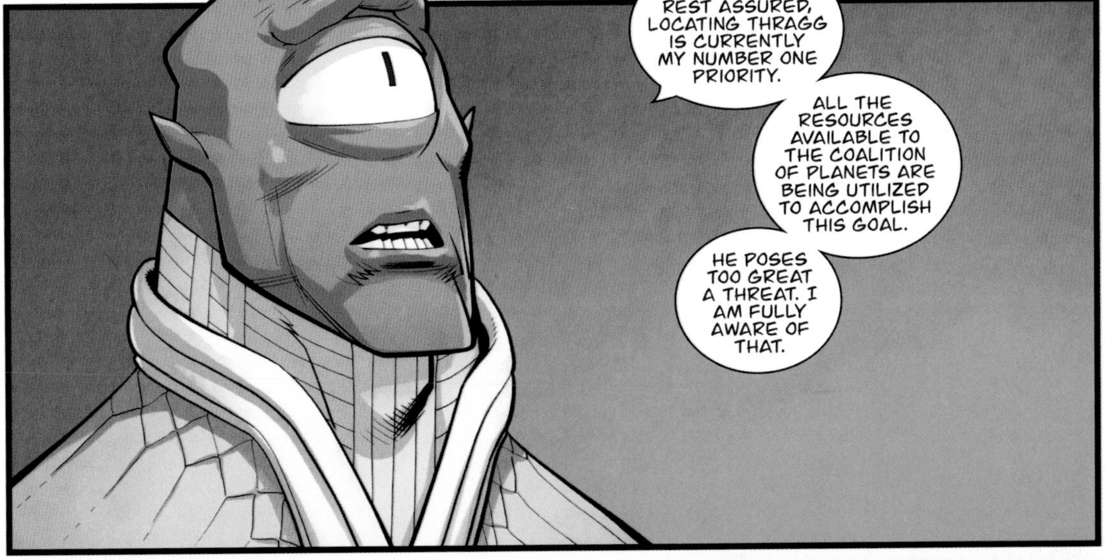
REST ASSURED, LOCATING THRAGG IS CURRENTLY MY NUMBER ONE PRIORITY.
ALL THE RESOURCES AVAILABLE TO THE COALITION OF PLANETS ARE BEING UTILIZED TO ACCOMPLISH THIS GOAL.
HE POSES TOO GREAT A THREAT. I AM FULLY AWARE OF THAT.

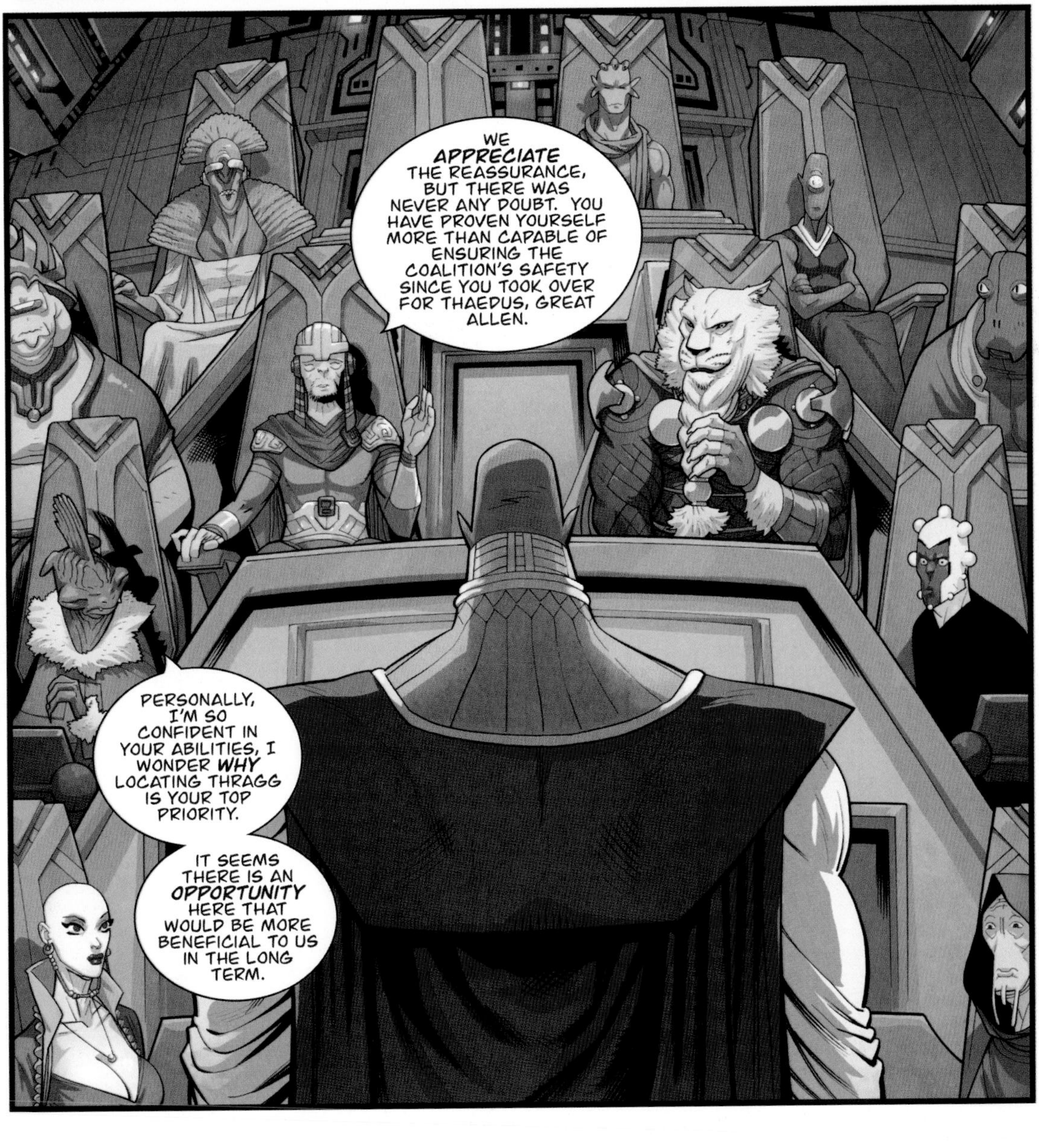
WE APPRECIATE THE REASSURANCE, BUT THERE WAS NEVER ANY DOUBT. YOU HAVE PROVEN YOURSELF MORE THAN CAPABLE OF ENSURING THE COALITION'S SAFETY SINCE YOU TOOK OVER FOR THAEDUS, GREAT ALLEN.
PERSONALLY, I'M SO CONFIDENT IN YOUR ABILITIES, I WONDER WHY LOCATING THRAGG IS YOUR TOP PRIORITY.
IT SEEMS THERE IS AN OPPORTUNITY HERE THAT WOULD BE MORE BENEFICIAL TO US IN THE LONG TERM.

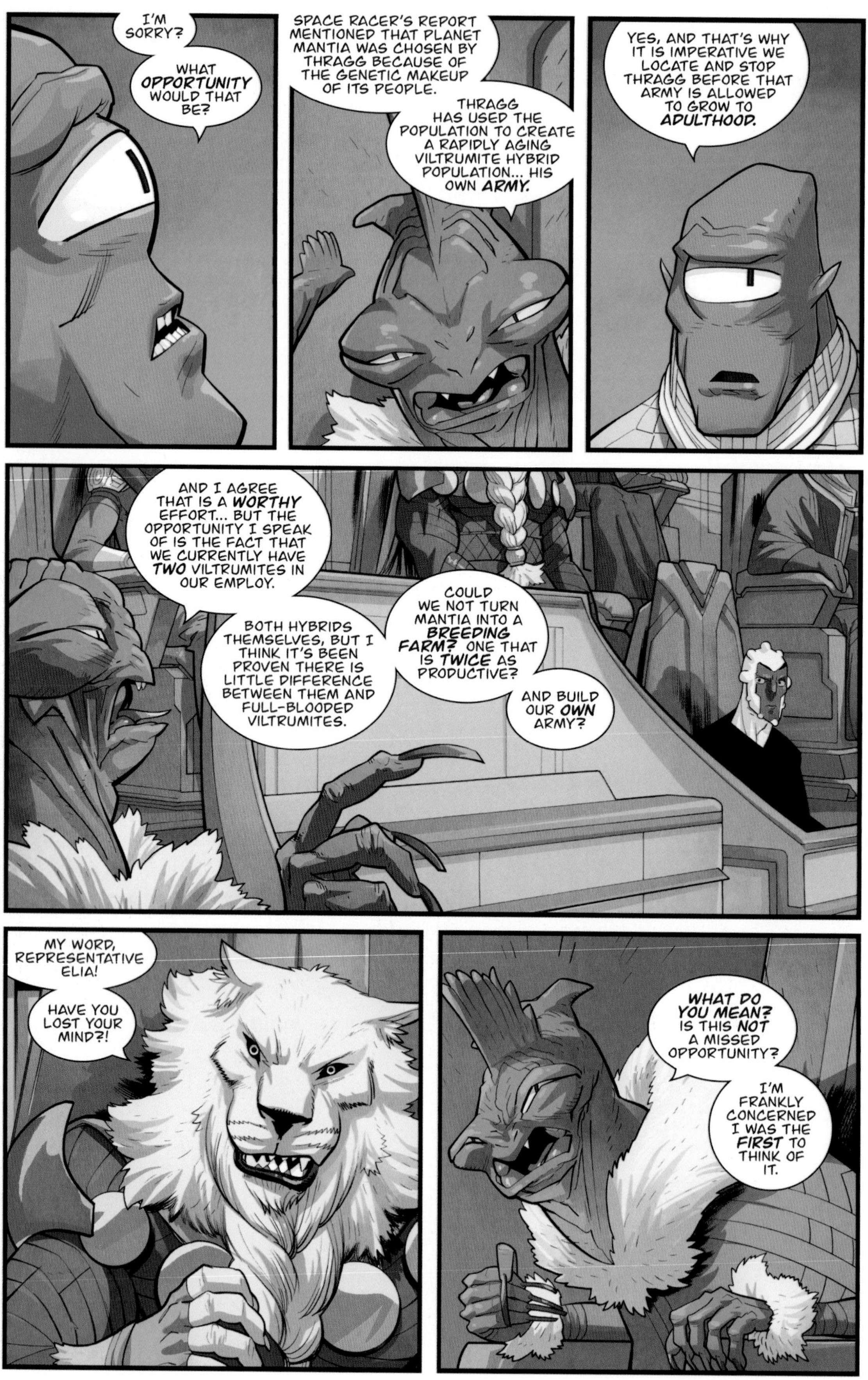
I'M SORRY?
WHAT OPPORTUNITY WOULD THAT BE?
SPACE RACER'S REPORT MENTIONED THAT PLANET MANTIA WAS CHOSEN BY THRAGG BECAUSE OF THE GENETIC MAKEUP OF ITS PEOPLE.
THRAGG HAS USED THE POPULATION TO CREATE A RAPIDLY AGING VILTRUMITE HYBRID POPULATION... HIS OWN ARMY.
YES, AND THAT'S WHY IT IS IMPERATIVE WE LOCATE AND STOP THRAGG BEFORE THAT ARMY IS ALLOWED TO GROW TO ADULTHOOD.
AND I AGREE THAT IS A WORTHY EFFORT... BUT THE OPPORTUNITY I SPEAK OF IS THE FACT THAT WE CURRENTLY HAVE TWO VILTRUMITES IN OUR EMPLOY.
BOTH HYBRIDS THEMSELVES, BUT I THINK IT'S BEEN PROVEN THERE IS LITTLE DIFFERENCE BETWEEN THEM AND FULL-BLOODED VILTRUMITES.
COULD WE NOT TURN MANTIA INTO A BREEDING FARM? ONE THAT IS TWICE AS PRODUCTIVE?
AND BUILD OUR OWN ARMY?
MY WORD, REPRESENTATIVE ELIA!
HAVE YOU LOST YOUR MIND?!
WHAT DO YOU MEAN? IS THIS NOT A MISSED OPPORTUNITY?
I'M FRANKLY CONCERNED I WAS THE FIRST TO THINK OF IT.

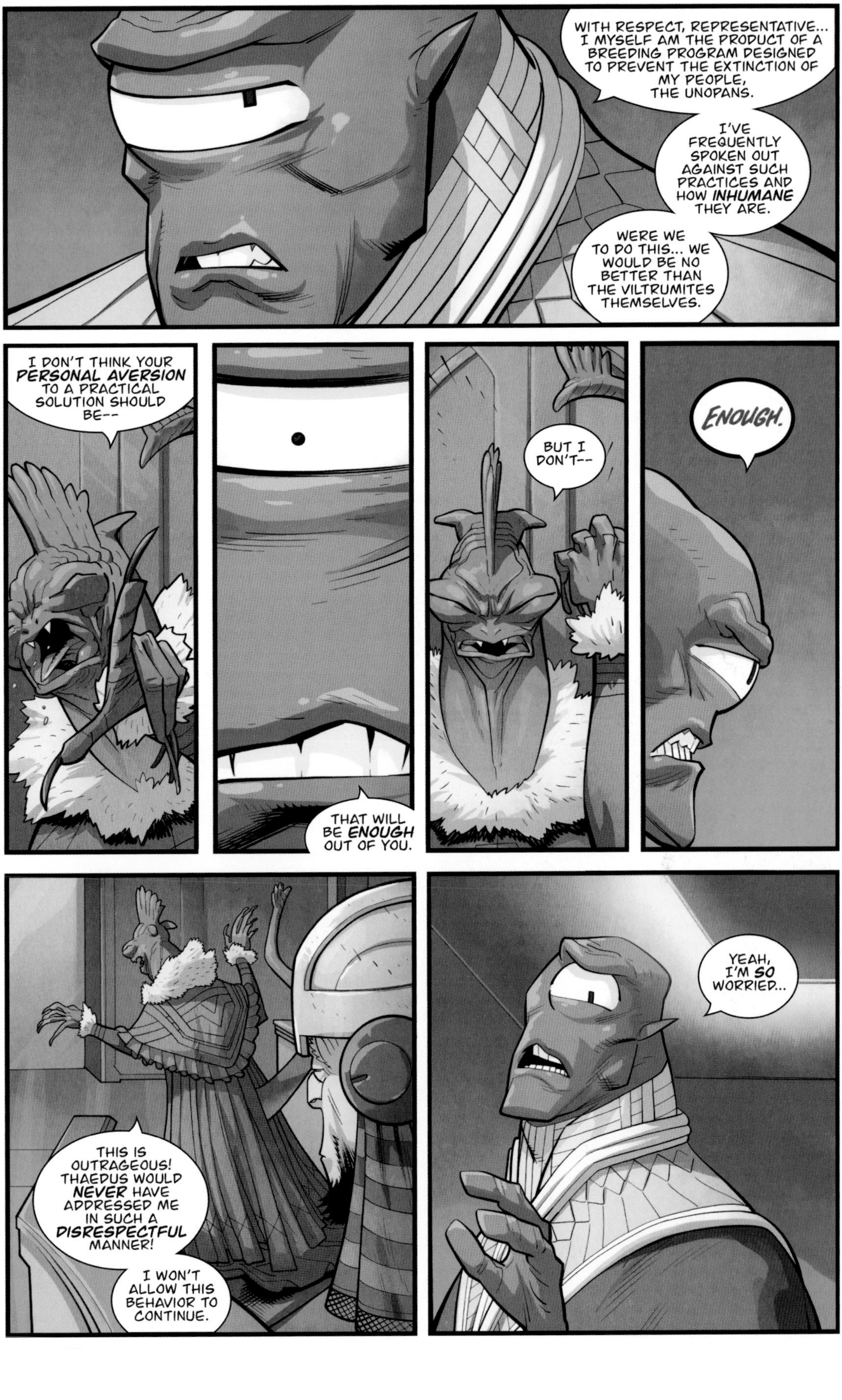

WITH RESPECT, REPRESENTATIVE... I MYSELF AM THE PRODUCT OF A BREEDING PROGRAM DESIGNED TO PREVENT THE EXTINCTION OF MY PEOPLE, THE UNOPANS.
I'VE FREQUENTLY SPOKEN OUT AGAINST SUCH PRACTICES AND HOW INHUMANE THEY ARE.
WERE WE TO DO THIS... WE WOULD BE NO BETTER THAN THE VILTRUMITES THEMSELVES.
I DON'T THINK YOUR PERSONAL AVERSION TO A PRACTICAL SOLUTION SHOULD BE--
THAT WILL BE ENOUGH OUT OF YOU.
BUT I DON'T--
ENOUGH.
THIS IS OUTRAGEOUS! THAEDUS WOULD NEVER HAVE ADDRESSED ME IN SUCH A DISRESPECTFUL MANNER!
I WON'T ALLOW THIS BEHAVIOR TO CONTINUE.
YEAH, I'M SO WORRIED...

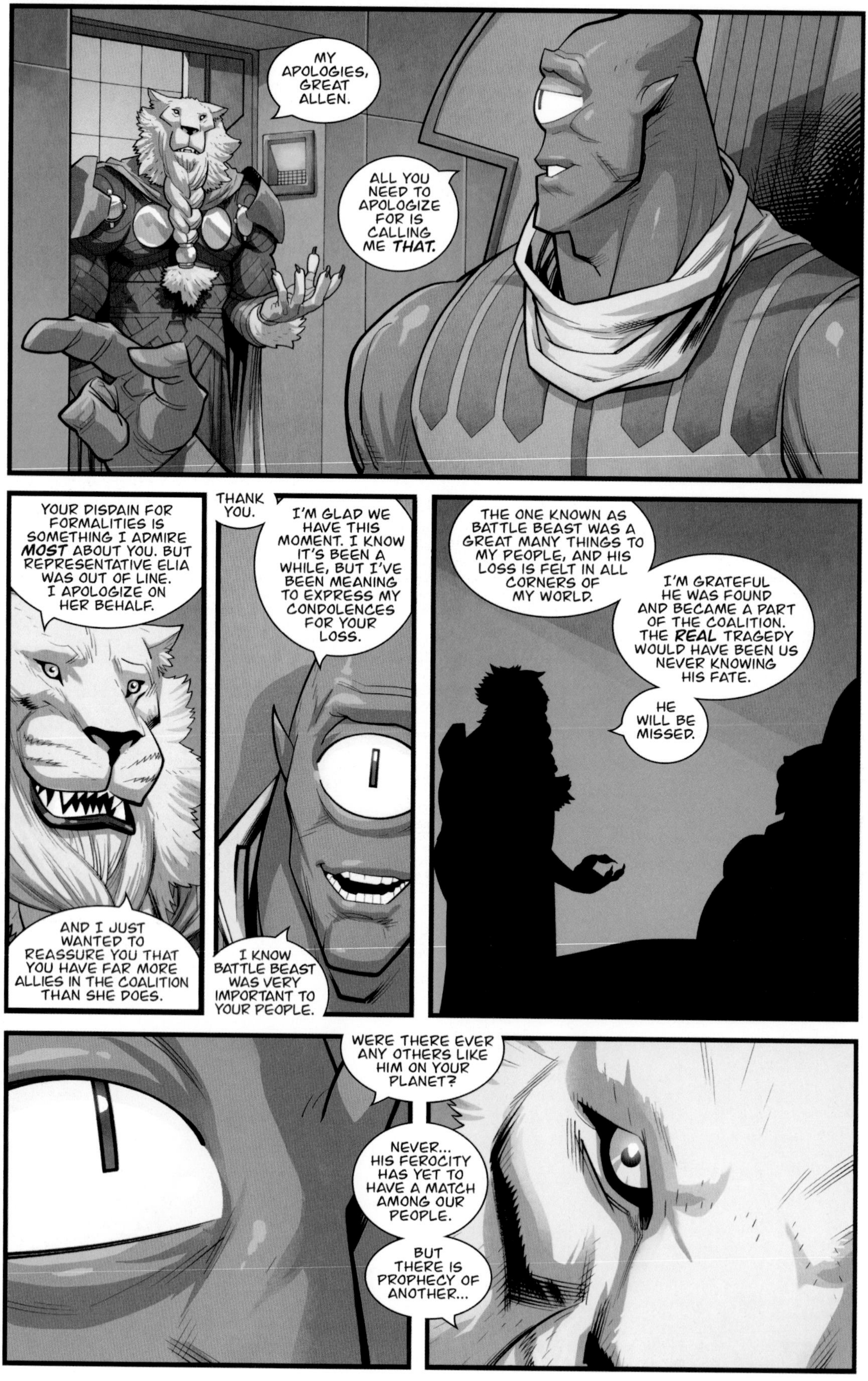
MY APOLOGIES, GREAT ALLEN.
ALL YOU NEED TO APOLOGIZE FOR IS CALLING ME *THAT.*
YOUR DISPAIN FOR FORMALITIES IS SOMETHING I ADMIRE *MOST* ABOUT YOU. BUT REPRESENTATIVE ELIA WAS OUT OF LINE. I APOLOGIZE ON HER BEHALF.
AND I JUST WANTED TO REASSURE YOU THAT YOU HAVE FAR MORE ALLIES IN THE COALITION THAN SHE DOES.
THANK YOU.
I'M GLAD WE HAVE THIS MOMENT. I KNOW IT'S BEEN A WHILE, BUT I'VE BEEN MEANING TO EXPRESS MY CONDOLENCES FOR YOUR LOSS.
I KNOW BATTLE BEAST WAS VERY IMPORTANT TO YOUR PEOPLE.
THE ONE KNOWN AS BATTLE BEAST WAS A GREAT MANY THINGS TO MY PEOPLE, AND HIS LOSS IS FELT IN ALL CORNERS OF MY WORLD.
I'M GRATEFUL HE WAS FOUND AND BECAME A PART OF THE COALITION. THE *REAL* TRAGEDY WOULD HAVE BEEN US NEVER KNOWING HIS FATE.
HE WILL BE MISSED.
WERE THERE EVER ANY OTHERS LIKE HIM ON YOUR PLANET?
NEVER... HIS FEROCITY HAS YET TO HAVE A MATCH AMONG OUR PEOPLE.
BUT THERE IS PROPHECY OF ANOTHER...

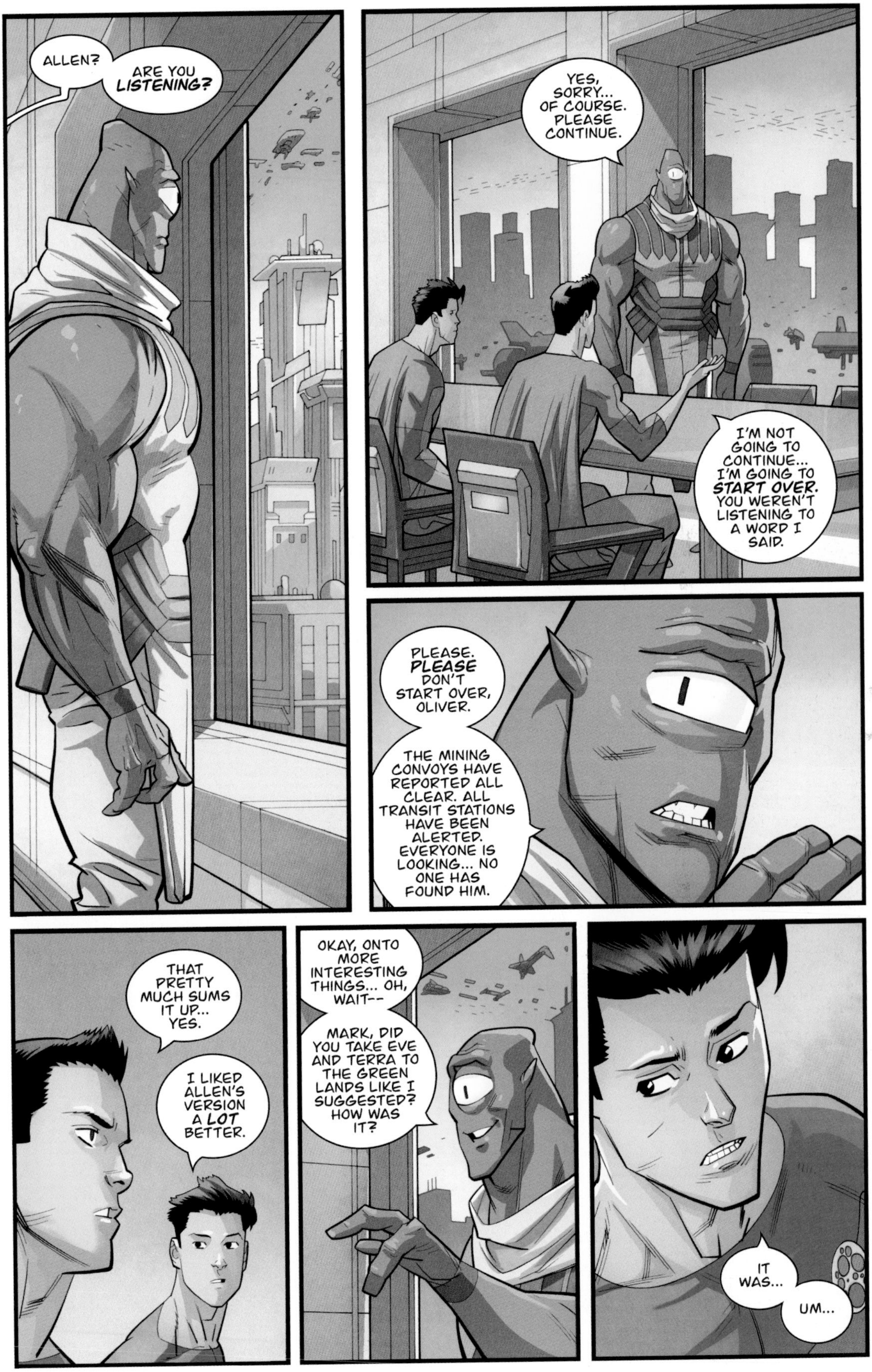

ALLEN?
ARE YOU LISTENING?
YES, SORRY... OF COURSE. PLEASE CONTINUE.
I'M NOT GOING TO CONTINUE... I'M GOING TO START OVER. YOU WEREN'T LISTENING TO A WORD I SAID.
PLEASE. PLEASE DON'T START OVER, OLIVER.
THE MINING CONVOYS HAVE REPORTED ALL CLEAR. ALL TRANSIT STATIONS HAVE BEEN ALERTED. EVERYONE IS LOOKING... NO ONE HAS FOUND HIM.
THAT PRETTY MUCH SUMS IT UP... YES.
I LIKED ALLEN'S VERSION A LOT BETTER.
OKAY, ONTO MORE INTERESTING THINGS... OH, WAIT--
MARK, DID YOU TAKE EVE AND TERRA TO THE GREEN LANDS LIKE I SUGGESTED? HOW WAS IT?
IT WAS...
UM...

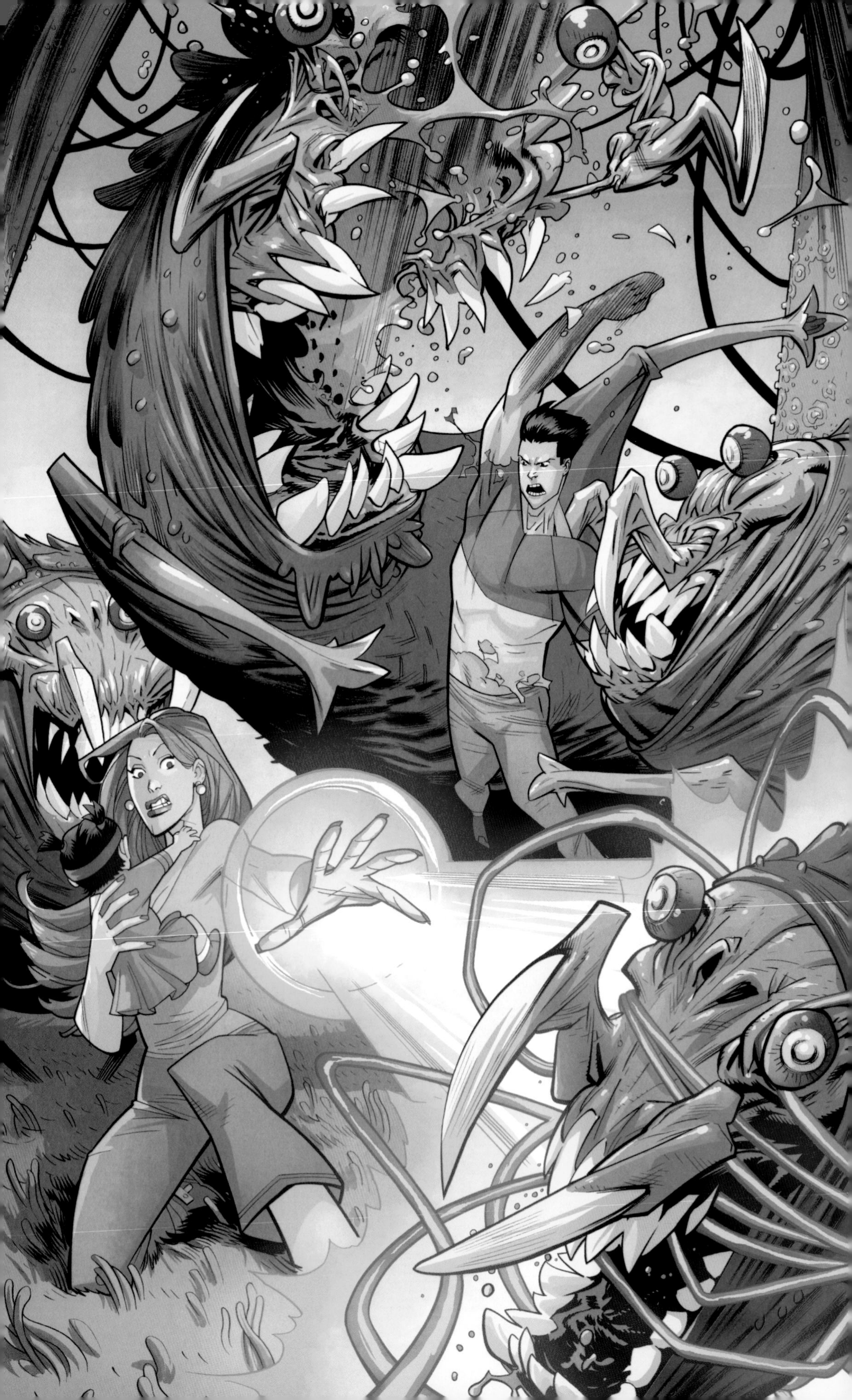

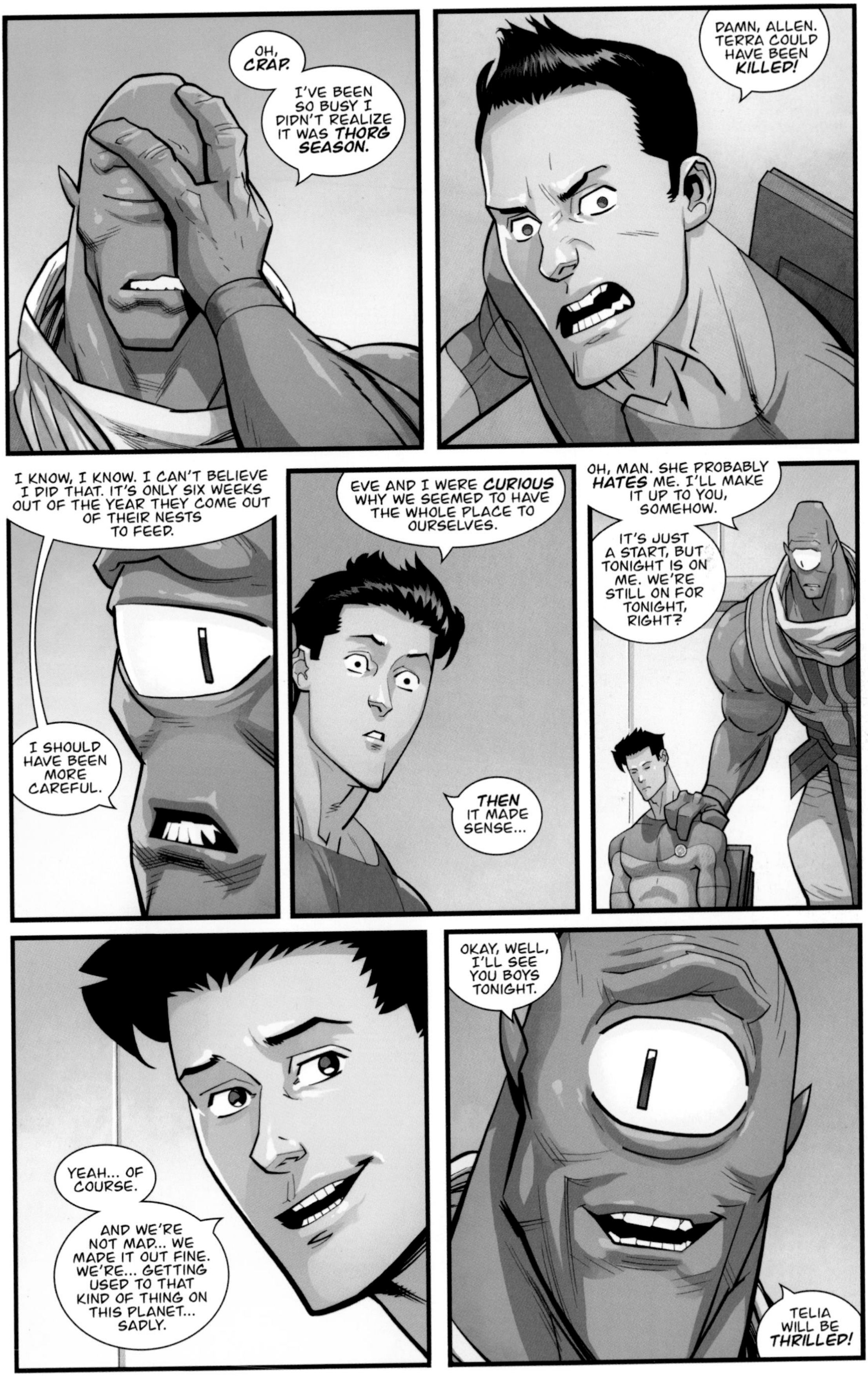
OH, CRAP.
I'VE BEEN SO BUSY I DIDN'T REALIZE IT WAS THORG SEASON.
DAMN, ALLEN. TERRA COULD HAVE BEEN KILLED!
I KNOW, I KNOW. I CAN'T BELIEVE I DID THAT. IT'S ONLY SIX WEEKS OUT OF THE YEAR THEY COME OUT OF THEIR NESTS TO FEED.
I SHOULD HAVE BEEN MORE CAREFUL.
EVE AND I WERE CURIOUS WHY WE SEEMED TO HAVE THE WHOLE PLACE TO OURSELVES.
THEN IT MADE SENSE...
OH, MAN. SHE PROBABLY HATES ME. I'LL MAKE IT UP TO YOU, SOMEHOW.
IT'S JUST A START, BUT TONIGHT IS ON ME. WE'RE STILL ON FOR TONIGHT, RIGHT?
YEAH... OF COURSE.
AND WE'RE NOT MAD... WE MADE IT OUT FINE. WE'RE... GETTING USED TO THAT KIND OF THING ON THIS PLANET... SADLY.
OKAY, WELL, I'LL SEE YOU BOYS TONIGHT.
TELIA WILL BE THRILLED!

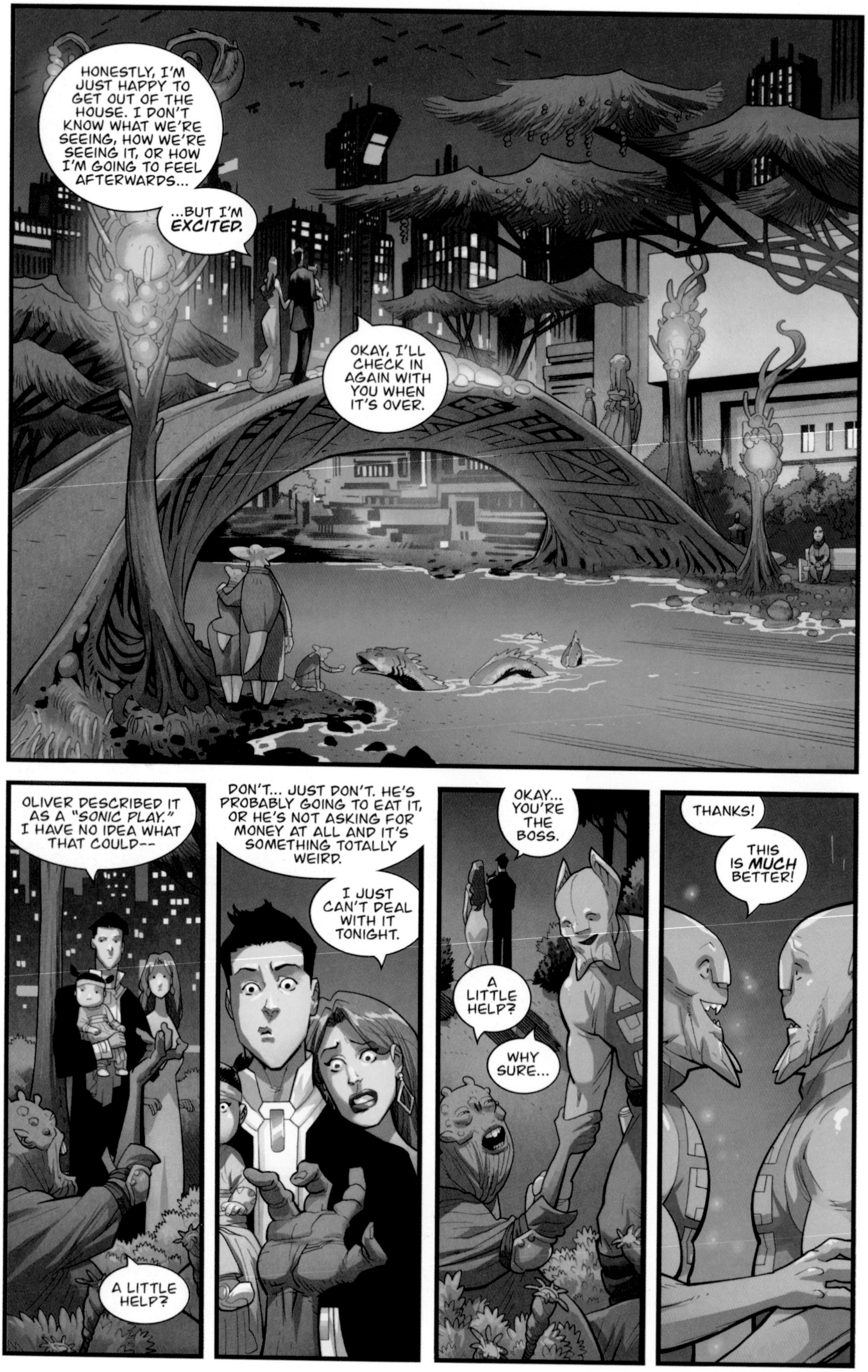
HONESTLY, I'M JUST HAPPY TO GET OUT OF THE HOUSE. I DON'T KNOW WHAT WE'RE SEEING, HOW WE'RE SEEING IT, OR HOW I'M GOING TO FEEL AFTERWARDS...
...BUT I'M EXCITED.
OKAY, I'LL CHECK IN AGAIN WITH YOU WHEN IT'S OVER.
OLIVER DESCRIBED IT AS A "SONIC PLAY." I HAVE NO IDEA WHAT THAT COULD--
A LITTLE HELP?
DON'T... JUST DON'T. HE'S PROBABLY GOING TO EAT IT, OR HE'S NOT ASKING FOR MONEY AT ALL AND IT'S SOMETHING TOTALLY WEIRD.
I JUST CAN'T DEAL WITH IT TONIGHT.
OKAY... YOU'RE THE BOSS.
A LITTLE HELP?
WHY SURE...
THANKS!
THIS IS MUCH BETTER!

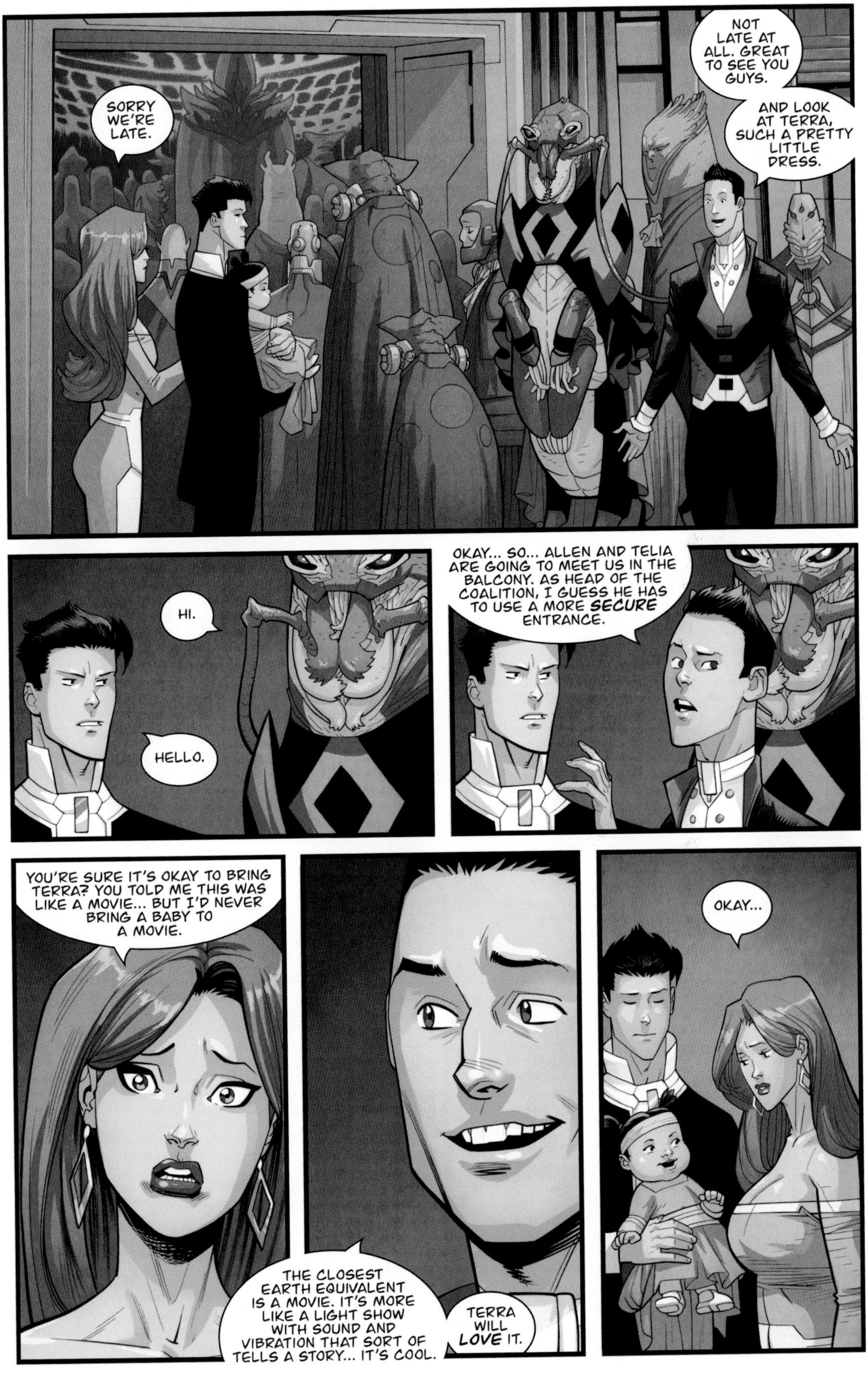
SORRY WE'RE LATE.
NOT LATE AT ALL. GREAT TO SEE YOU GUYS.
AND LOOK AT TERRA, SUCH A PRETTY LITTLE DRESS.
HI.
HELLO.
OKAY... SO... ALLEN AND TELIA ARE GOING TO MEET US IN THE BALCONY. AS HEAD OF THE COALITION, I GUESS HE HAS TO USE A MORE SECURE ENTRANCE.
YOU'RE SURE IT'S OKAY TO BRING TERRA? YOU TOLD ME THIS WAS LIKE A MOVIE... BUT I'D NEVER BRING A BABY TO A MOVIE.
THE CLOSEST EARTH EQUIVALENT IS A MOVIE. IT'S MORE LIKE A LIGHT SHOW WITH SOUND AND VIBRATION THAT SORT OF TELLS A STORY... IT'S COOL.
TERRA WILL LOVE IT.
OKAY...

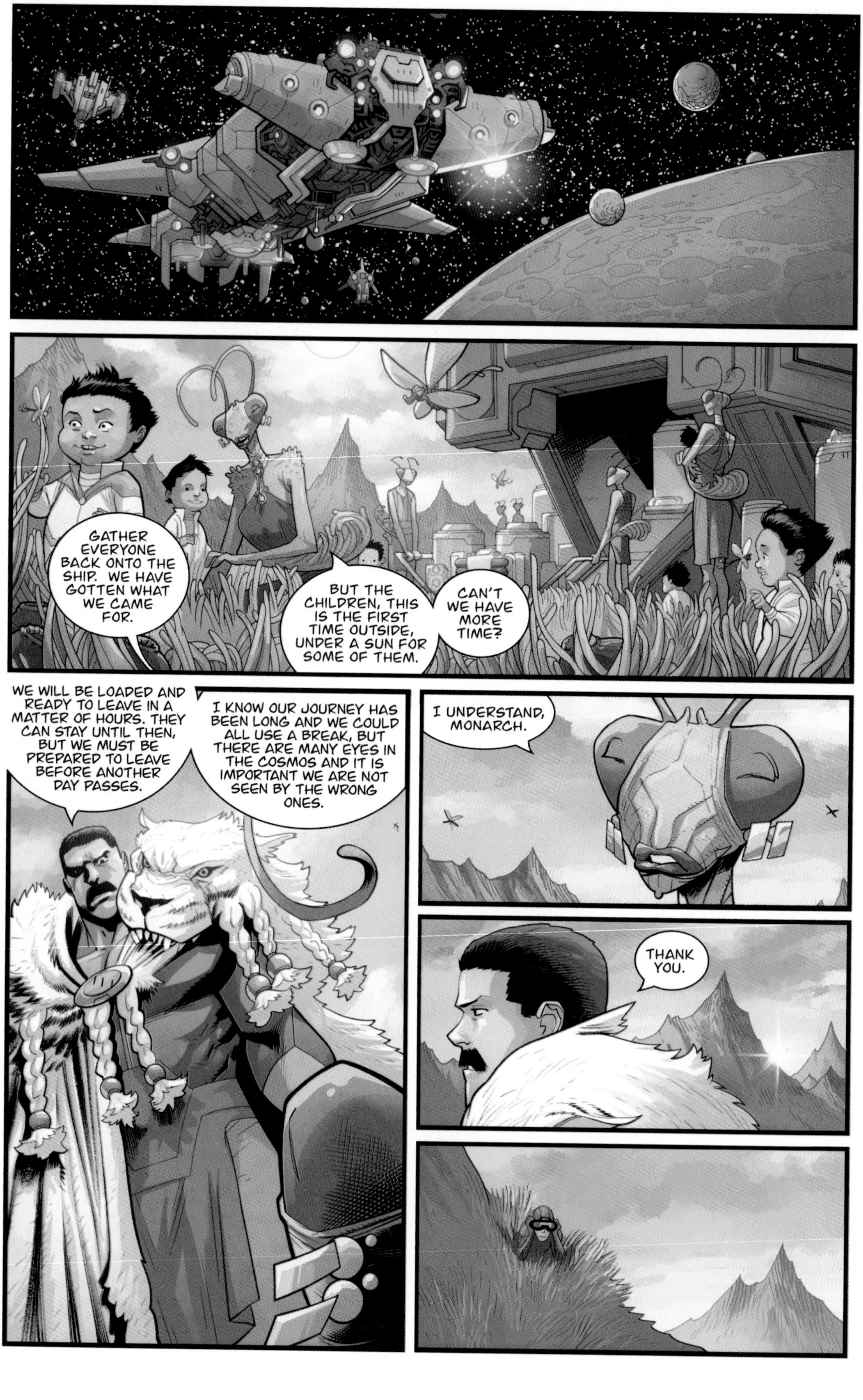
GATHER EVERYONE BACK ONTO THE SHIP. WE HAVE GOTTEN WHAT WE CAME FOR.
BUT THE CHILDREN, THIS IS THE FIRST TIME OUTSIDE, UNDER A SUN FOR SOME OF THEM.
CAN'T WE HAVE MORE TIME?
WE WILL BE LOADED AND READY TO LEAVE IN A MATTER OF HOURS. THEY CAN STAY UNTIL THEN, BUT WE MUST BE PREPARED TO LEAVE BEFORE ANOTHER DAY PASSES.
I KNOW OUR JOURNEY HAS BEEN LONG AND WE COULD ALL USE A BREAK, BUT THERE ARE MANY EYES IN THE COSMOS AND IT IS IMPORTANT WE ARE NOT SEEN BY THE WRONG ONES.
I UNDERSTAND, MONARCH.
THANK YOU.

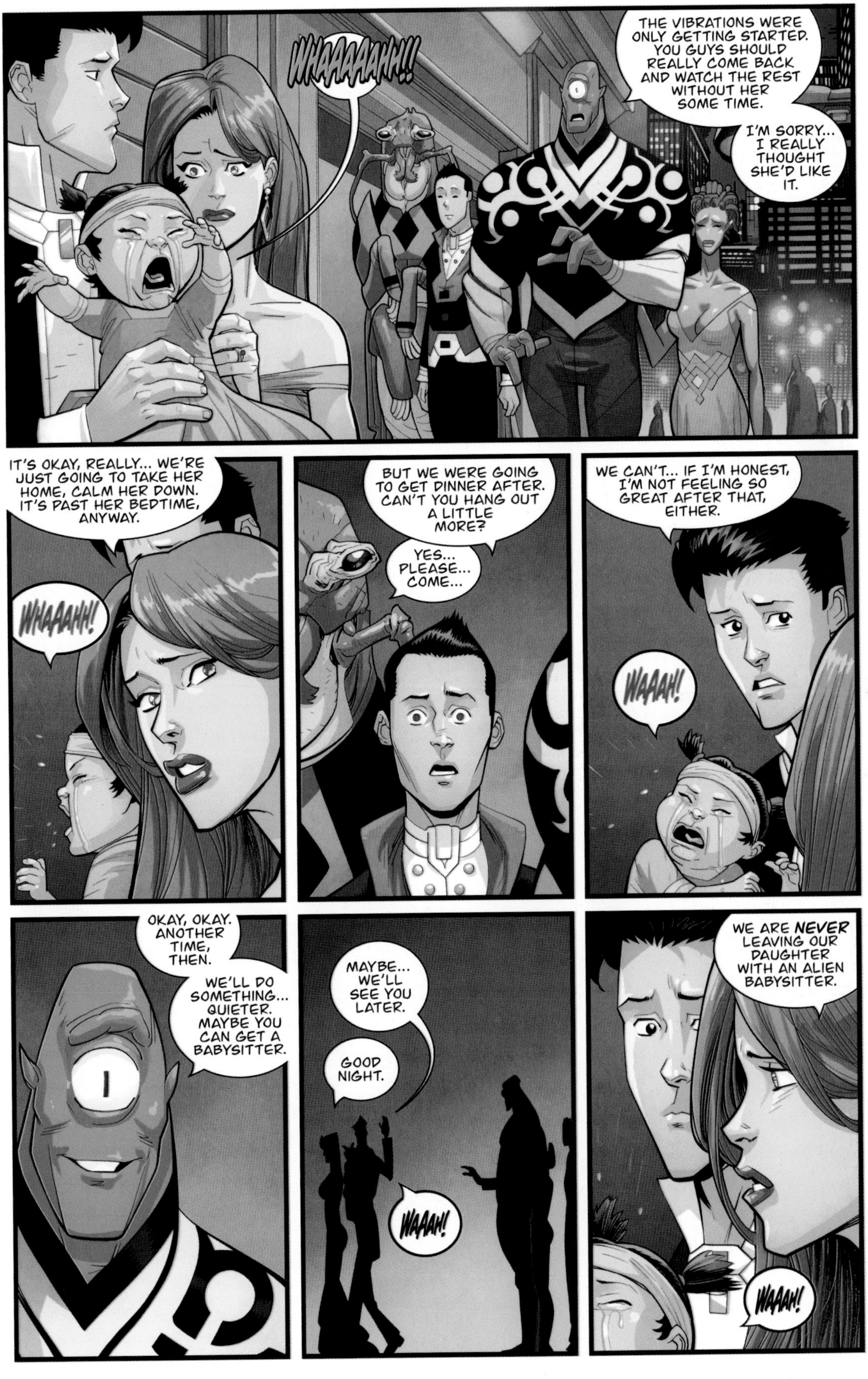
WHAAAAAAHH!!
THE VIBRATIONS WERE ONLY GETTING STARTED. YOU GUYS SHOULD REALLY COME BACK AND WATCH THE REST WITHOUT HER SOME TIME.
I'M SORRY... I REALLY THOUGHT SHE'D LIKE IT.
IT'S OKAY, REALLY... WE'RE JUST GOING TO TAKE HER HOME, CALM HER DOWN. IT'S PAST HER BEDTIME, ANYWAY.
WHAAAHH!
BUT WE WERE GOING TO GET DINNER AFTER. CAN'T YOU HANG OUT A LITTLE MORE?
YES... PLEASE... COME...
WE CAN'T... IF I'M HONEST, I'M NOT FEELING SO GREAT AFTER THAT, EITHER.
WAAAH!
OKAY, OKAY. ANOTHER TIME, THEN.
WE'LL DO SOMETHING... QUIETER. MAYBE YOU CAN GET A BABYSITTER.
MAYBE... WE'LL SEE YOU LATER.
GOOD NIGHT.
WAAAH!
WE ARE NEVER LEAVING OUR DAUGHTER WITH AN ALIEN BABYSITTER.
WAAAH!

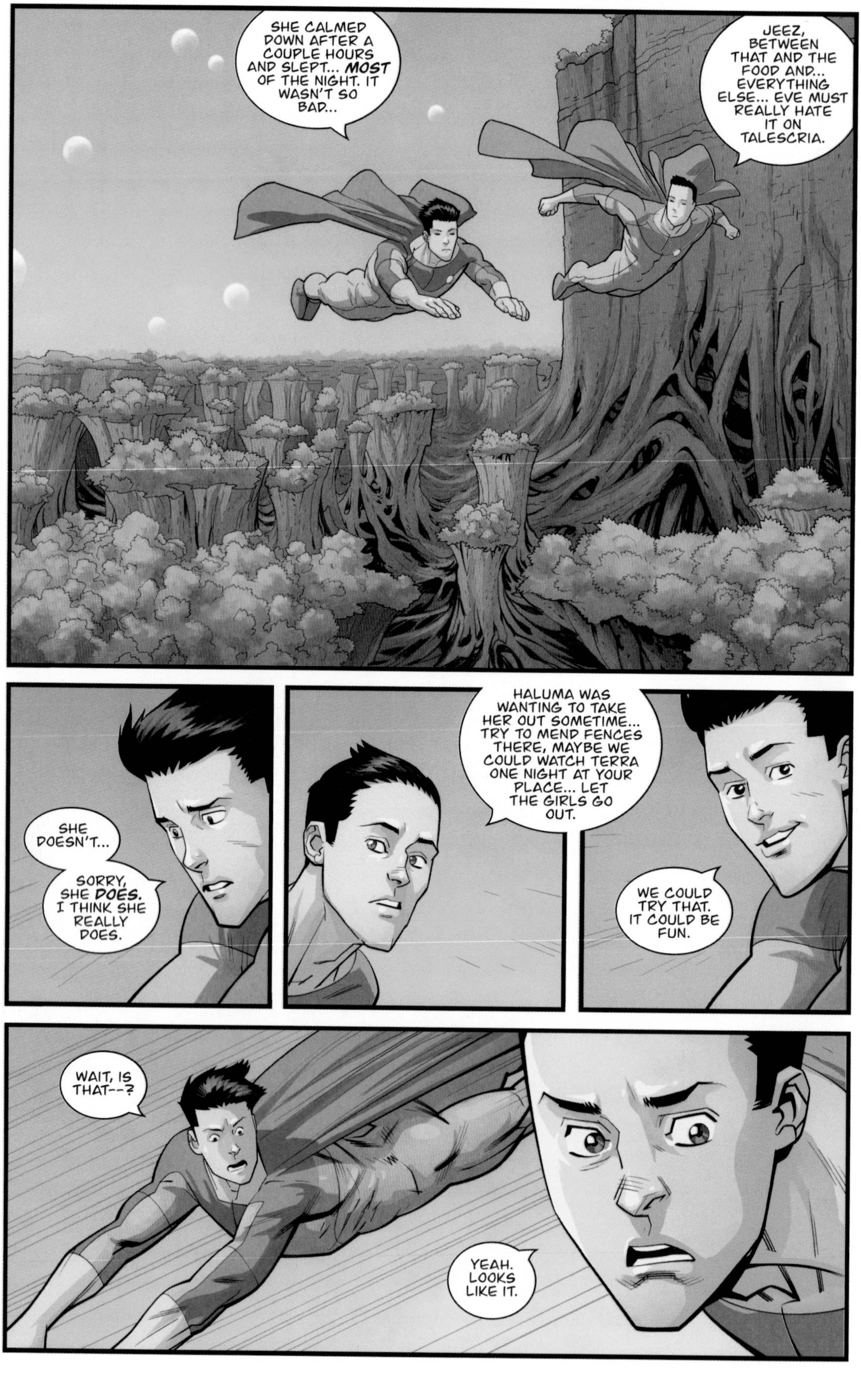
SHE CALMED DOWN AFTER A COUPLE HOURS AND SLEPT... **MOST** OF THE NIGHT. IT WASN'T SO BAD...
JEEZ, BETWEEN THAT AND THE FOOD AND... EVERYTHING ELSE... EVE MUST REALLY HATE IT ON TALESCRIA.
SHE DOESN'T...
SORRY, SHE **DOES.** I THINK SHE REALLY DOES.
HALUMA WAS WANTING TO TAKE HER OUT SOMETIME... TRY TO MEND FENCES THERE, MAYBE WE COULD WATCH TERRA ONE NIGHT AT YOUR PLACE... LET THE GIRLS GO OUT.
WE COULD TRY THAT. IT COULD BE FUN.
WAIT, IS THAT--?
YEAH. LOOKS LIKE IT.

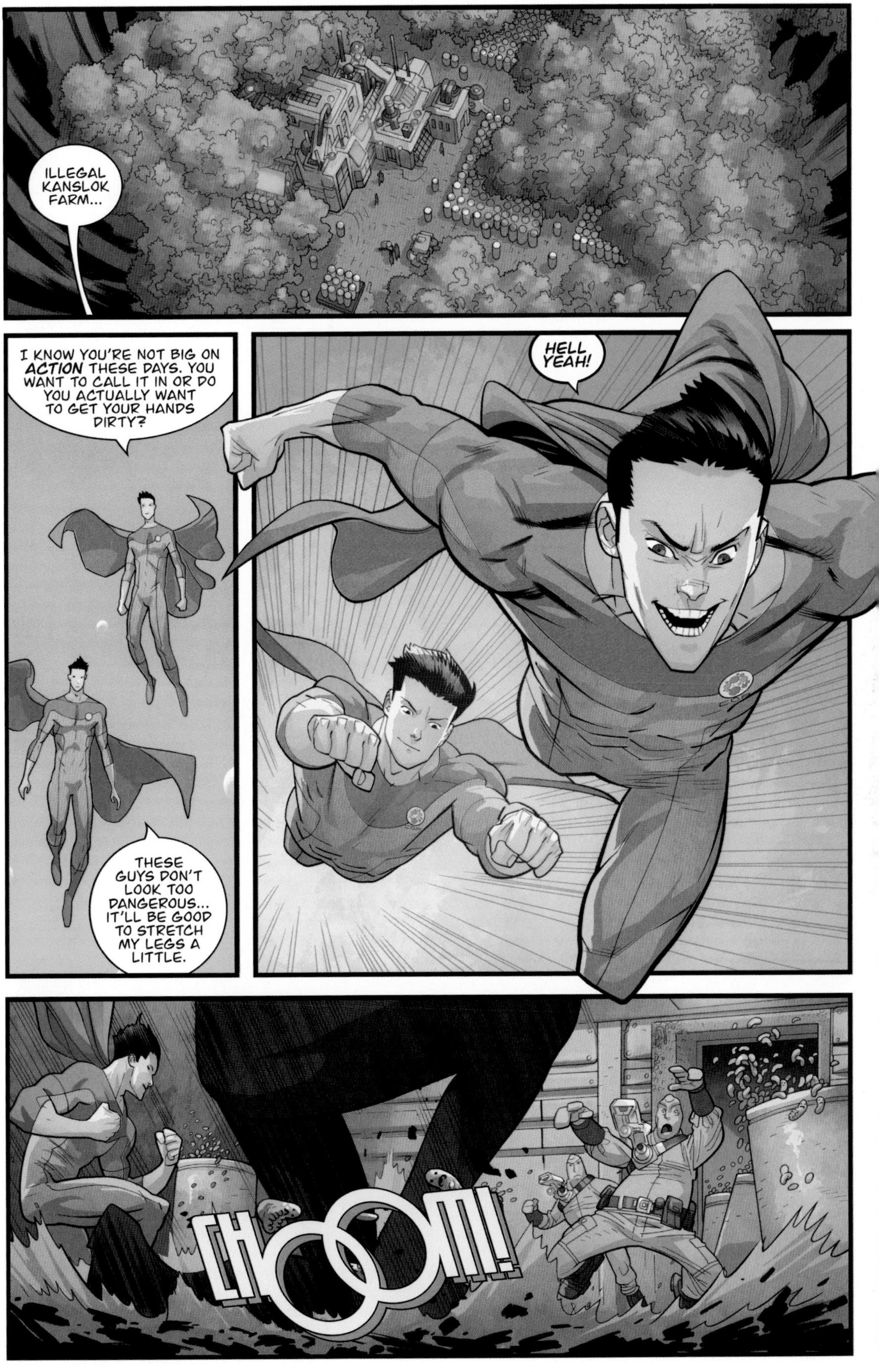
ILLEGAL KANSLOK FARM...
I KNOW YOU'RE NOT BIG ON ACTION THESE DAYS. YOU WANT TO CALL IT IN OR DO YOU ACTUALLY WANT TO GET YOUR HANDS DIRTY?
THESE GUYS DON'T LOOK TOO DANGEROUS... IT'LL BE GOOD TO STRETCH MY LEGS A LITTLE.
HELL YEAH!
CHOOM!

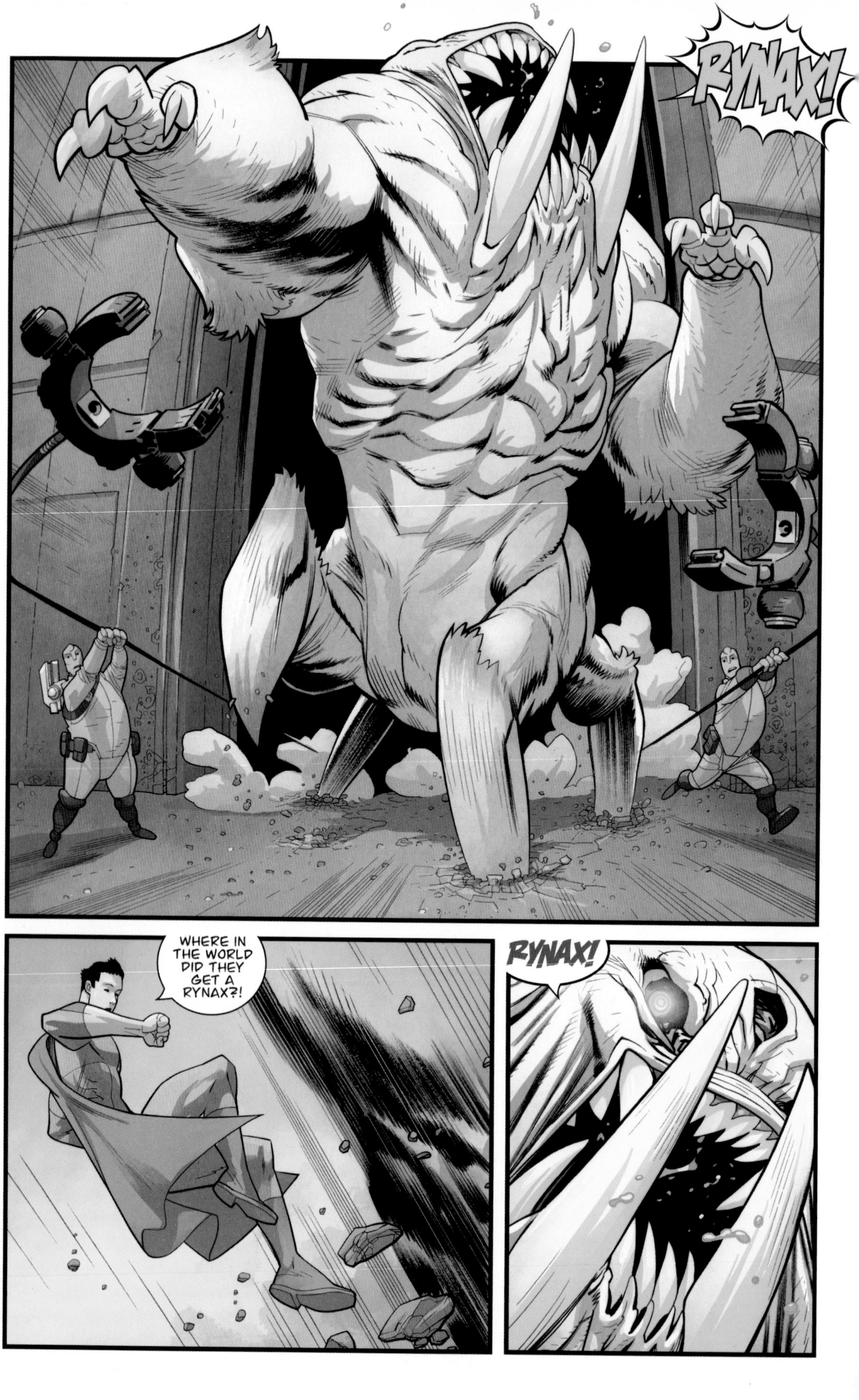
RYNAX!
WHERE IN THE WORLD DID THEY GET A RYNAX?!
RYNAX!

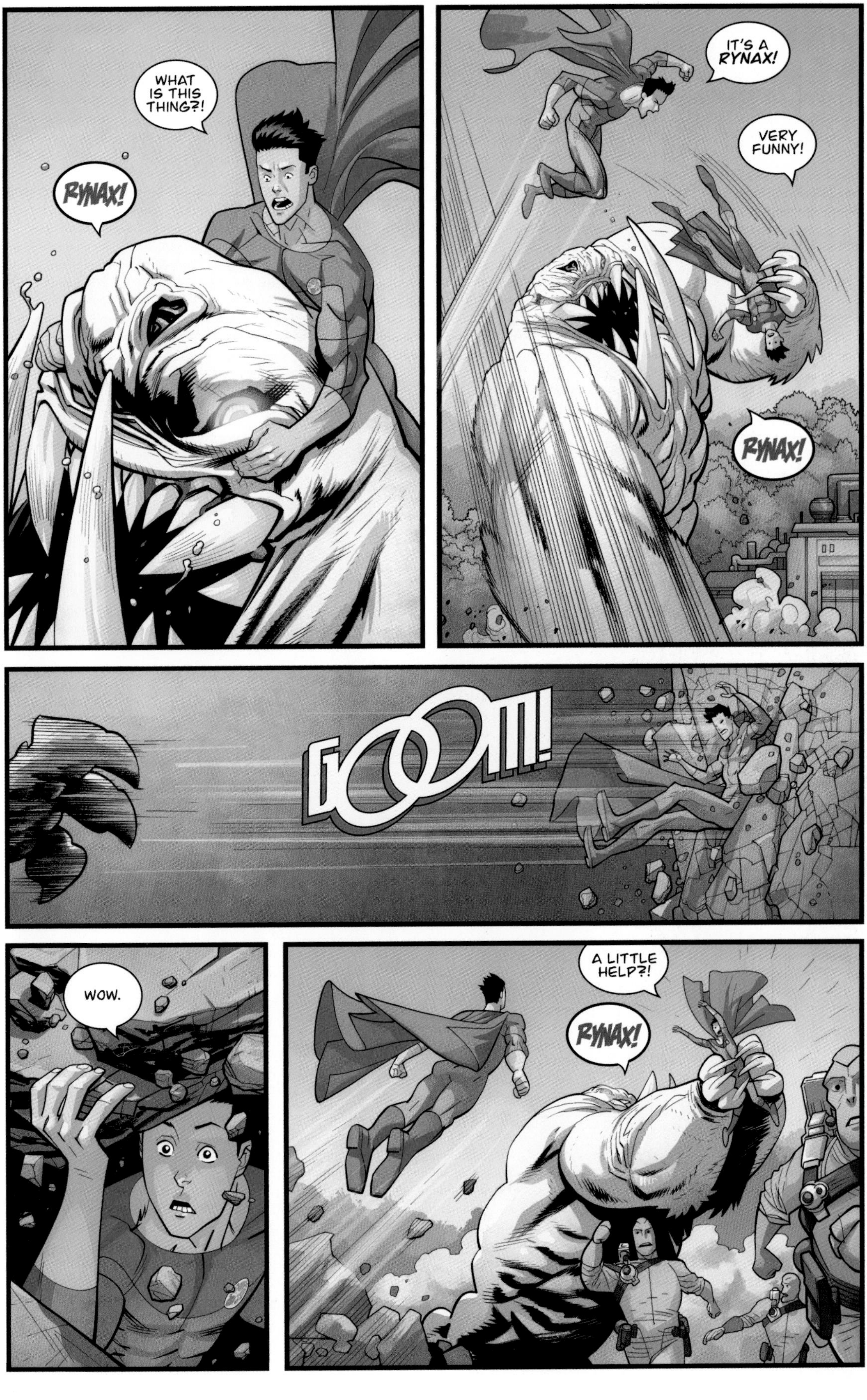
WHAT IS THIS THING?!
RYNAX!
IT'S A RYNAX!
VERY FUNNY!
RYNAX!
GOOM!
WOW.
A LITTLE HELP?!
RYNAX!

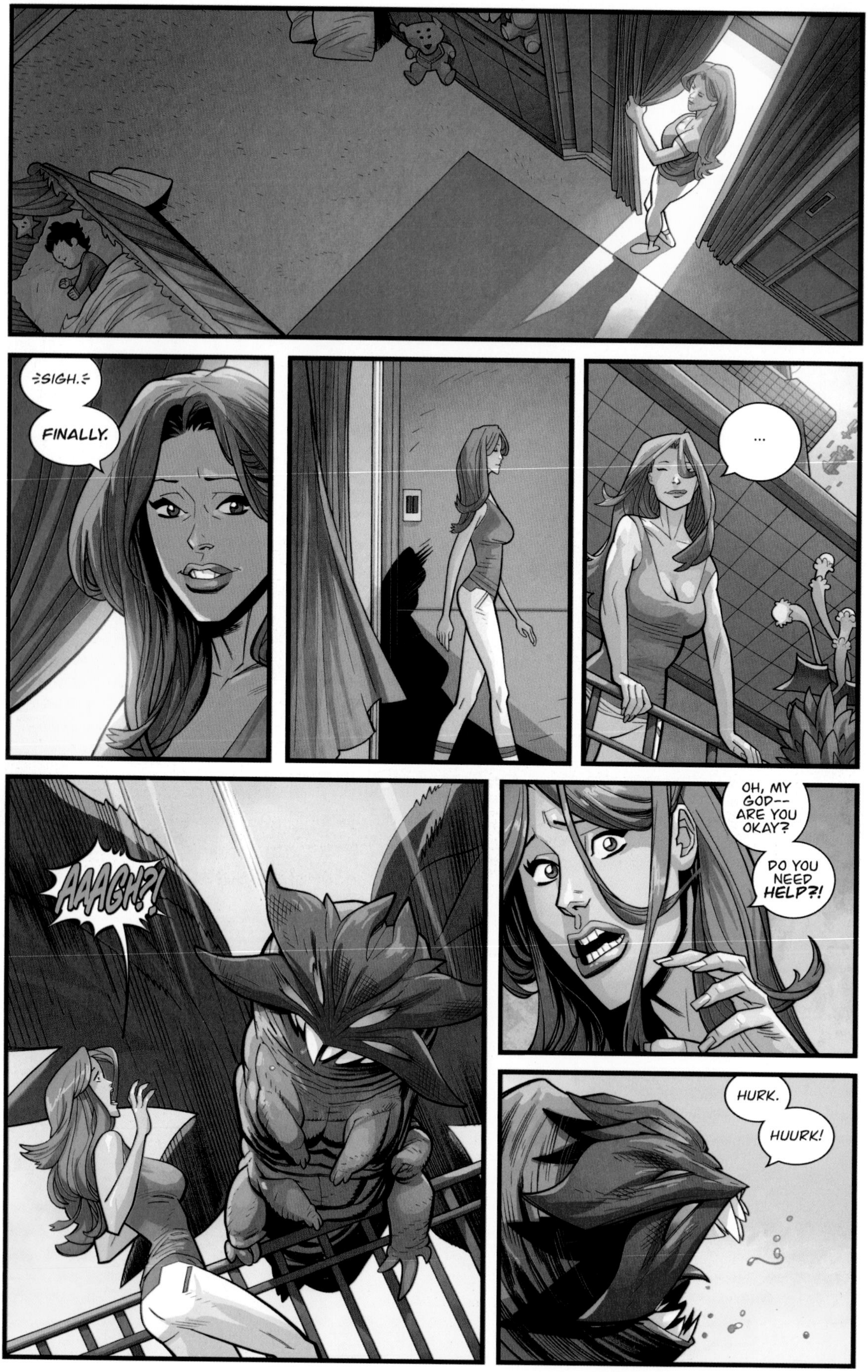

=SIGH.=
FINALLY.
...
AAAGH?!
OH, MY GOD-- ARE YOU OKAY?
DO YOU NEED HELP?!
HURK.
HUURK!

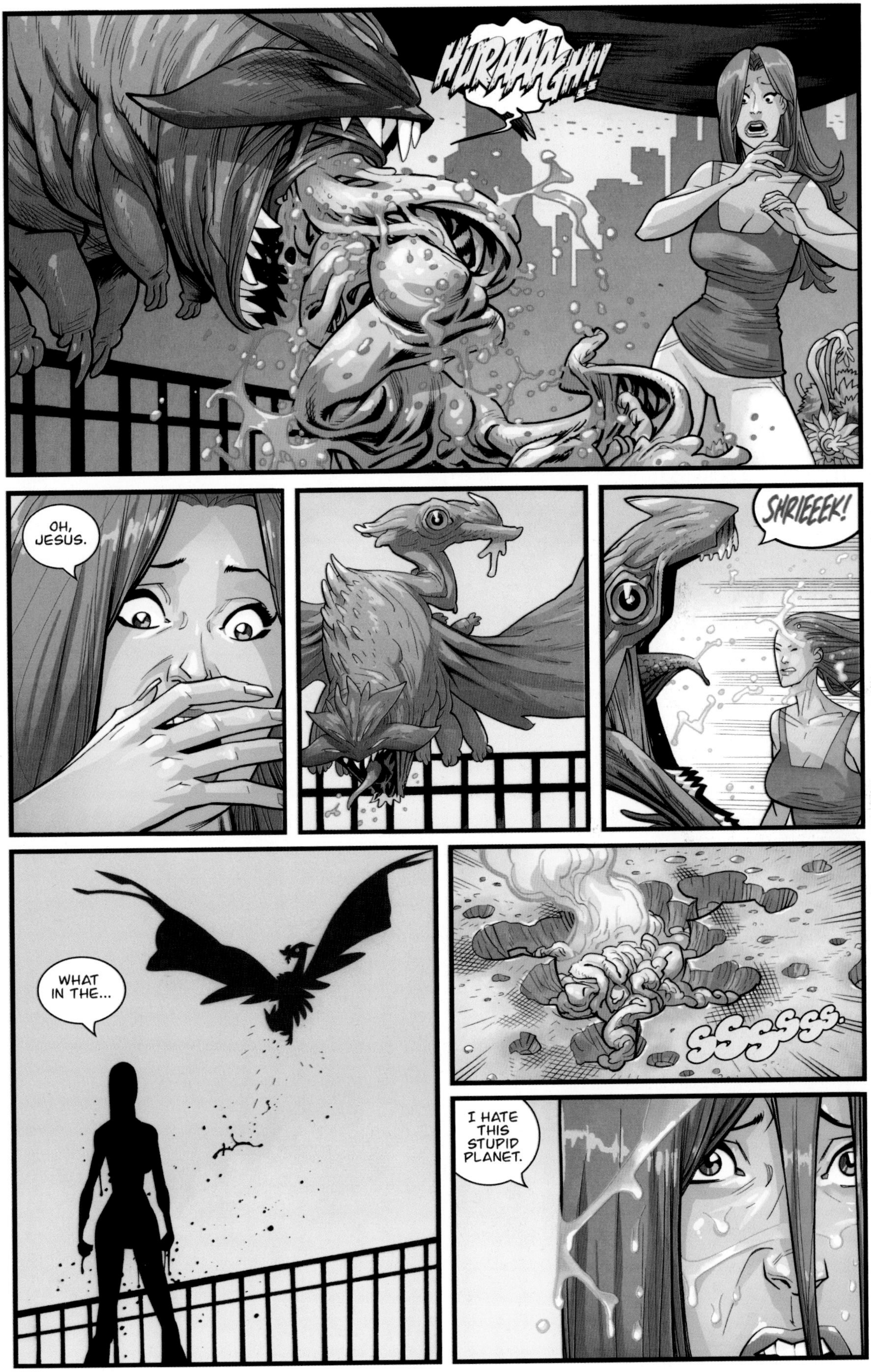
HURAAAGH!!
OH, JESUS.
SHRIEEEK!
WHAT IN THE...
SSSSSS
I HATE THIS STUPID PLANET.

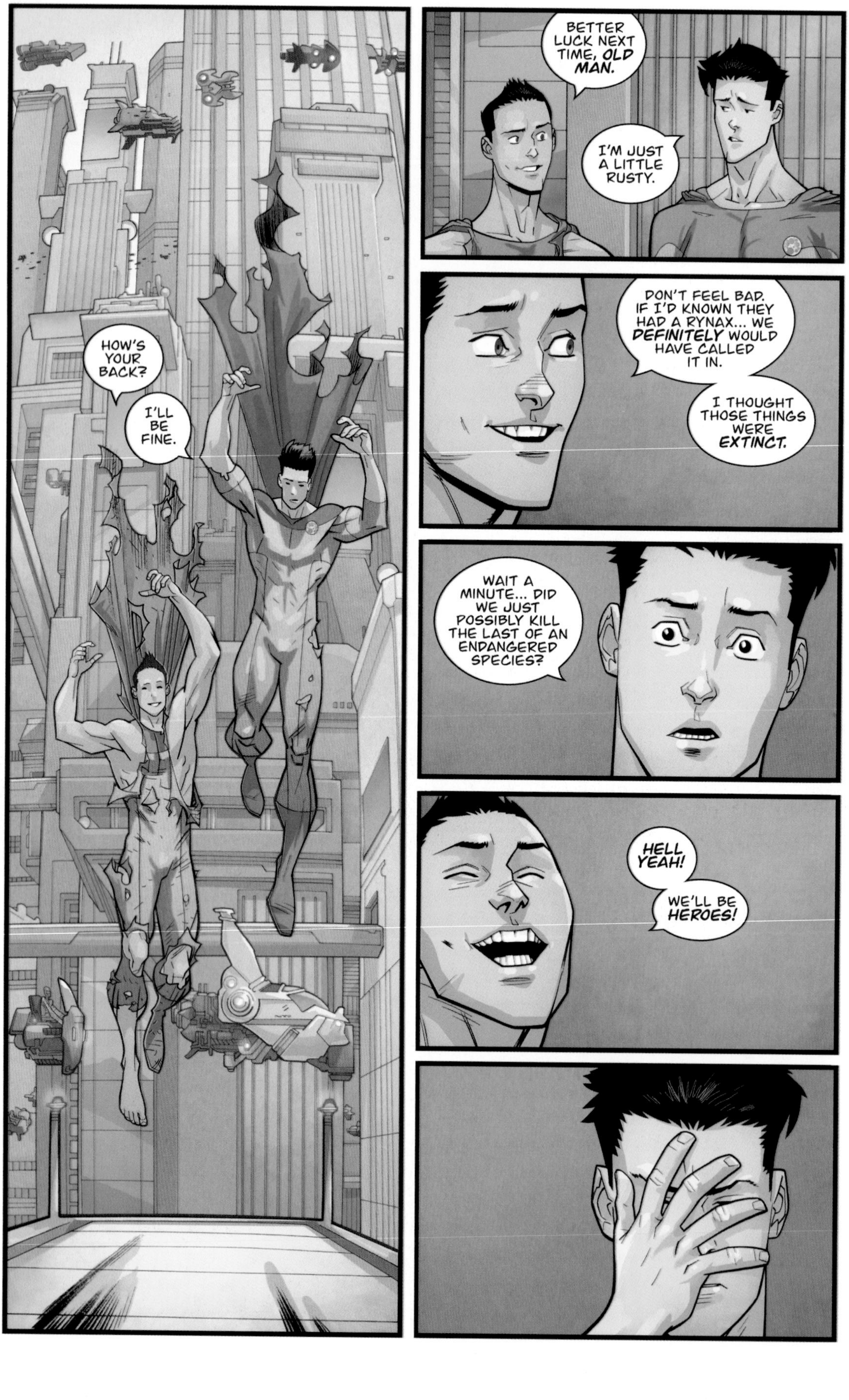
HOW'S YOUR BACK?
I'LL BE FINE.
BETTER LUCK NEXT TIME, OLD MAN.
I'M JUST A LITTLE RUSTY.
DON'T FEEL BAD. IF I'D KNOWN THEY HAD A RYNAX... WE DEFINITELY WOULD HAVE CALLED IT IN.
I THOUGHT THOSE THINGS WERE EXTINCT.
WAIT A MINUTE... DID WE JUST POSSIBLY KILL THE LAST OF AN ENDANGERED SPECIES?
HELL YEAH!
WE'LL BE HEROES!

I WAS KIDDING ABOUT THEM BEING EXTINCT, YOU BIG SOFTY.

YOU'RE A JERK.

MAN... *EVE* WOULD HAVE KILLED ME IF SHE FOUND OUT.

YOU'RE SO GULLIBLE.

GREAT ALLEN WILL SEE YOU NOW.

HE APOLOGIZES FOR THE DELAY.

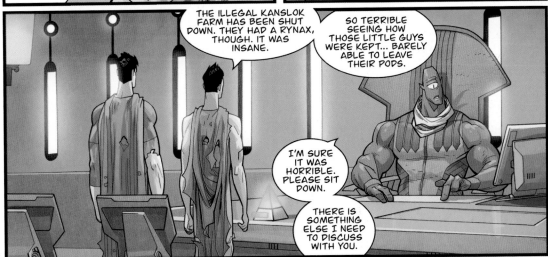

THE ILLEGAL KANSLOK FARM HAS BEEN SHUT DOWN. THEY HAD A RYNAX, THOUGH. IT WAS INSANE.

SO TERRIBLE SEEING HOW THOSE LITTLE GUYS WERE KEPT... BARELY ABLE TO LEAVE THEIR PODS.

I'M SURE IT WAS HORRIBLE. PLEASE SIT DOWN.

THERE IS SOMETHING ELSE I NEED TO DISCUSS WITH YOU.

WE'VE LOCATED *THRAGG.*

SPACE RACER IS INTERCEPTING WITH A TEAM. HE'S BEEN DIRECTED TO MONITOR HIM, WITHOUT GIVING AWAY HIS POSITION. HE'LL KEEP TABS ON HIM... HE'S BEEN ON PLANET FOR A WHILE.

WE'RE HOPING HE REMAINS *UNDETECTED.*

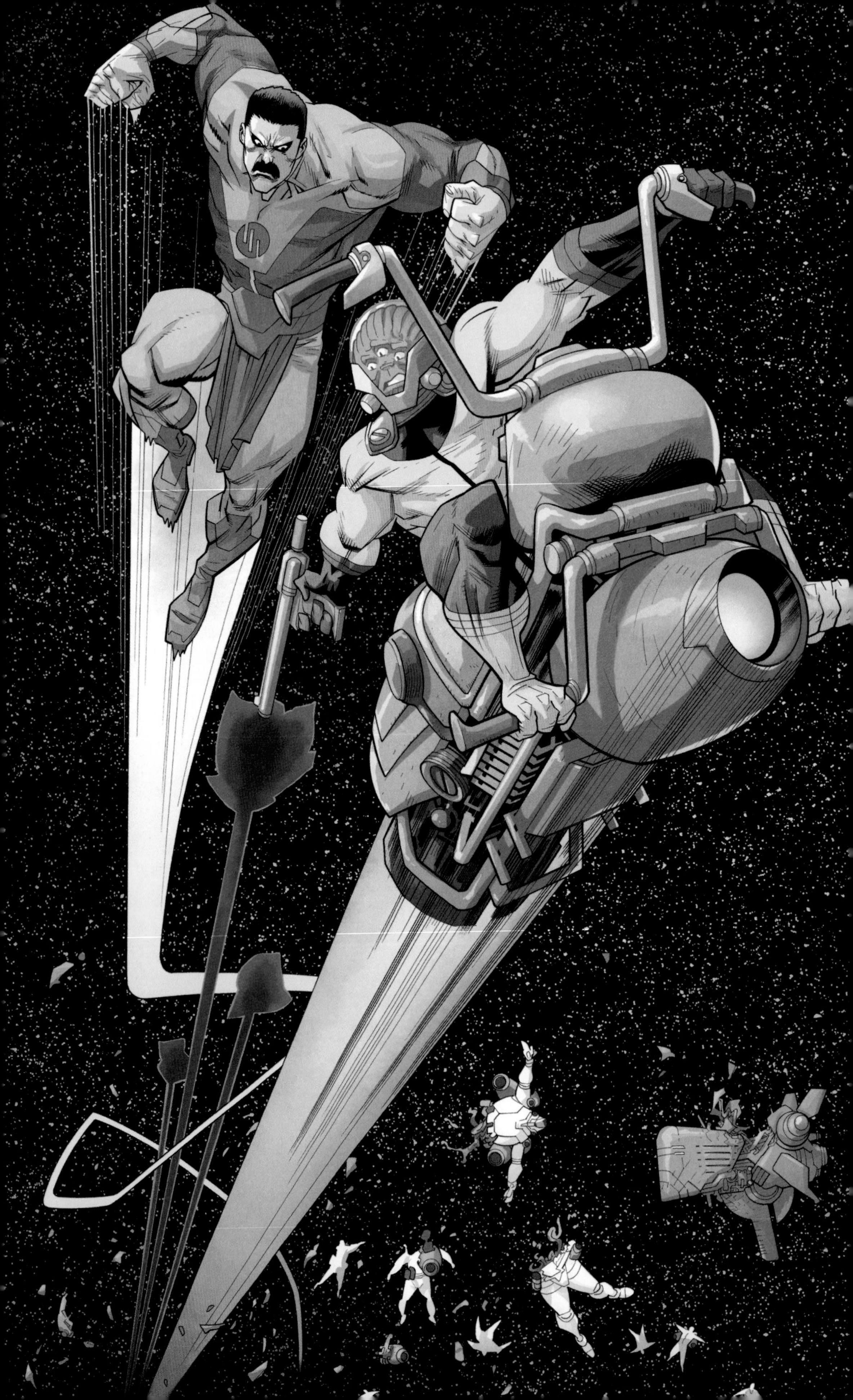

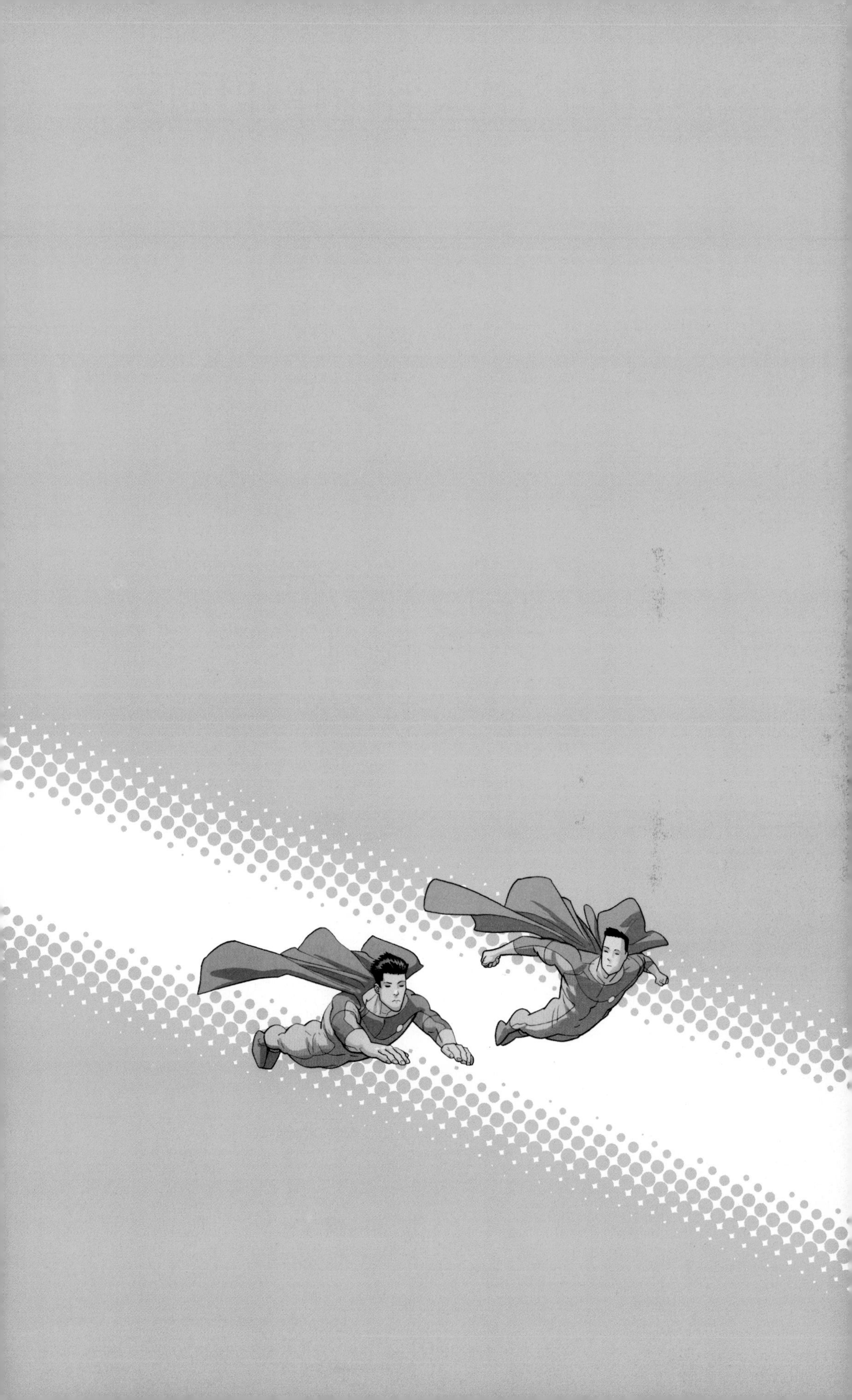

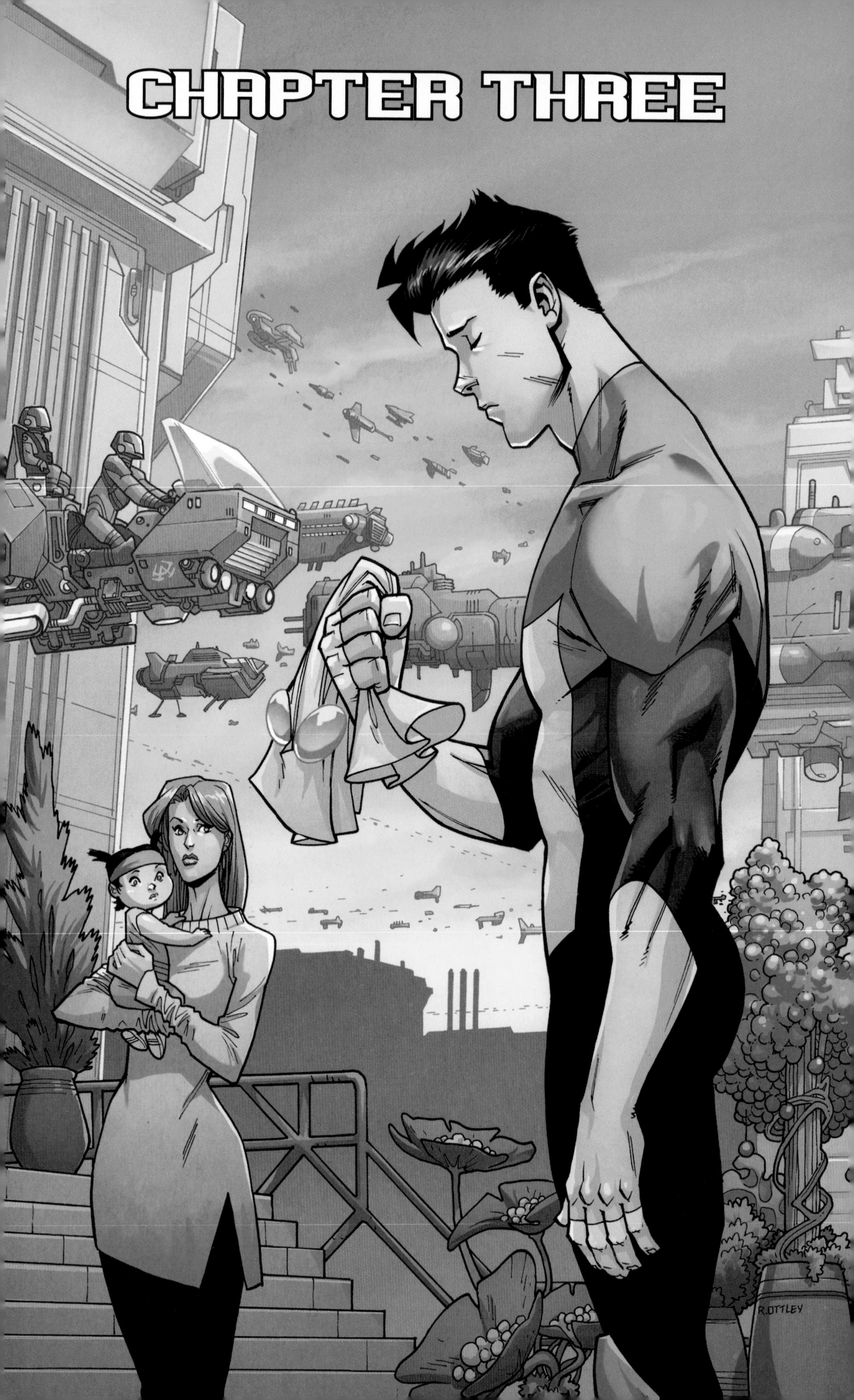
CHAPTER THREE
R.OTTLEY

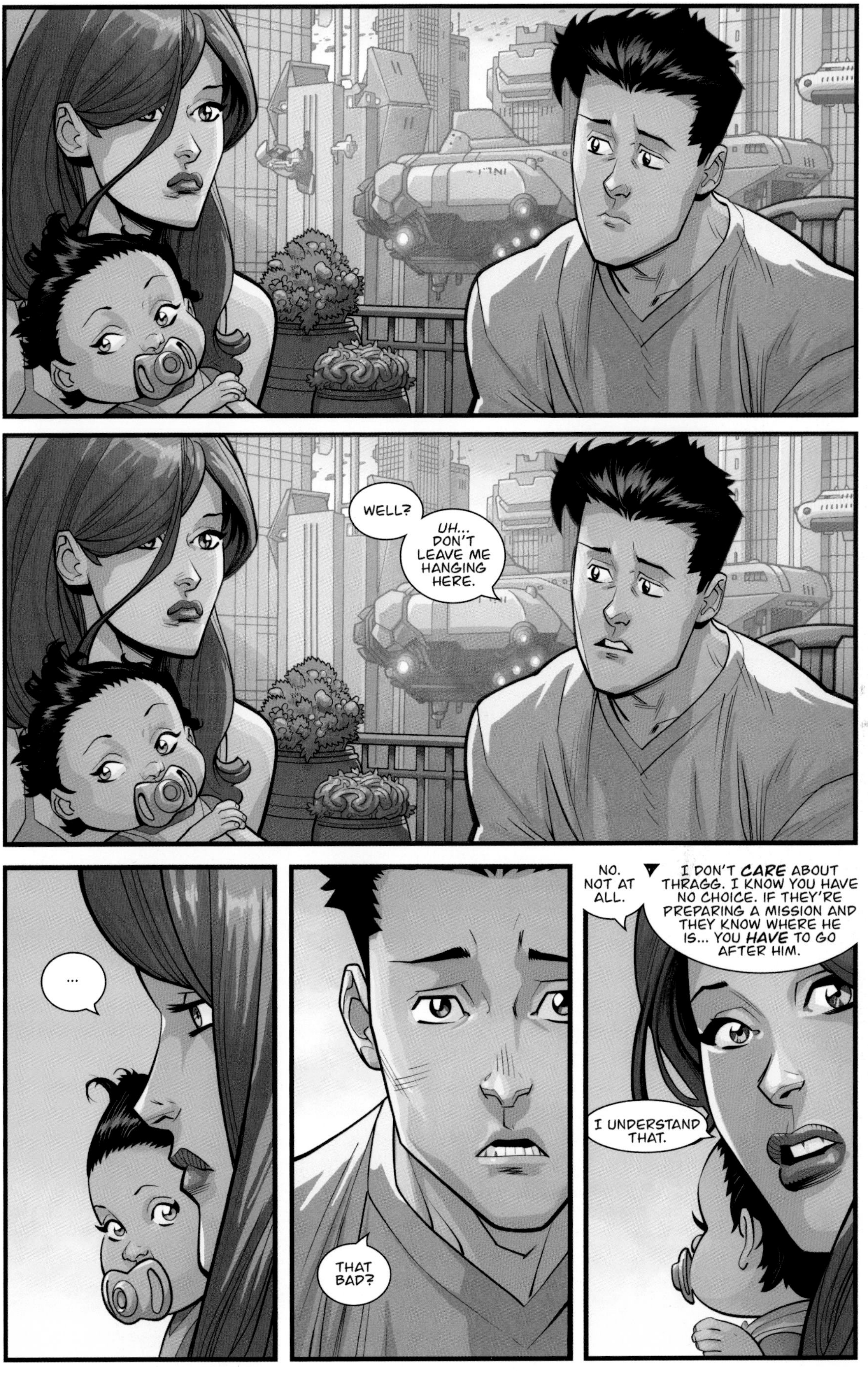
WELL?
UH... DON'T LEAVE ME HANGING HERE.
...
THAT BAD?
NO. NOT AT ALL.
I DON'T CARE ABOUT THRAGG. I KNOW YOU HAVE NO CHOICE. IF THEY'RE PREPARING A MISSION AND THEY KNOW WHERE HE IS... YOU HAVE TO GO AFTER HIM.
I UNDERSTAND THAT.

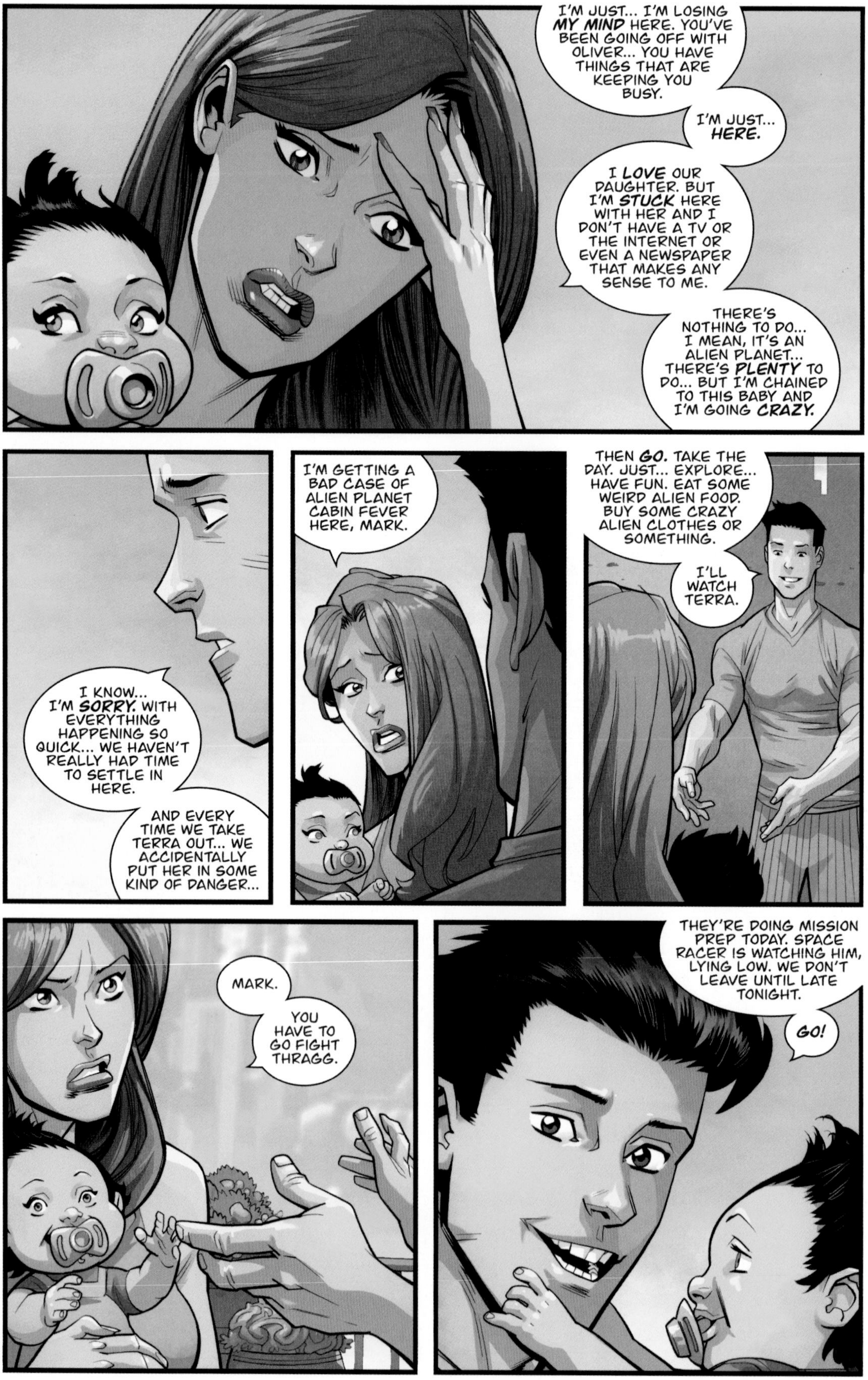
I'M JUST... I'M LOSING MY MIND HERE. YOU'VE BEEN GOING OFF WITH OLIVER... YOU HAVE THINGS THAT ARE KEEPING YOU BUSY.
I'M JUST... HERE.
I LOVE OUR DAUGHTER. BUT I'M STUCK HERE WITH HER AND I DON'T HAVE A TV OR THE INTERNET OR EVEN A NEWSPAPER THAT MAKES ANY SENSE TO ME.
THERE'S NOTHING TO DO... I MEAN, IT'S AN ALIEN PLANET... THERE'S PLENTY TO DO... BUT I'M CHAINED TO THIS BABY AND I'M GOING CRAZY.
I KNOW... I'M SORRY. WITH EVERYTHING HAPPENING SO QUICK... WE HAVEN'T REALLY HAD TIME TO SETTLE IN HERE.
AND EVERY TIME WE TAKE TERRA OUT... WE ACCIDENTALLY PUT HER IN SOME KIND OF DANGER...
I'M GETTING A BAD CASE OF ALIEN PLANET CABIN FEVER HERE, MARK.
THEN GO. TAKE THE DAY. JUST... EXPLORE... HAVE FUN. EAT SOME WEIRD ALIEN FOOD. BUY SOME CRAZY ALIEN CLOTHES OR SOMETHING.
I'LL WATCH TERRA.
MARK.
YOU HAVE TO GO FIGHT THRAGG.
THEY'RE DOING MISSION PREP TODAY. SPACE RACER IS WATCHING HIM, LYING LOW. WE DON'T LEAVE UNTIL LATE TONIGHT.
GO!

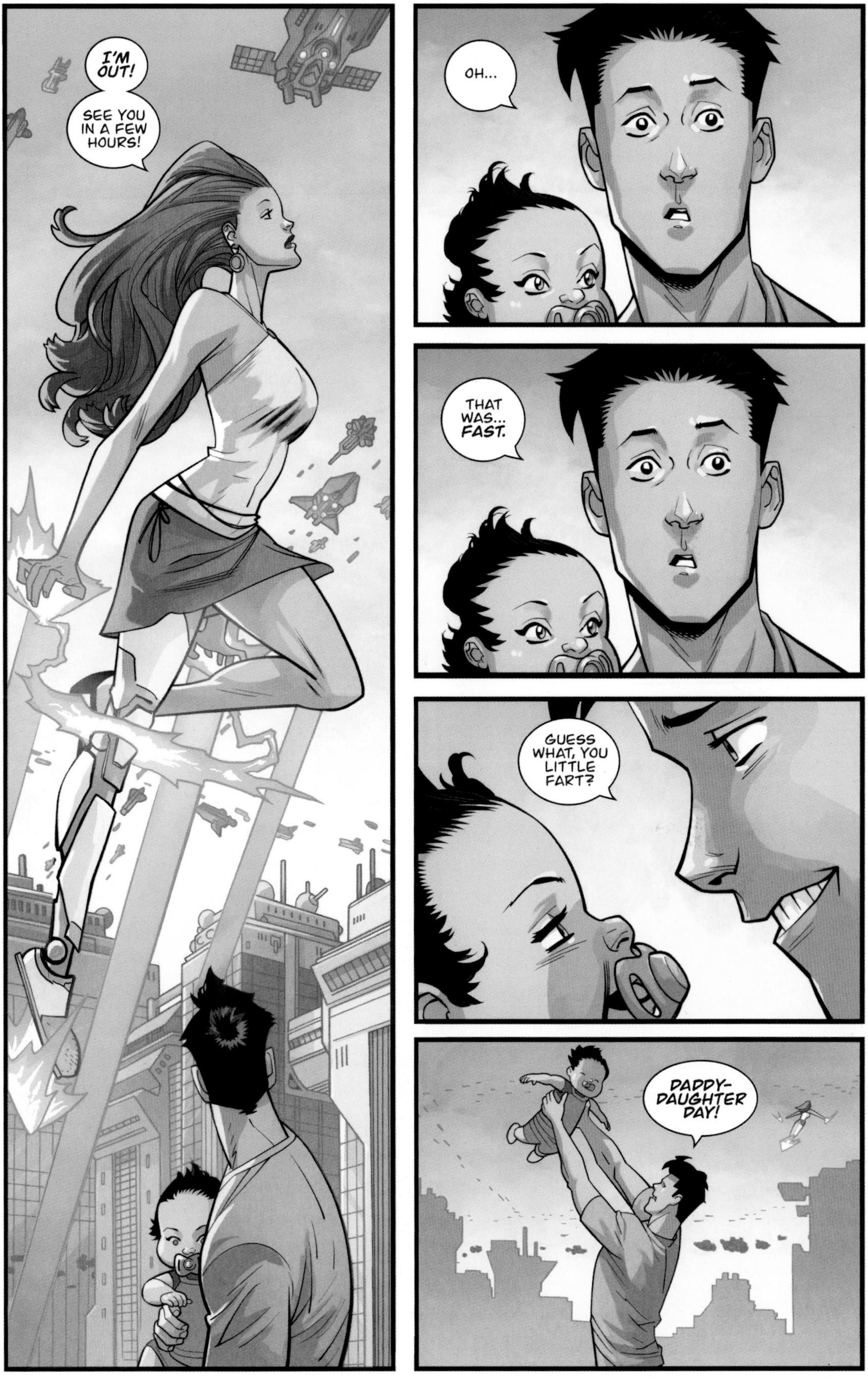
I'M OUT!
SEE YOU IN A FEW HOURS!
OH...
THAT WAS... FAST.
GUESS WHAT, YOU LITTLE FART?
DADDY-DAUGHTER DAY!

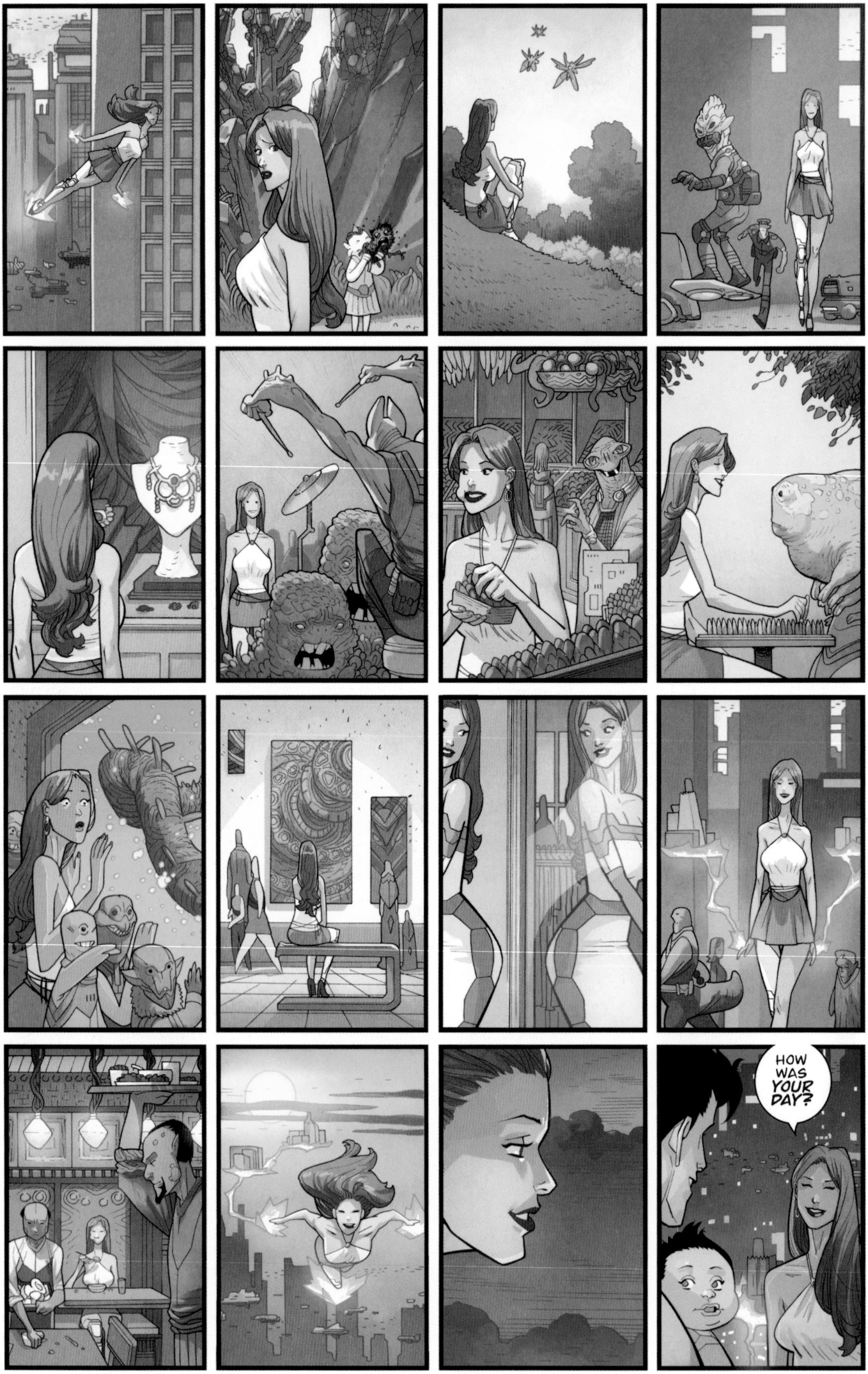
HOW WAS YOUR DAY?

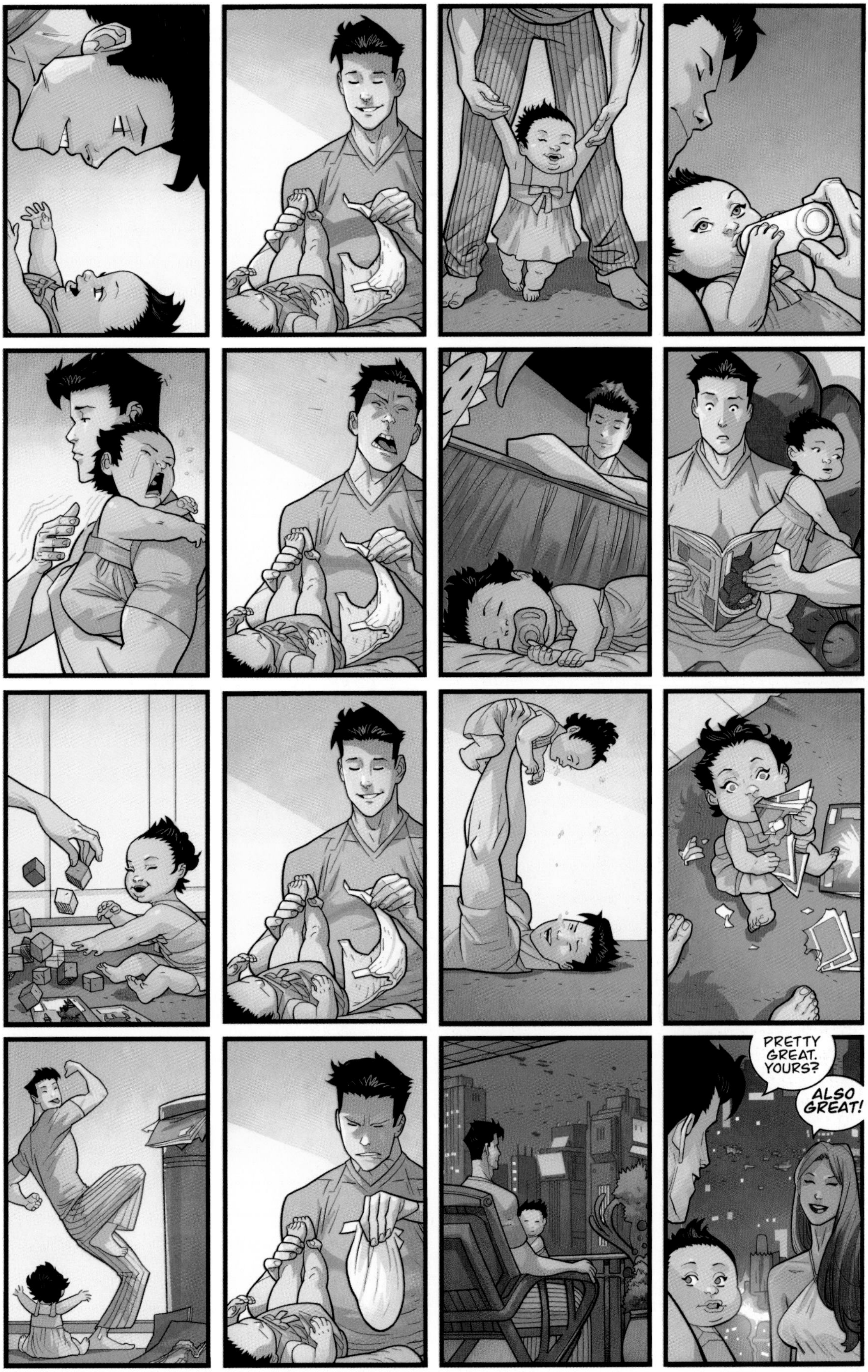
PRETTY GREAT. YOURS?
ALSO GREAT!

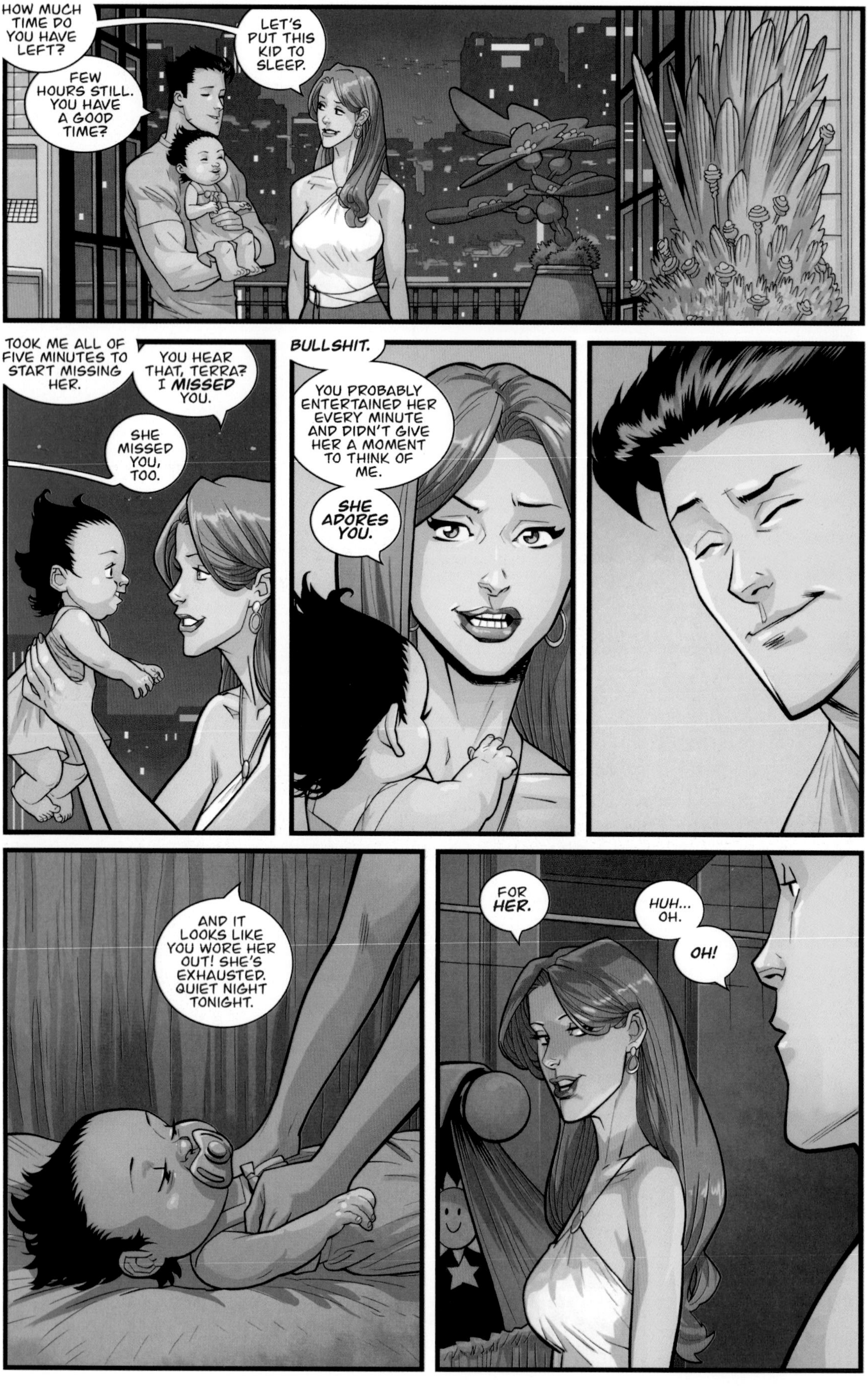
HOW MUCH TIME DO YOU HAVE LEFT?
FEW HOURS STILL. YOU HAVE A GOOD TIME?
LET'S PUT THIS KID TO SLEEP.
TOOK ME ALL OF FIVE MINUTES TO START MISSING HER.
YOU HEAR THAT, TERRA? I MISSED YOU.
SHE MISSED YOU, TOO.
BULLSHIT.
YOU PROBABLY ENTERTAINED HER EVERY MINUTE AND DIDN'T GIVE HER A MOMENT TO THINK OF ME.
SHE ADORES YOU.
AND IT LOOKS LIKE YOU WORE HER OUT! SHE'S EXHAUSTED. QUIET NIGHT TONIGHT.
FOR HER.
HUH... OH.
OH!

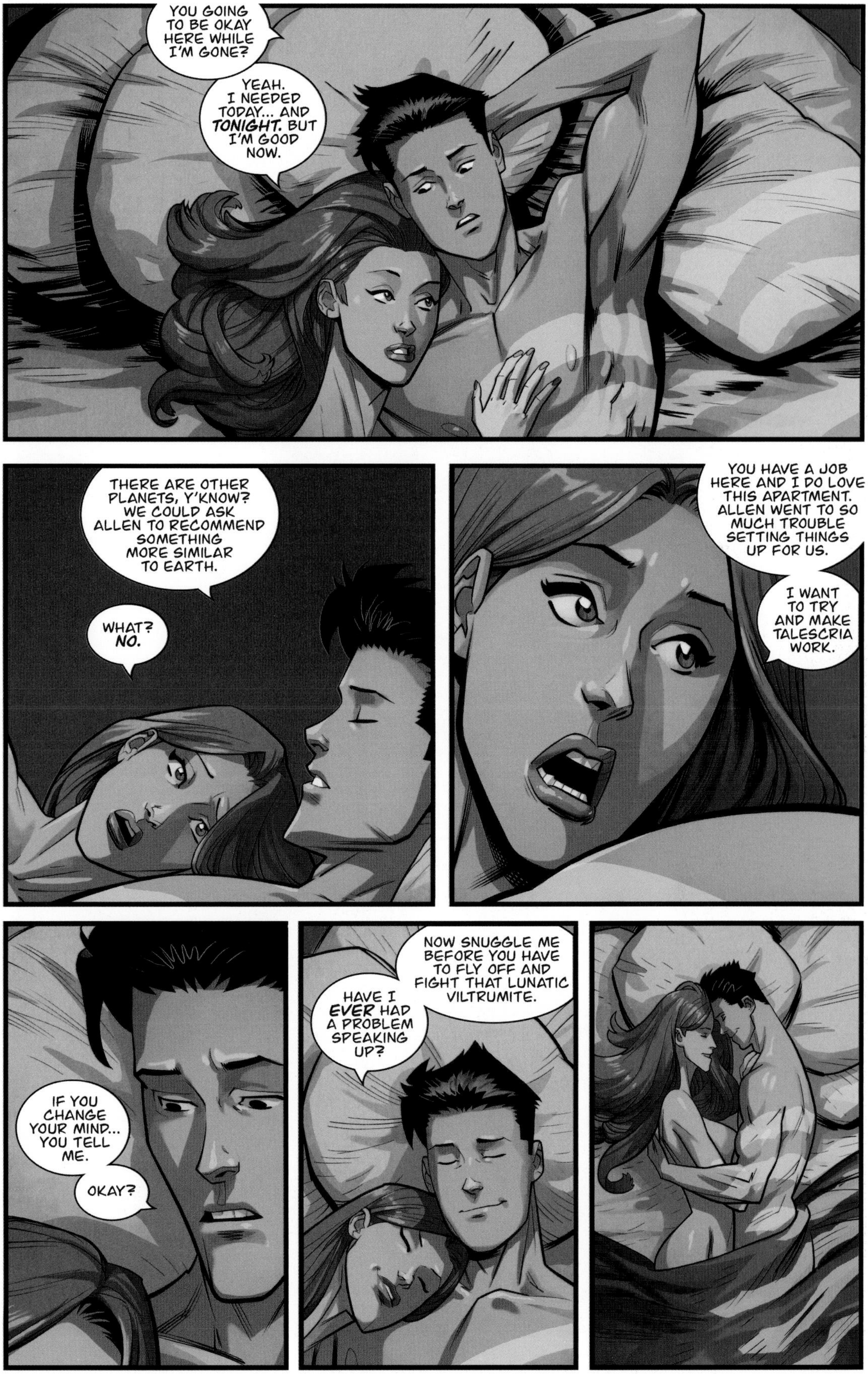
YOU GOING TO BE OKAY HERE WHILE I'M GONE?
YEAH. I NEEDED TODAY... AND TONIGHT. BUT I'M GOOD NOW.
THERE ARE OTHER PLANETS, Y'KNOW? WE COULD ASK ALLEN TO RECOMMEND SOMETHING MORE SIMILAR TO EARTH.
WHAT? NO.
YOU HAVE A JOB HERE AND I DO LOVE THIS APARTMENT. ALLEN WENT TO SO MUCH TROUBLE SETTING THINGS UP FOR US.
I WANT TO TRY AND MAKE TALESCRIA WORK.
IF YOU CHANGE YOUR MIND... YOU TELL ME.
OKAY?
HAVE I EVER HAD A PROBLEM SPEAKING UP?
NOW SNUGGLE ME BEFORE YOU HAVE TO FLY OFF AND FIGHT THAT LUNATIC VILTRUMITE.

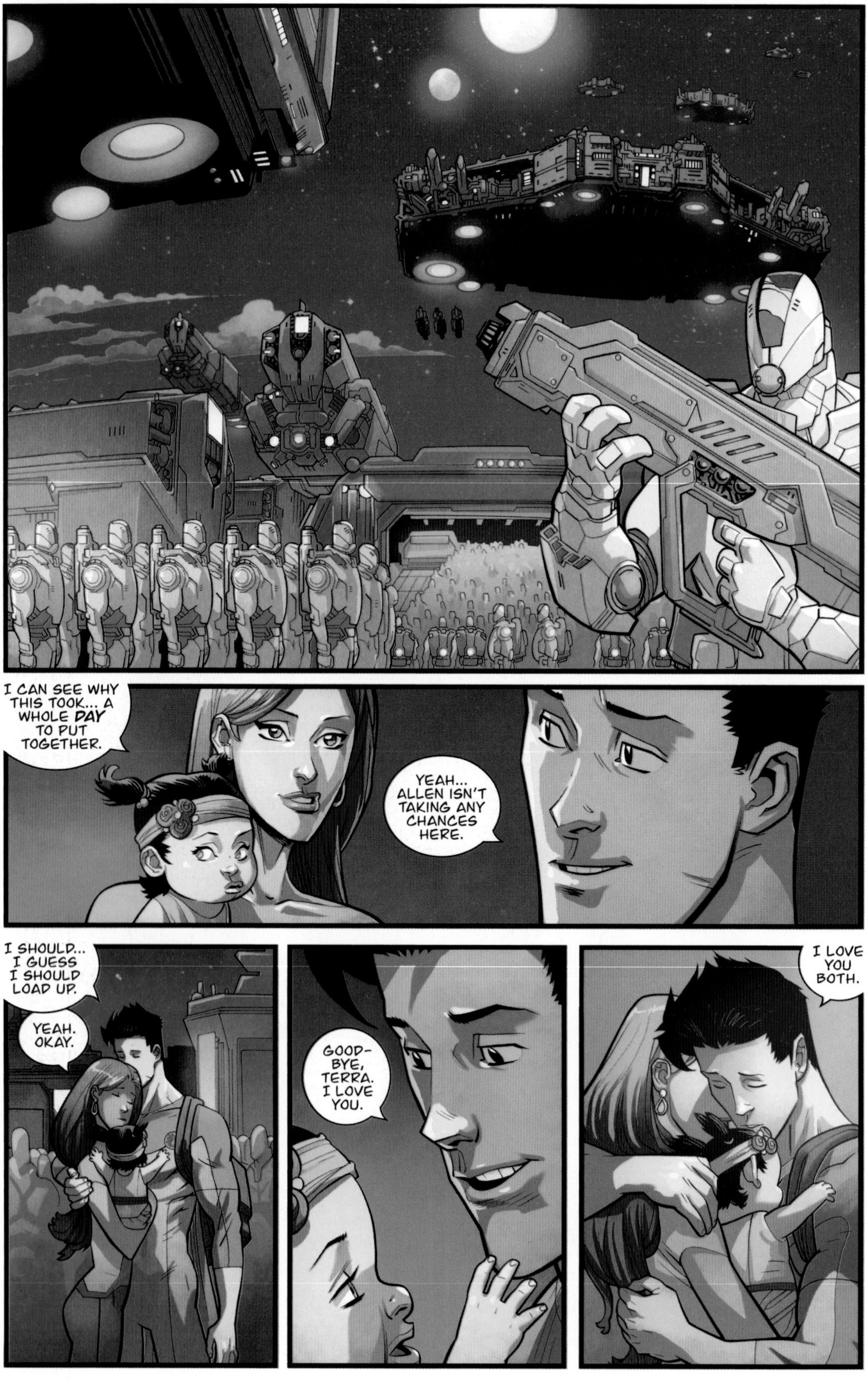
I CAN SEE WHY THIS TOOK... A WHOLE DAY TO PUT TOGETHER.
YEAH... ALLEN ISN'T TAKING ANY CHANCES HERE.
I SHOULD... I GUESS I SHOULD LOAD UP.
YEAH. OKAY.
GOOD-BYE, TERRA. I LOVE YOU.
I LOVE YOU BOTH.

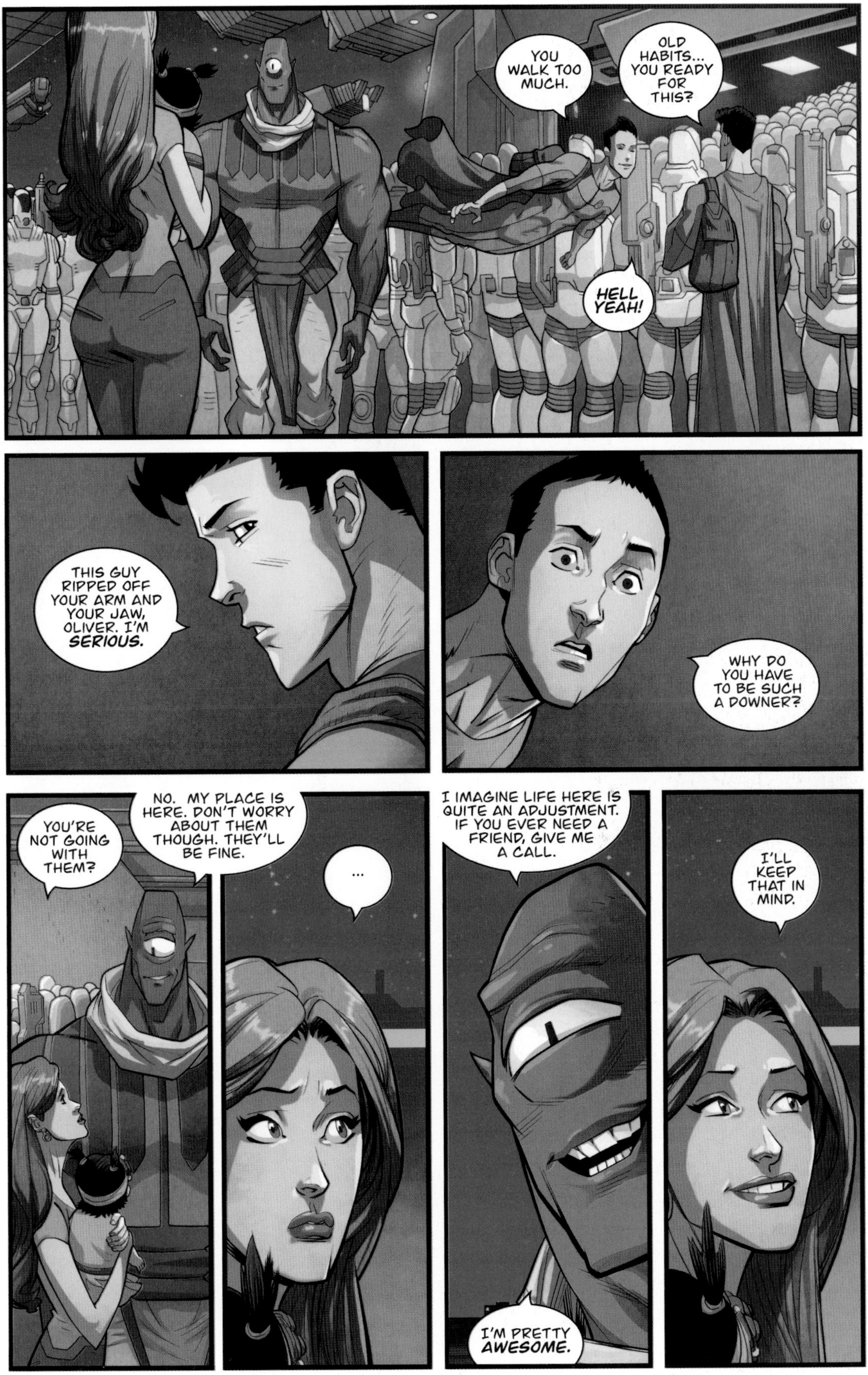
YOU WALK TOO MUCH.
OLD HABITS... YOU READY FOR THIS?
HELL YEAH!
THIS GUY RIPPED OFF YOUR ARM AND YOUR JAW, OLIVER. I'M SERIOUS.
WHY DO YOU HAVE TO BE SUCH A DOWNER?
YOU'RE NOT GOING WITH THEM?
NO. MY PLACE IS HERE. DON'T WORRY ABOUT THEM THOUGH. THEY'LL BE FINE.
...
I IMAGINE LIFE HERE IS QUITE AN ADJUSTMENT. IF YOU EVER NEED A FRIEND, GIVE ME A CALL.
I'M PRETTY AWESOME.
I'LL KEEP THAT IN MIND.

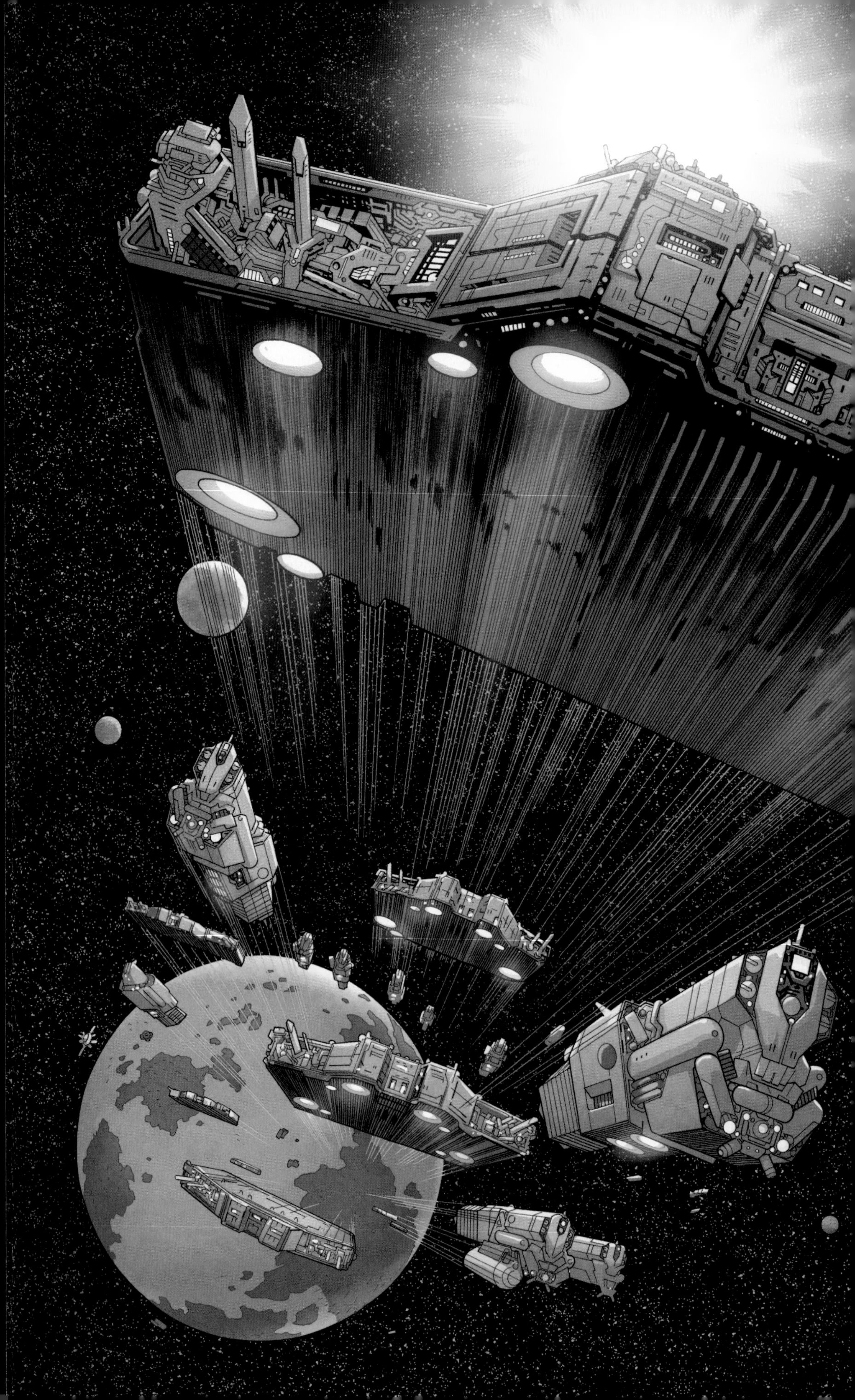

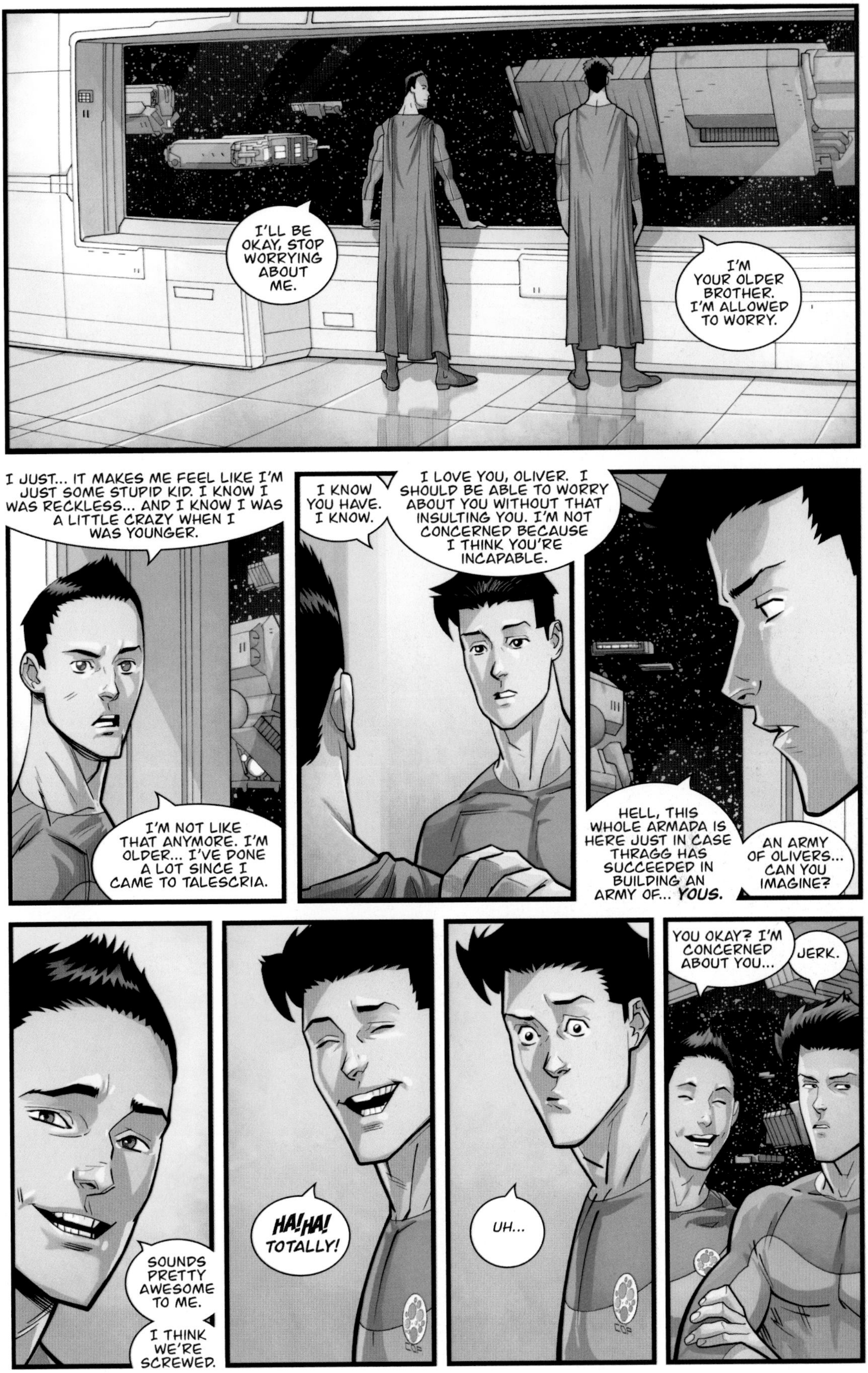
I'LL BE OKAY, STOP WORRYING ABOUT ME.
I'M YOUR OLDER BROTHER. I'M ALLOWED TO WORRY.
I JUST... IT MAKES ME FEEL LIKE I'M JUST SOME STUPID KID. I KNOW I WAS RECKLESS... AND I KNOW I WAS A LITTLE CRAZY WHEN I WAS YOUNGER.
I'M NOT LIKE THAT ANYMORE. I'M OLDER... I'VE DONE A LOT SINCE I CAME TO TALESCRIA.
I KNOW YOU HAVE. I KNOW.
I LOVE YOU, OLIVER. I SHOULD BE ABLE TO WORRY ABOUT YOU WITHOUT THAT INSULTING YOU. I'M NOT CONCERNED BECAUSE I THINK YOU'RE INCAPABLE.
HELL, THIS WHOLE ARMADA IS HERE JUST IN CASE THRAGG HAS SUCCEEDED IN BUILDING AN ARMY OF... YOUS.
AN ARMY OF OLIVERS... CAN YOU IMAGINE?
SOUNDS PRETTY AWESOME TO ME.
I THINK WE'RE SCREWED.
HA! HA! TOTALLY!
UH...
YOU OKAY? I'M CONCERNED ABOUT YOU...
JERK.

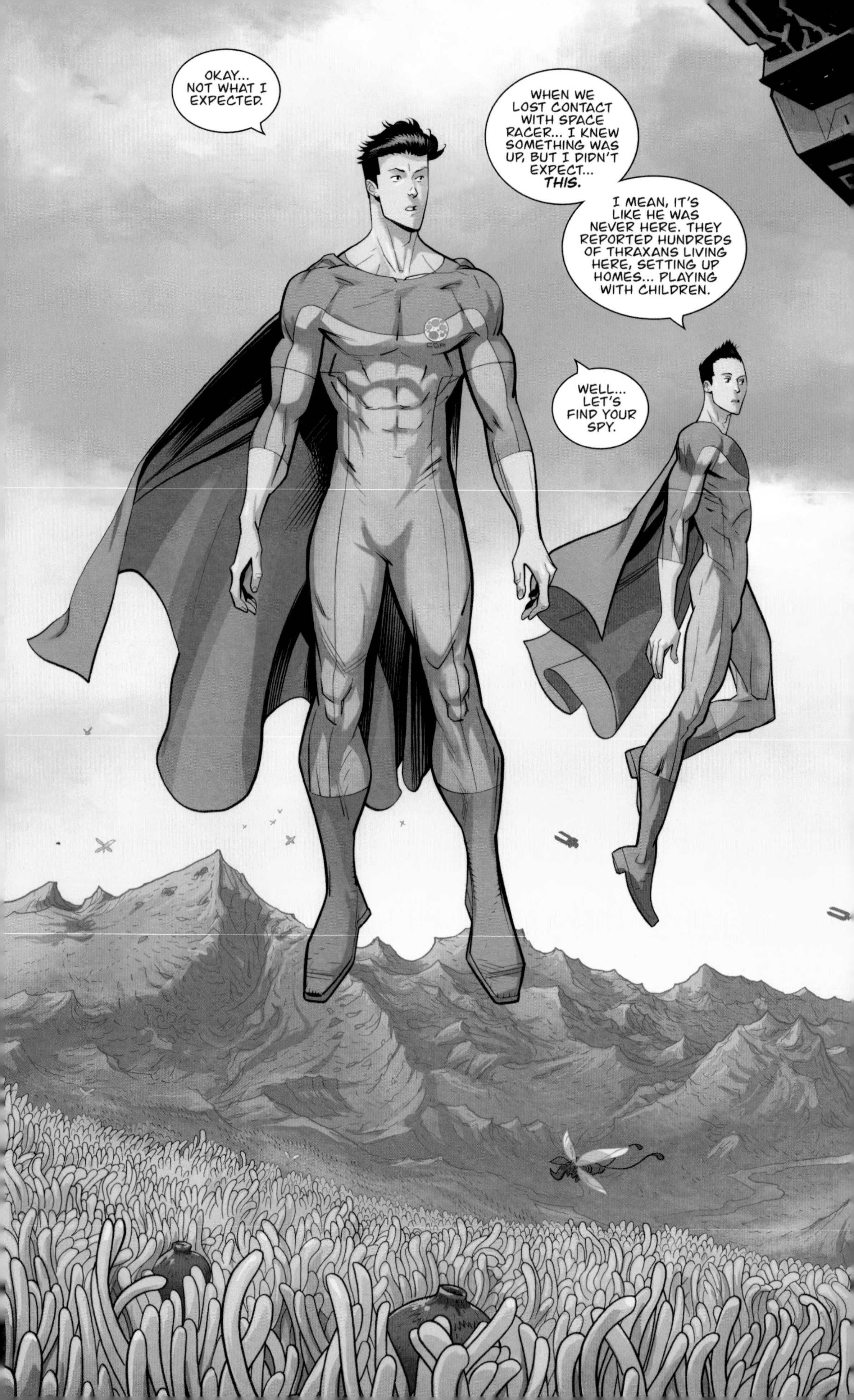
OKAY... NOT WHAT I EXPECTED.
WHEN WE LOST CONTACT WITH SPACE RACER... I KNEW SOMETHING WAS UP, BUT I DIDN'T EXPECT... THIS.
I MEAN, IT'S LIKE HE WAS NEVER HERE. THEY REPORTED HUNDREDS OF THRAXANS LIVING HERE, SETTING UP HOMES... PLAYING WITH CHILDREN.
WELL... LET'S FIND YOUR SPY.

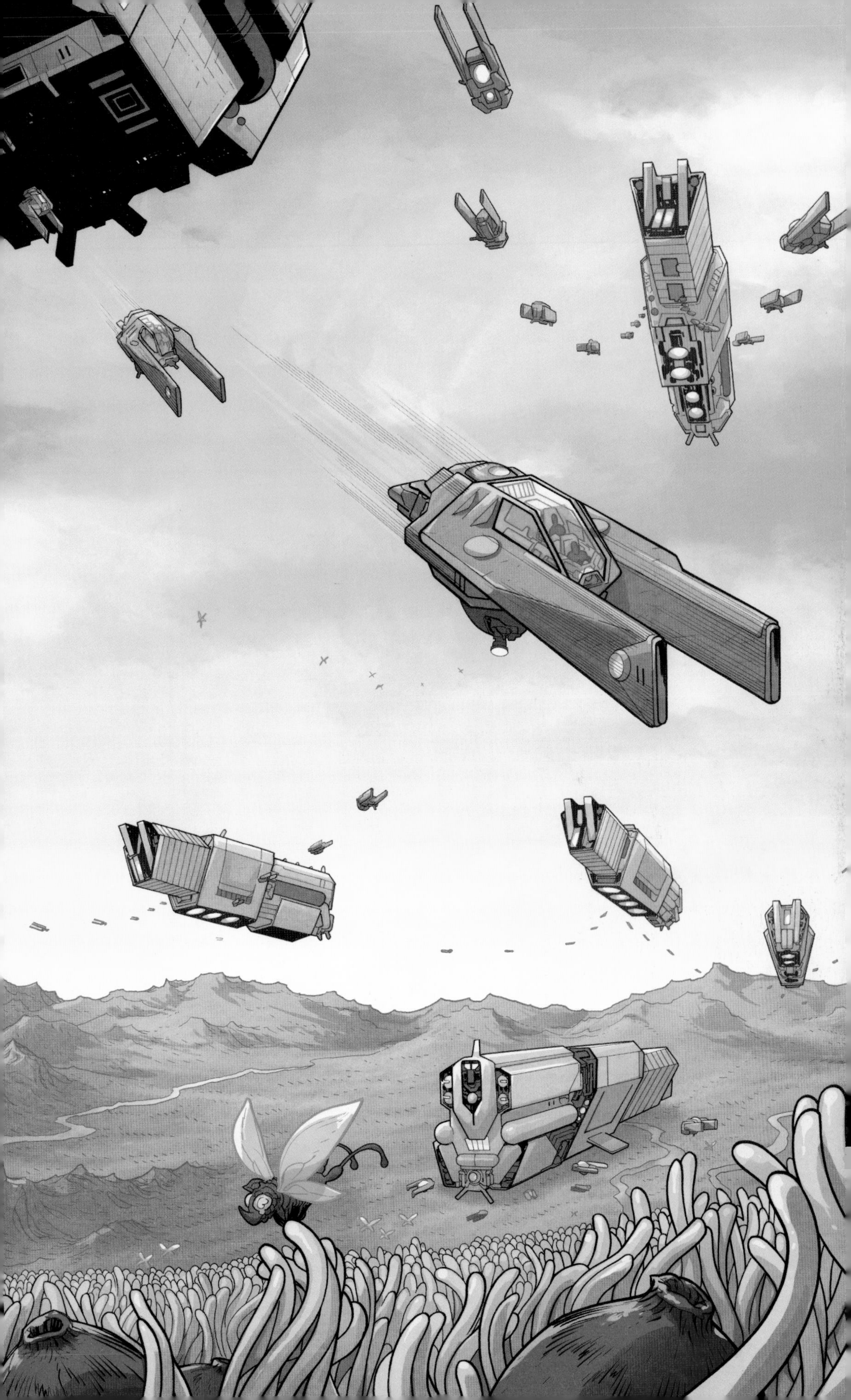

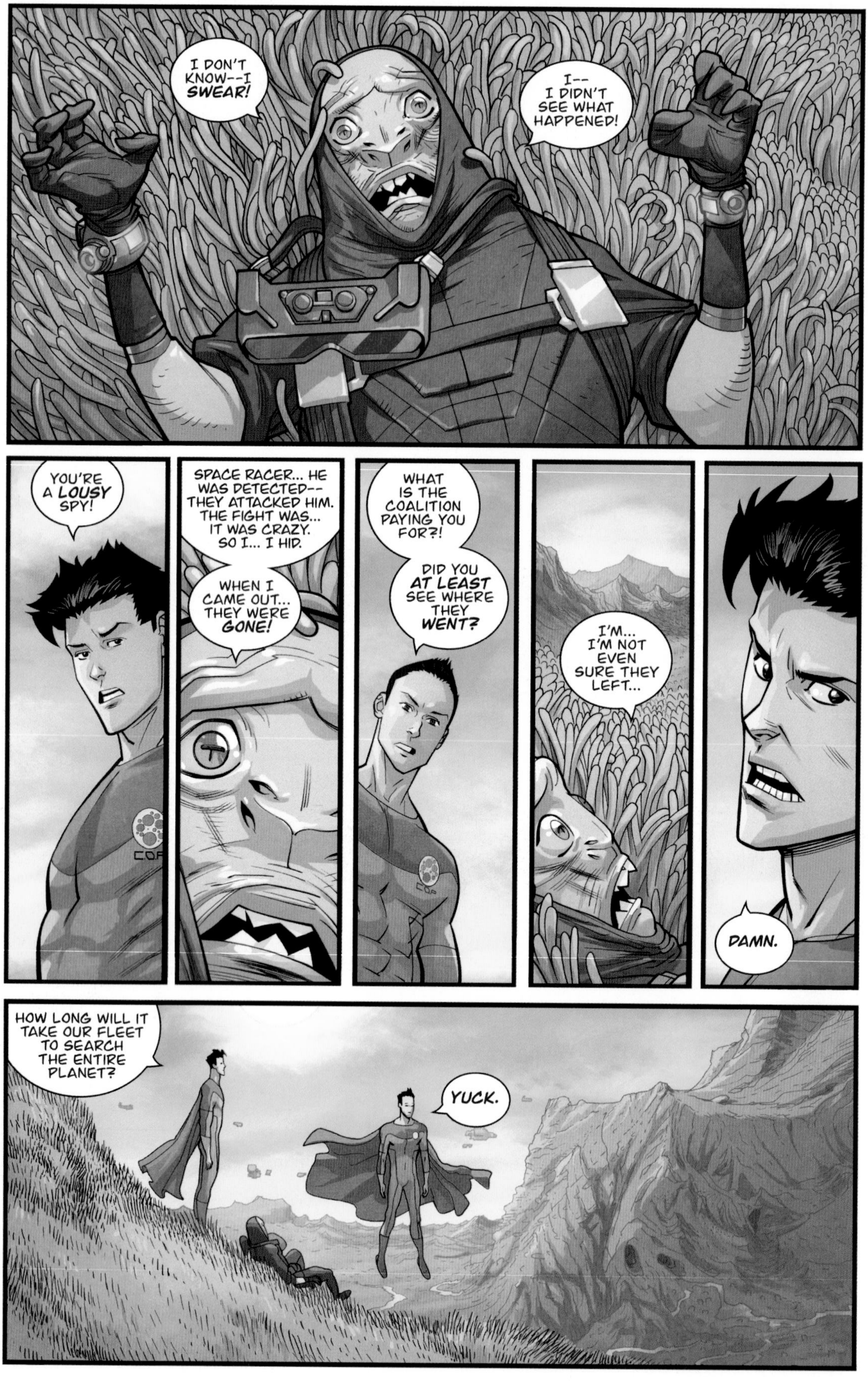
I DON'T KNOW--I SWEAR!
I-- I DIDN'T SEE WHAT HAPPENED!
YOU'RE A LOUSY SPY!
SPACE RACER... HE WAS DETECTED-- THEY ATTACKED HIM. THE FIGHT WAS... IT WAS CRAZY. SO I... I HID.
WHEN I CAME OUT... THEY WERE GONE!
WHAT IS THE COALITION PAYING YOU FOR?!
DID YOU AT LEAST SEE WHERE THEY WENT?
I'M... I'M NOT EVEN SURE THEY LEFT...
DAMN.
HOW LONG WILL IT TAKE OUR FLEET TO SEARCH THE ENTIRE PLANET?
YUCK.

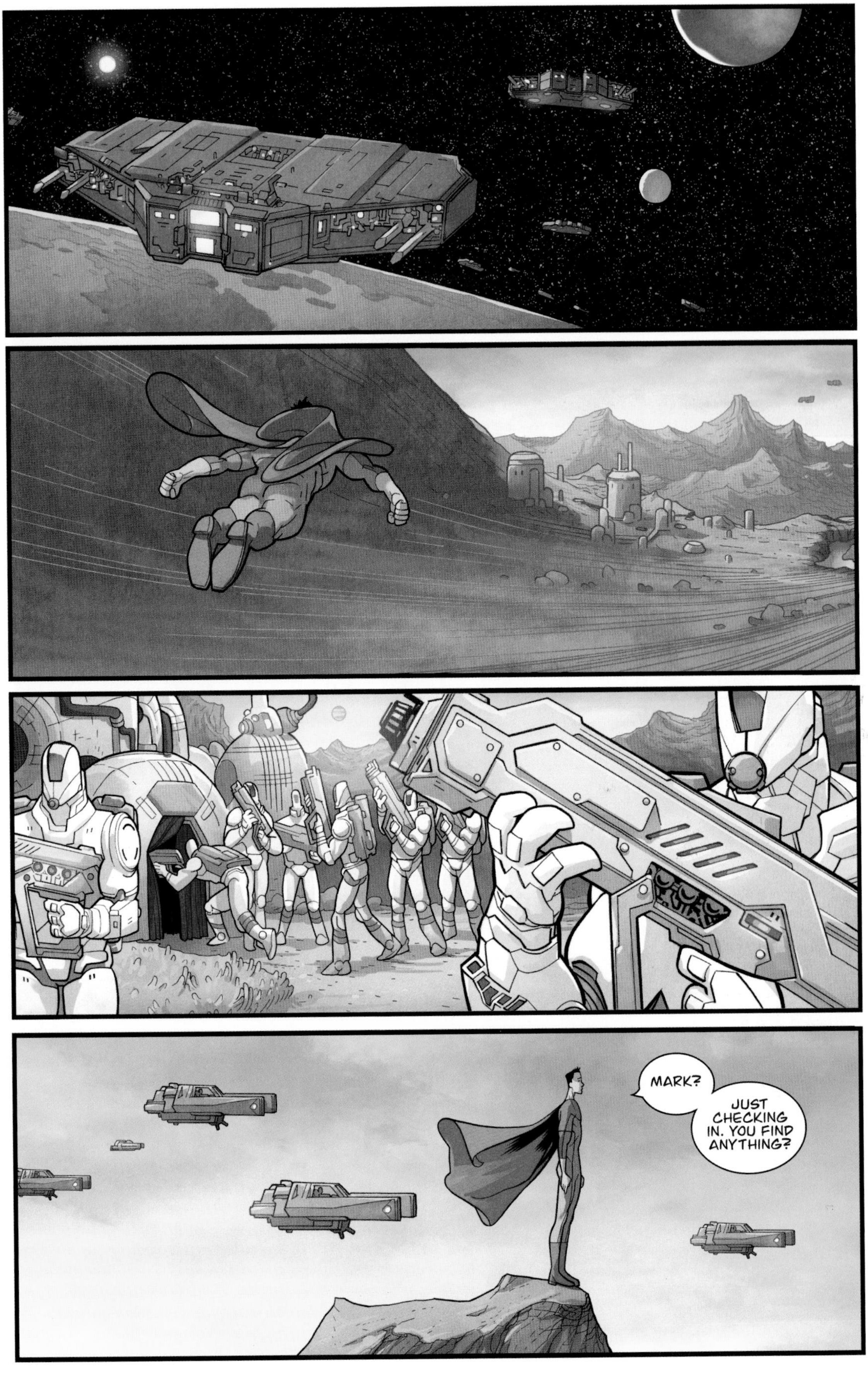
MARK?
JUST CHECKING IN. YOU FIND ANYTHING?

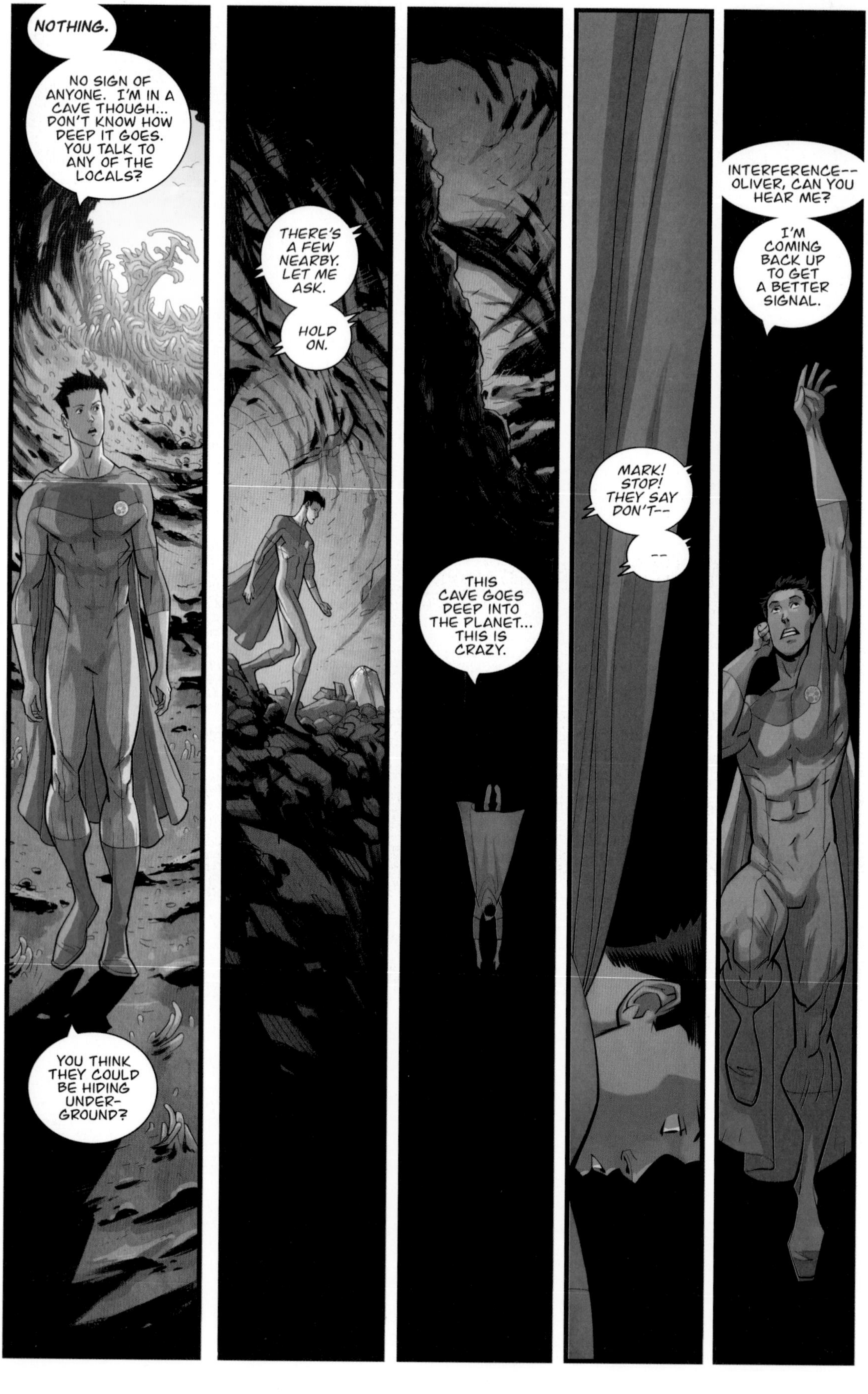
NOTHING.
NO SIGN OF ANYONE. I'M IN A CAVE THOUGH... DON'T KNOW HOW DEEP IT GOES. YOU TALK TO ANY OF THE LOCALS?
YOU THINK THEY COULD BE HIDING UNDER-GROUND?
THERE'S A FEW NEARBY. LET ME ASK.
HOLD ON.
THIS CAVE GOES DEEP INTO THE PLANET... THIS IS CRAZY.
MARK! STOP! THEY SAY DON'T--
--
INTERFERENCE--OLIVER, CAN YOU HEAR ME?
I'M COMING BACK UP TO GET A BETTER SIGNAL.

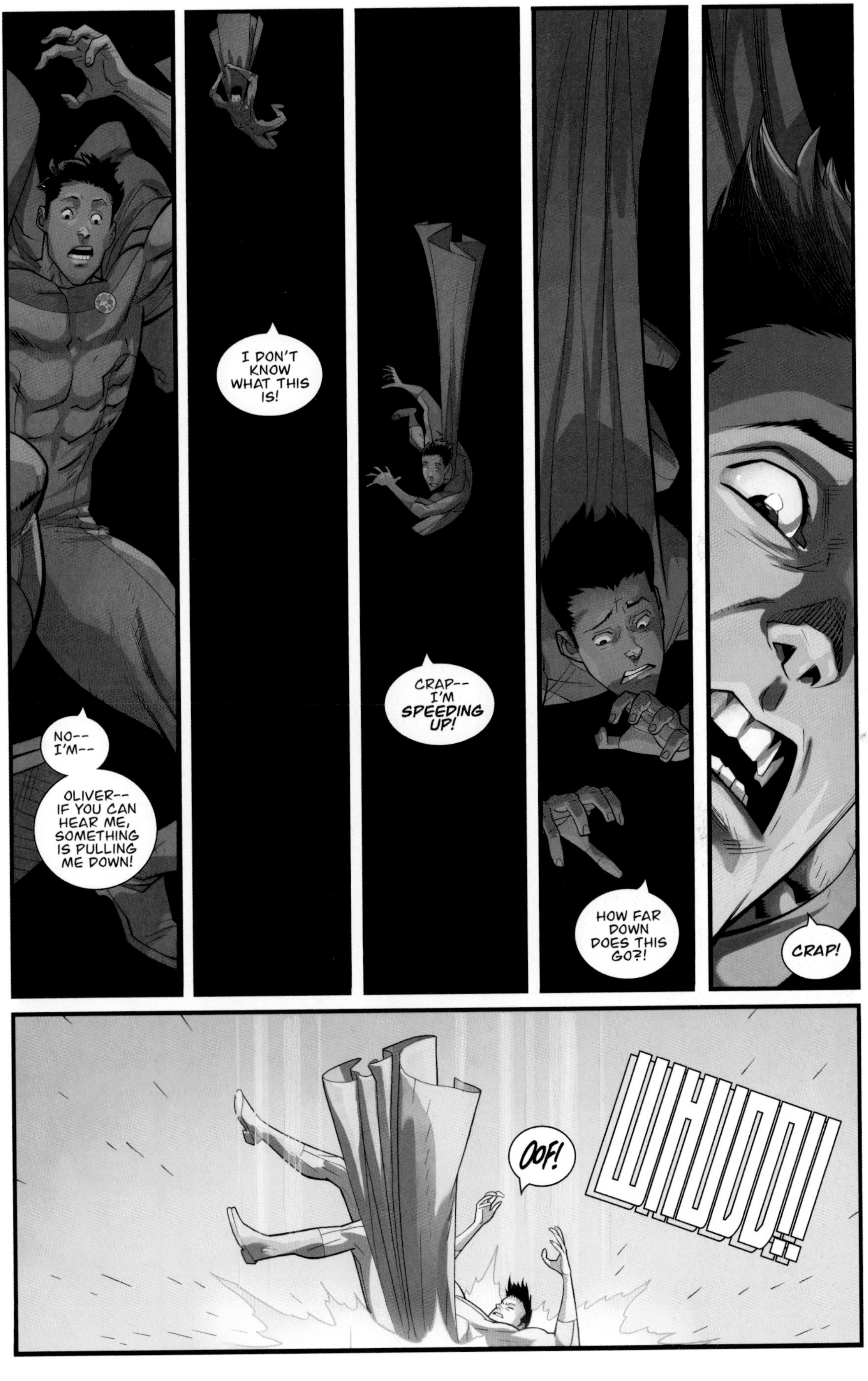
NO-- I'M--
OLIVER-- IF YOU CAN HEAR ME, SOMETHING IS PULLING ME DOWN!
I DON'T KNOW WHAT THIS IS!
CRAP-- I'M SPEEDING UP!
HOW FAR DOWN DOES THIS GO?!
CRAP!
OOF!

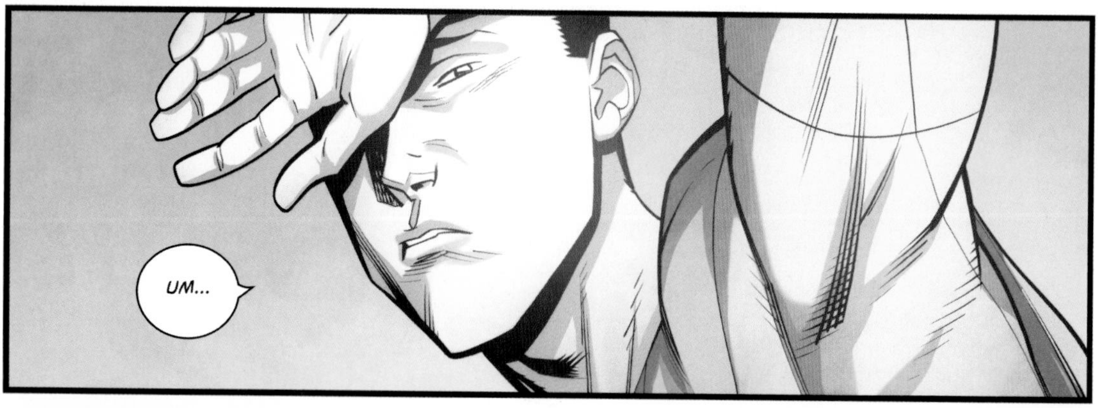
UM...

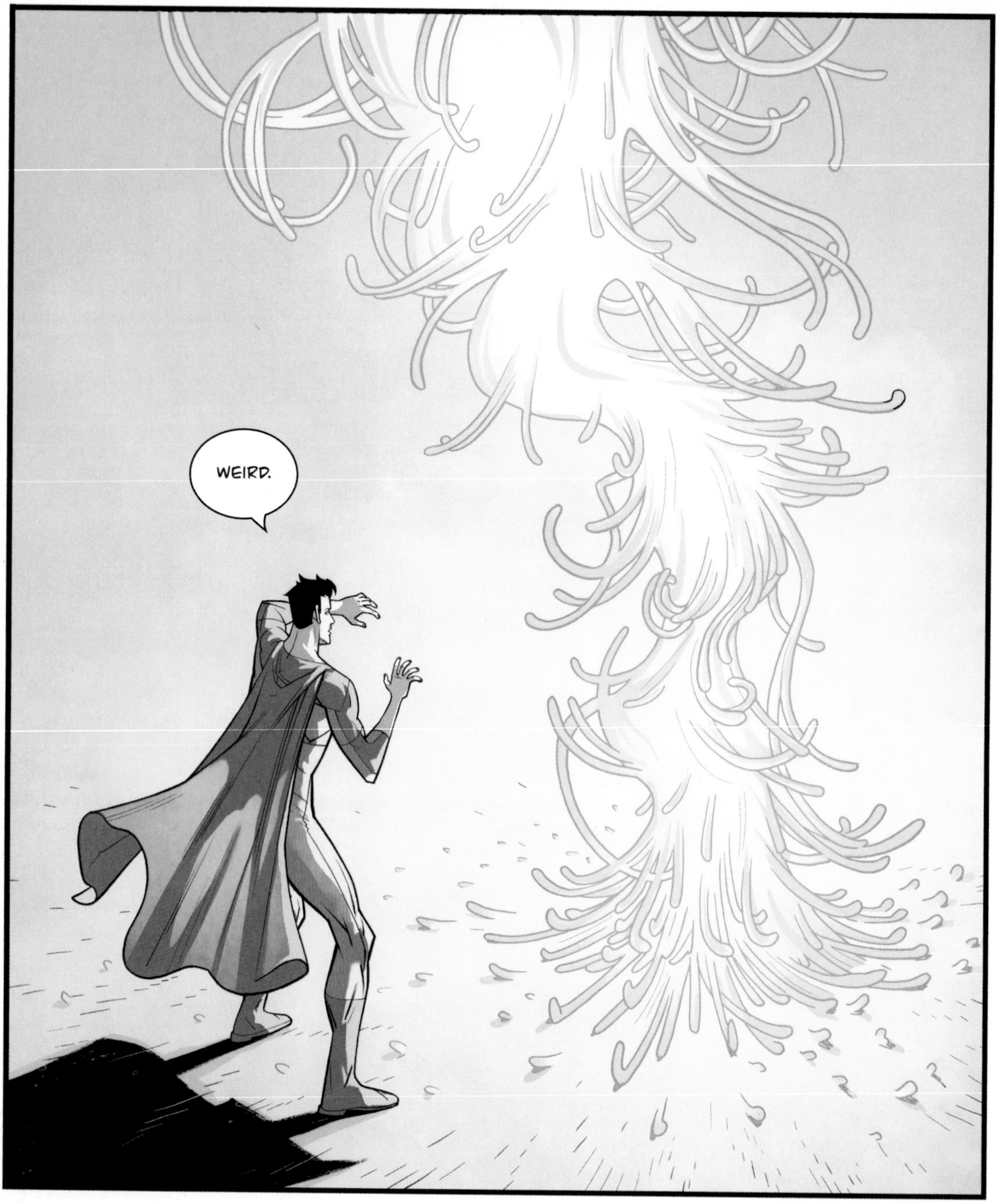
WEIRD.

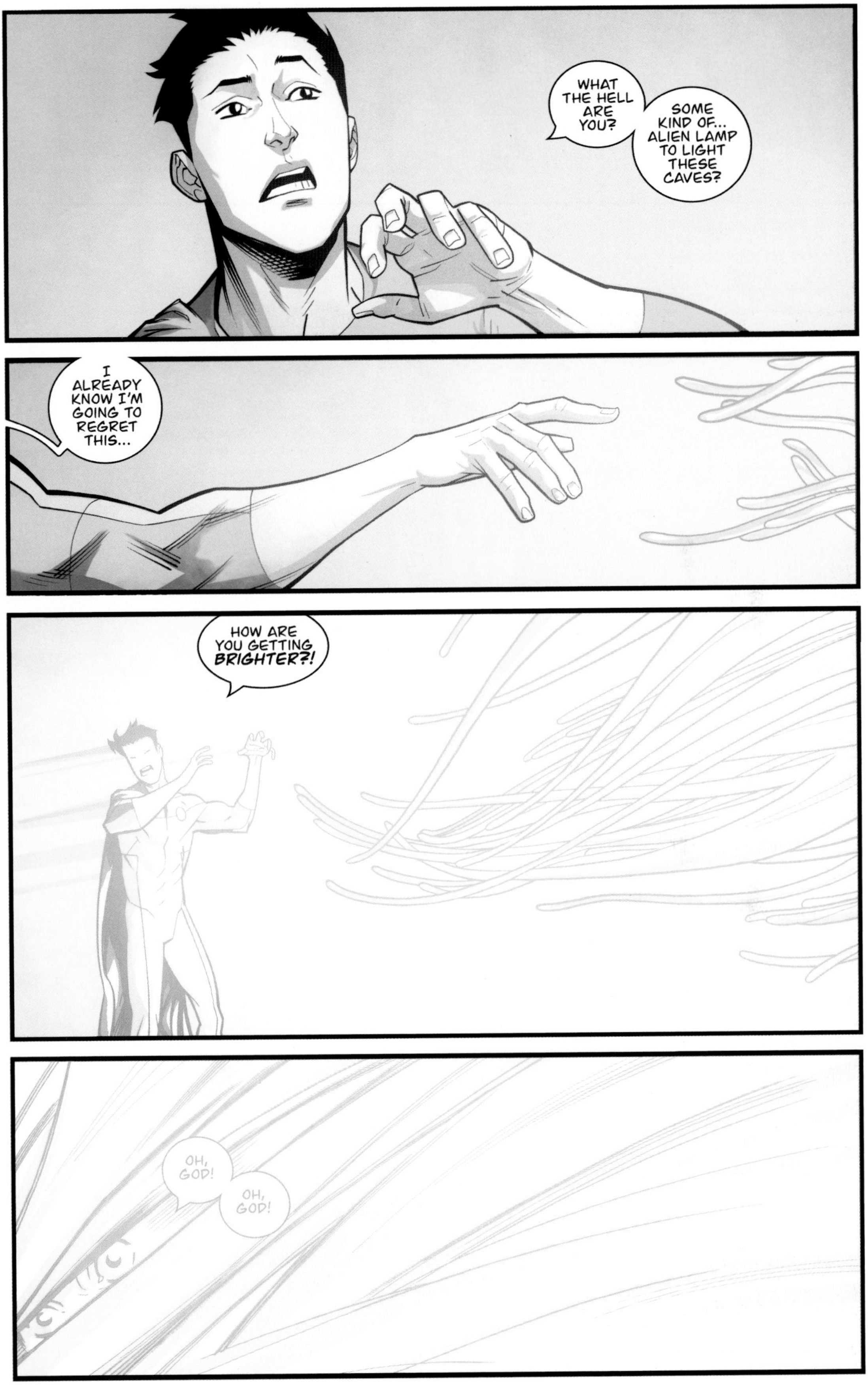
WHAT THE HELL ARE YOU?
SOME KIND OF... ALIEN LAMP TO LIGHT THESE CAVES?
I ALREADY KNOW I'M GOING TO REGRET THIS...
HOW ARE YOU GETTING BRIGHTER?!
OH, GOD!
OH, GOD!

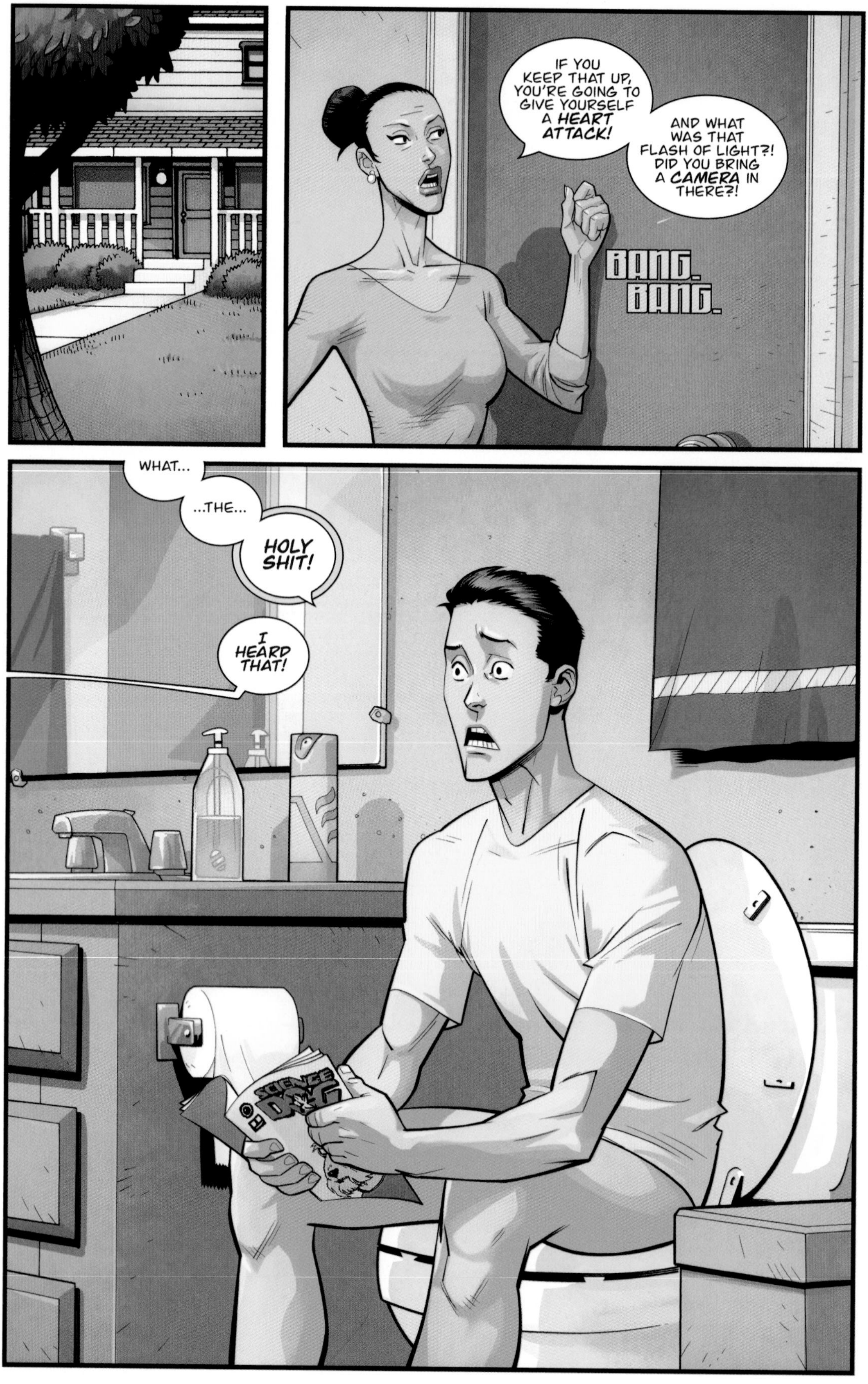
IF YOU KEEP THAT UP, YOU'RE GOING TO GIVE YOURSELF A **HEART ATTACK!**
AND WHAT WAS THAT FLASH OF LIGHT?! DID YOU BRING A **CAMERA** IN THERE?!
BANG. BANG.
WHAT...
...THE...
HOLY SHIT!
I HEARD THAT!

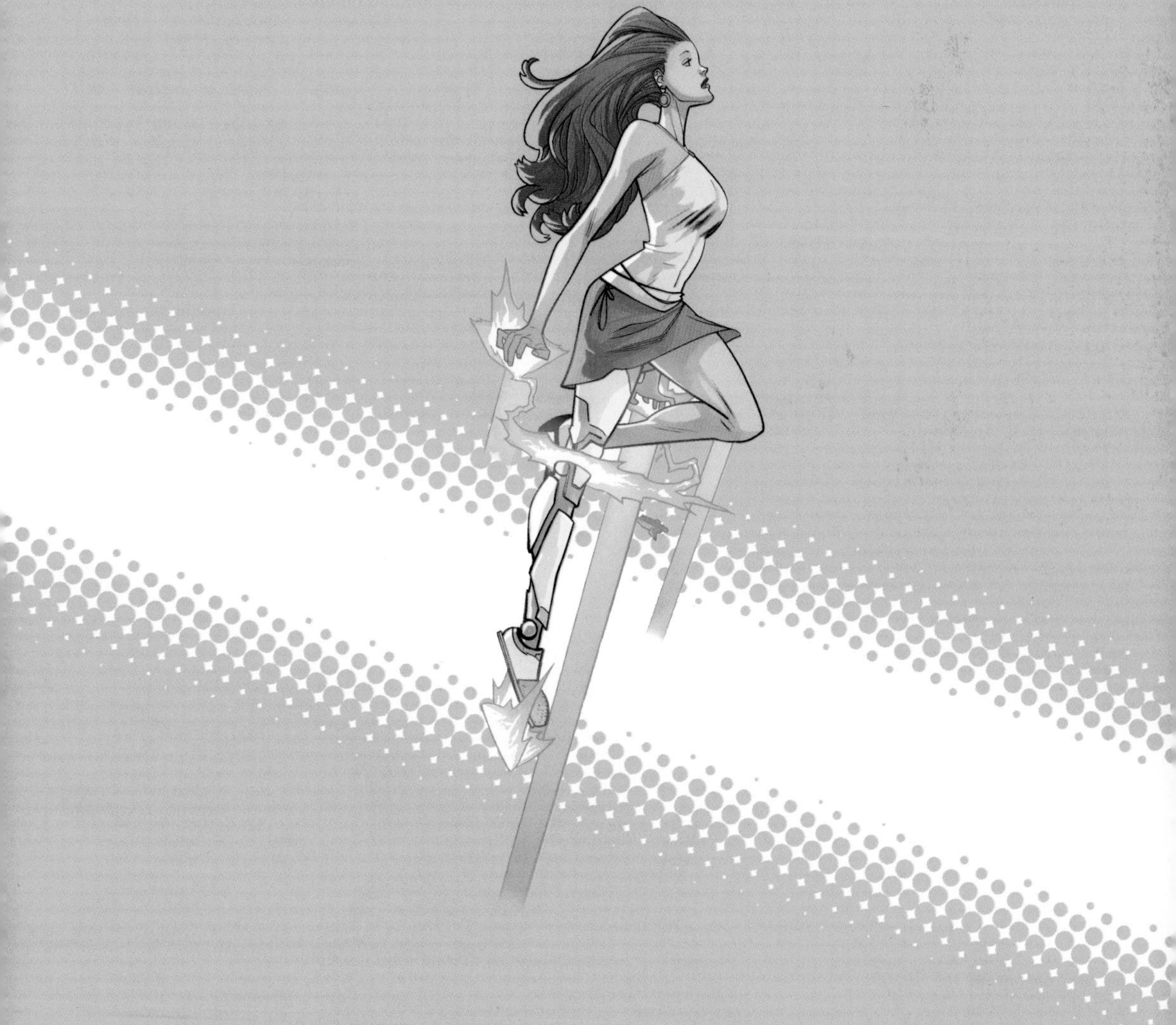

CHAPTER FOUR

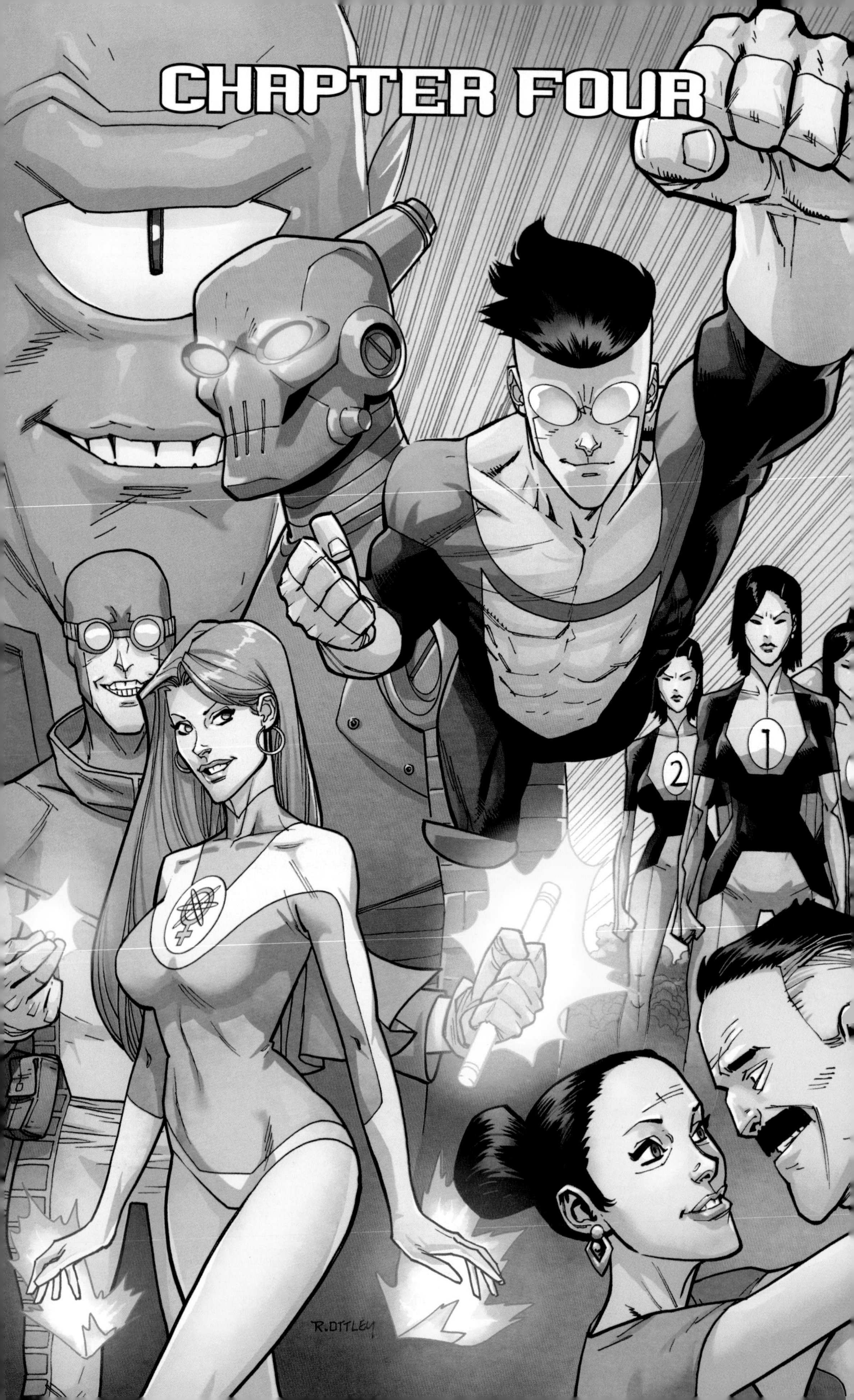

R.OTTLEY

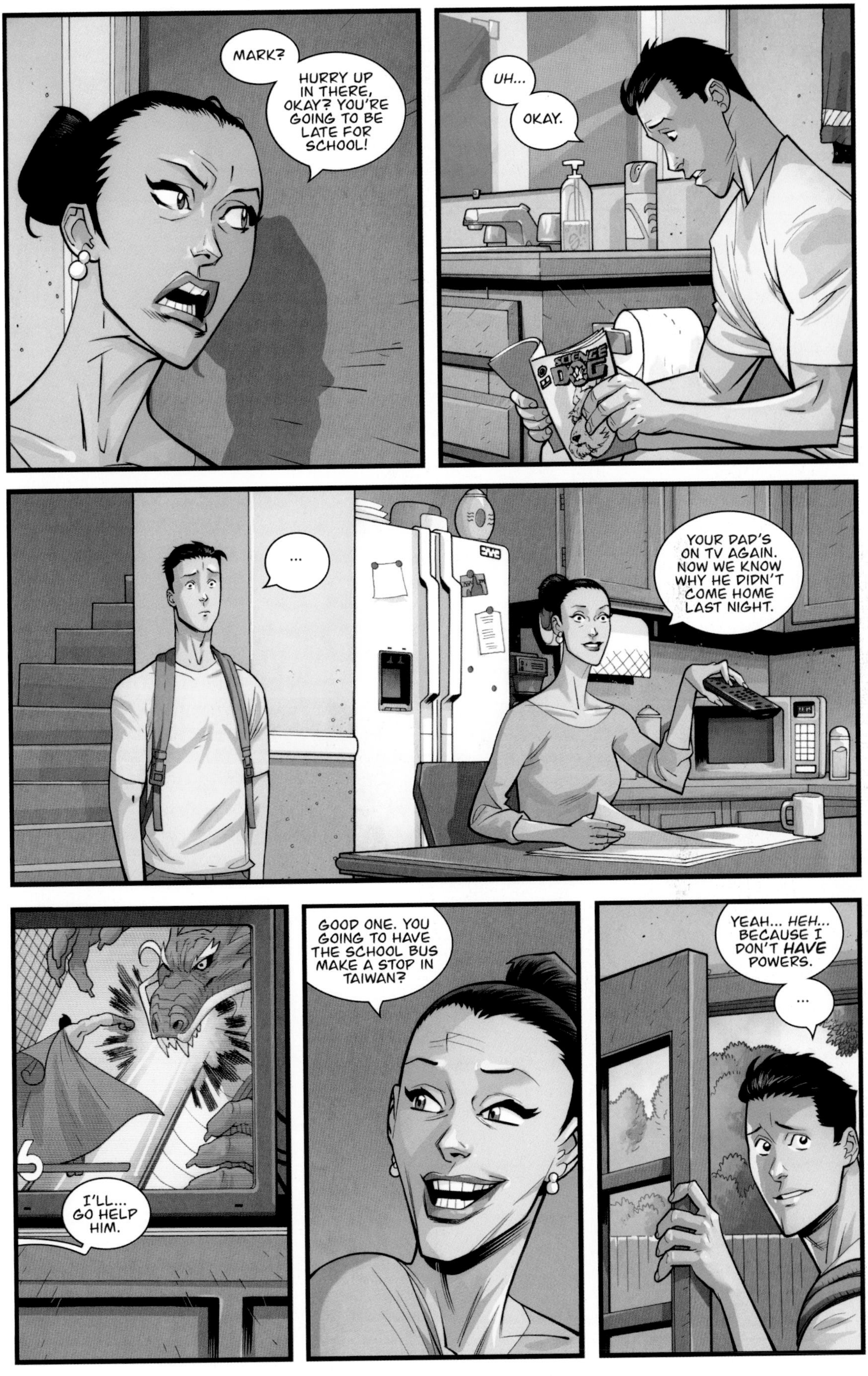

MARK?
HURRY UP IN THERE, OKAY? YOU'RE GOING TO BE LATE FOR SCHOOL!
UH...
OKAY.
SCIENCE DOG
...
YOUR DAD'S ON TV AGAIN. NOW WE KNOW WHY HE DIDN'T COME HOME LAST NIGHT.
I'LL... GO HELP HIM.
GOOD ONE. YOU GOING TO HAVE THE SCHOOL BUS MAKE A STOP IN TAIWAN?
YEAH... HEH... BECAUSE I DON'T HAVE POWERS.
...

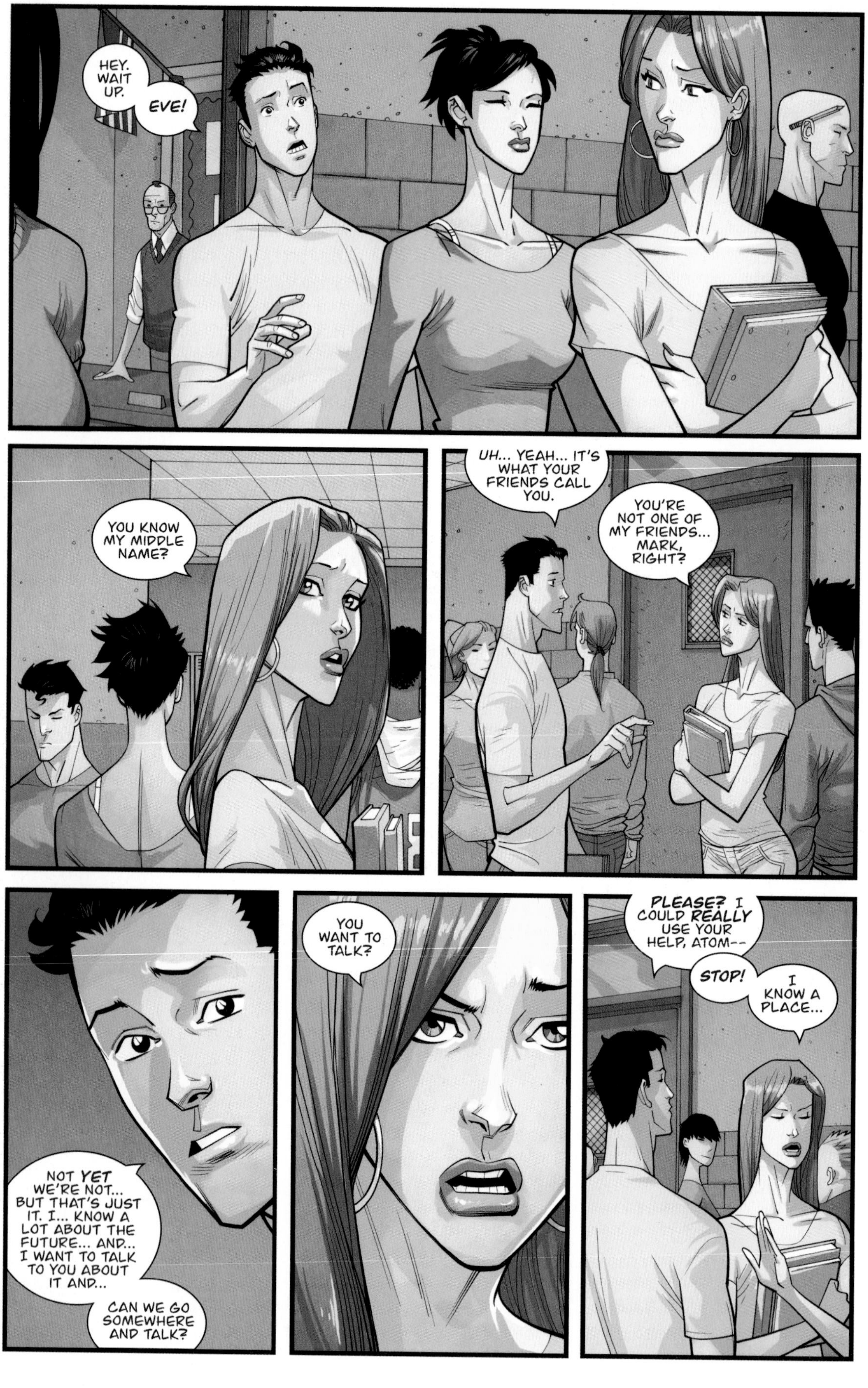
HEY. WAIT UP.
EVE!
YOU KNOW MY MIDDLE NAME?
UH... YEAH... IT'S WHAT YOUR FRIENDS CALL YOU.
YOU'RE NOT ONE OF MY FRIENDS... MARK, RIGHT?
NOT YET WE'RE NOT... BUT THAT'S JUST IT. I... KNOW A LOT ABOUT THE FUTURE... AND... I WANT TO TALK TO YOU ABOUT IT AND...
CAN WE GO SOMEWHERE AND TALK?
YOU WANT TO TALK?
PLEASE? I COULD REALLY USE YOUR HELP, ATOM--
STOP!
I KNOW A PLACE...

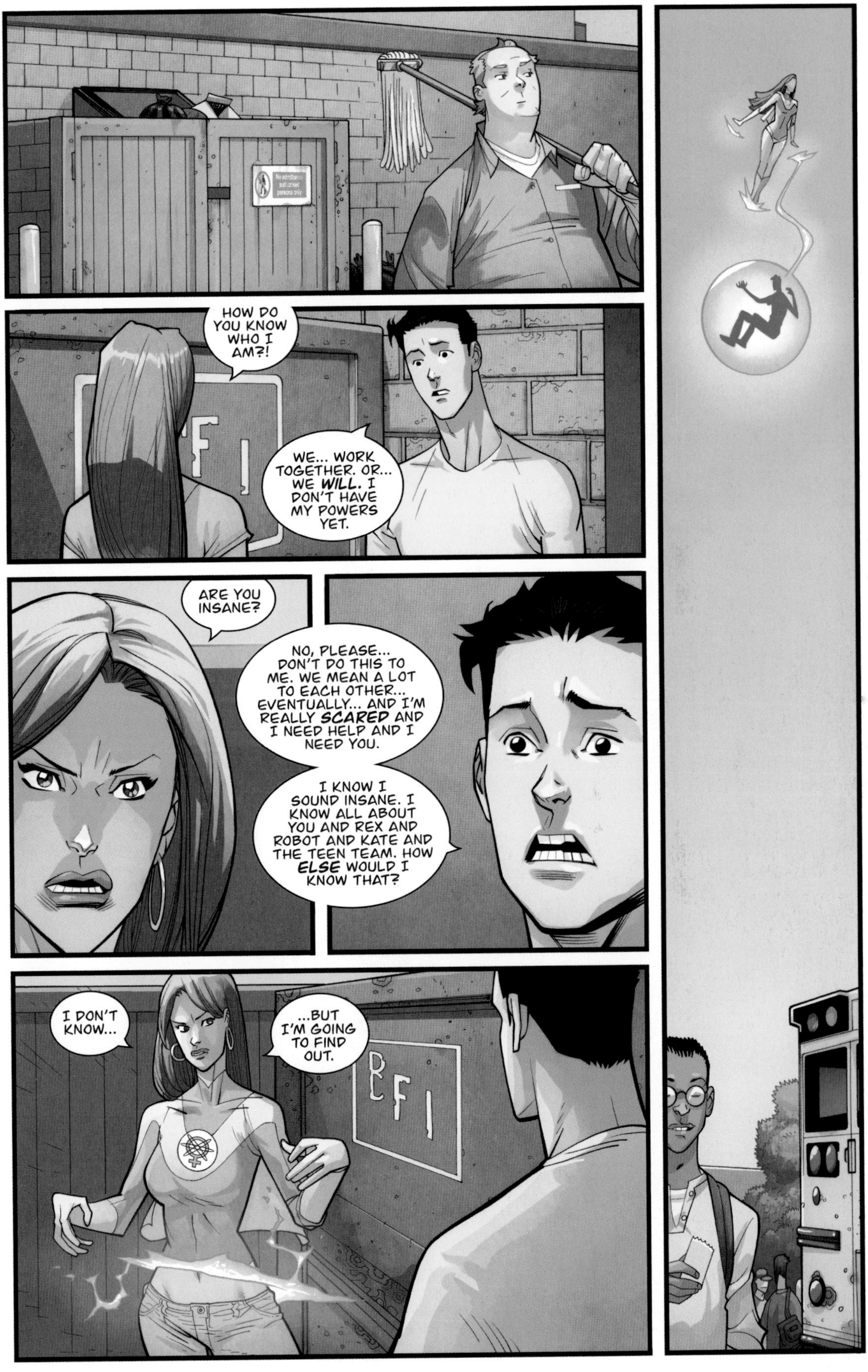
HOW DO YOU KNOW WHO I AM?!
WE... WORK TOGETHER. OR... WE *WILL.* I DON'T HAVE MY POWERS YET.
ARE YOU INSANE?
NO, PLEASE... DON'T DO THIS TO ME. WE MEAN A LOT TO EACH OTHER... EVENTUALLY... AND I'M REALLY *SCARED* AND I NEED HELP AND I NEED YOU.
I KNOW I SOUND INSANE. I KNOW ALL ABOUT YOU AND REX AND ROBOT AND KATE AND THE TEEN TEAM. HOW *ELSE* WOULD I KNOW THAT?
I DON'T KNOW...
...BUT I'M GOING TO FIND OUT.

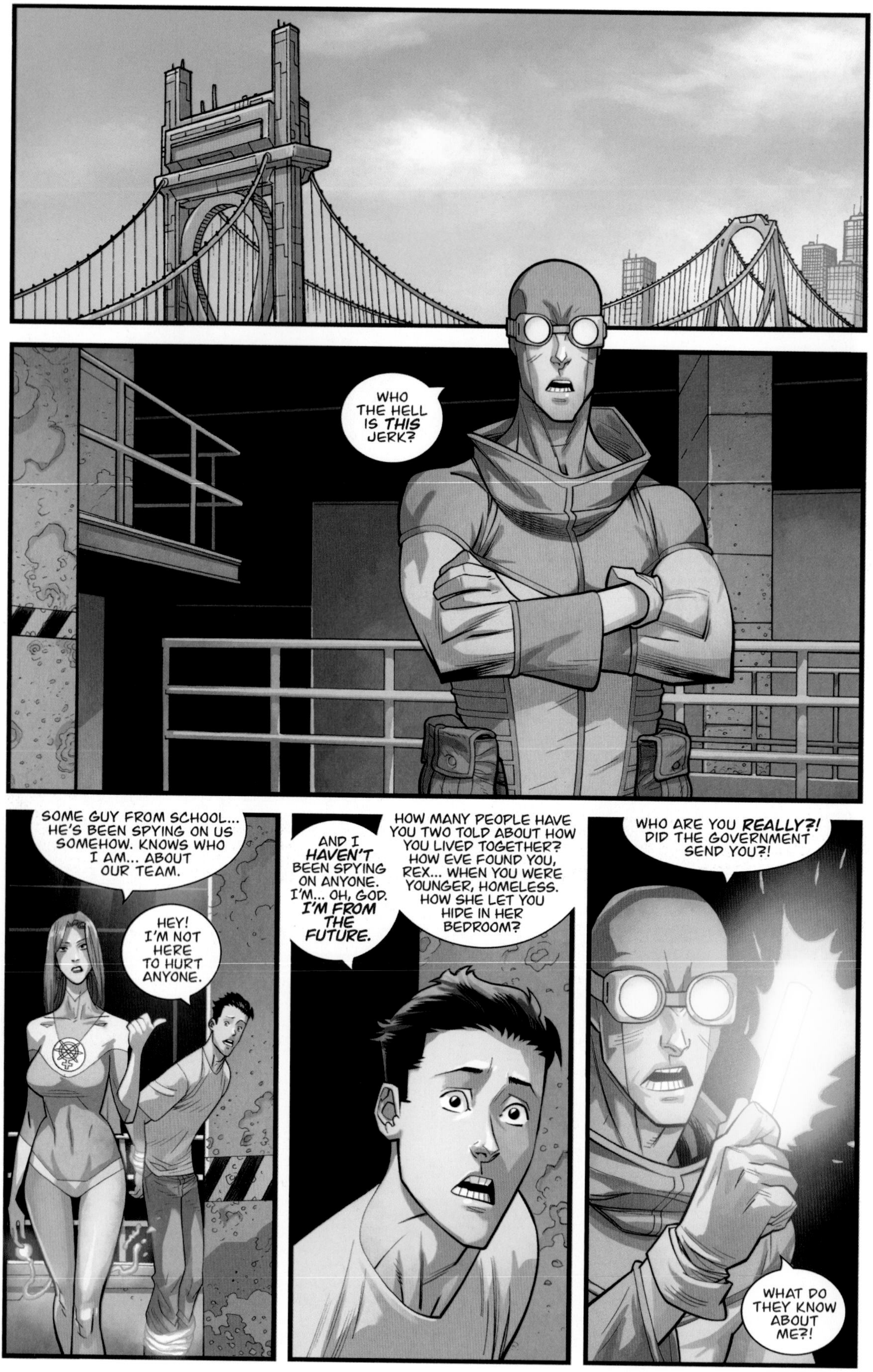
WHO THE HELL IS THIS JERK?
SOME GUY FROM SCHOOL... HE'S BEEN SPYING ON US SOMEHOW. KNOWS WHO I AM... ABOUT OUR TEAM.
HEY! I'M NOT HERE TO HURT ANYONE.
AND I HAVEN'T BEEN SPYING ON ANYONE. I'M... OH, GOD. I'M FROM THE FUTURE.
HOW MANY PEOPLE HAVE YOU TWO TOLD ABOUT HOW YOU LIVED TOGETHER? HOW EVE FOUND YOU, REX... WHEN YOU WERE YOUNGER, HOMELESS. HOW SHE LET YOU HIDE IN HER BEDROOM?
WHO ARE YOU REALLY?! DID THE GOVERNMENT SEND YOU?!
WHAT DO THEY KNOW ABOUT ME?!

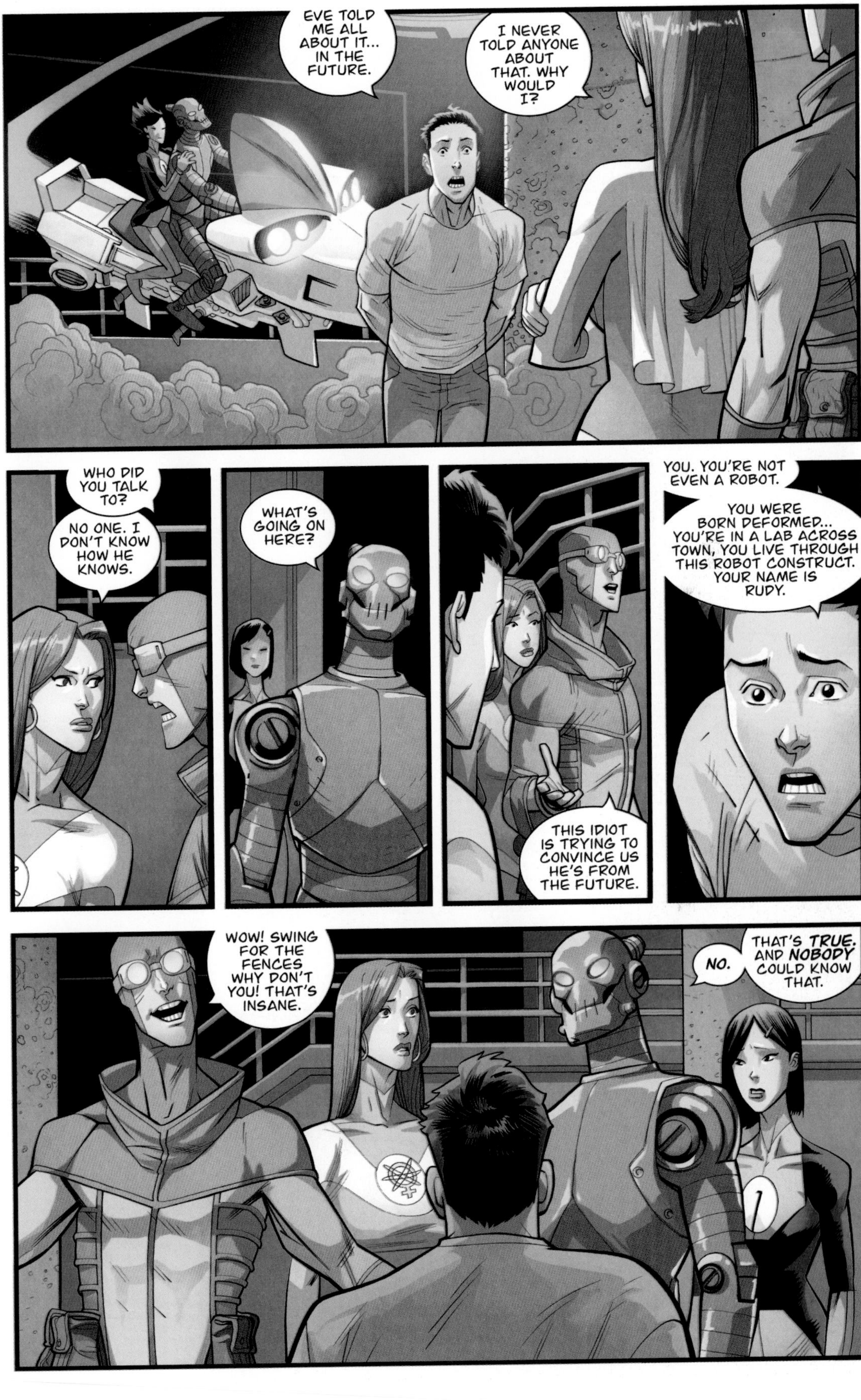
EVE TOLD ME ALL ABOUT IT... IN THE FUTURE.
I NEVER TOLD ANYONE ABOUT THAT. WHY WOULD I?
WHO DID YOU TALK TO?
NO ONE. I DON'T KNOW HOW HE KNOWS.
WHAT'S GOING ON HERE?
THIS IDIOT IS TRYING TO CONVINCE US HE'S FROM THE FUTURE.
YOU. YOU'RE NOT EVEN A ROBOT.
YOU WERE BORN DEFORMED... YOU'RE IN A LAB ACROSS TOWN, YOU LIVE THROUGH THIS ROBOT CONSTRUCT. YOUR NAME IS RUDY.
WOW! SWING FOR THE FENCES WHY DON'T YOU! THAT'S INSANE.
NO.
THAT'S TRUE. AND NOBODY COULD KNOW THAT.

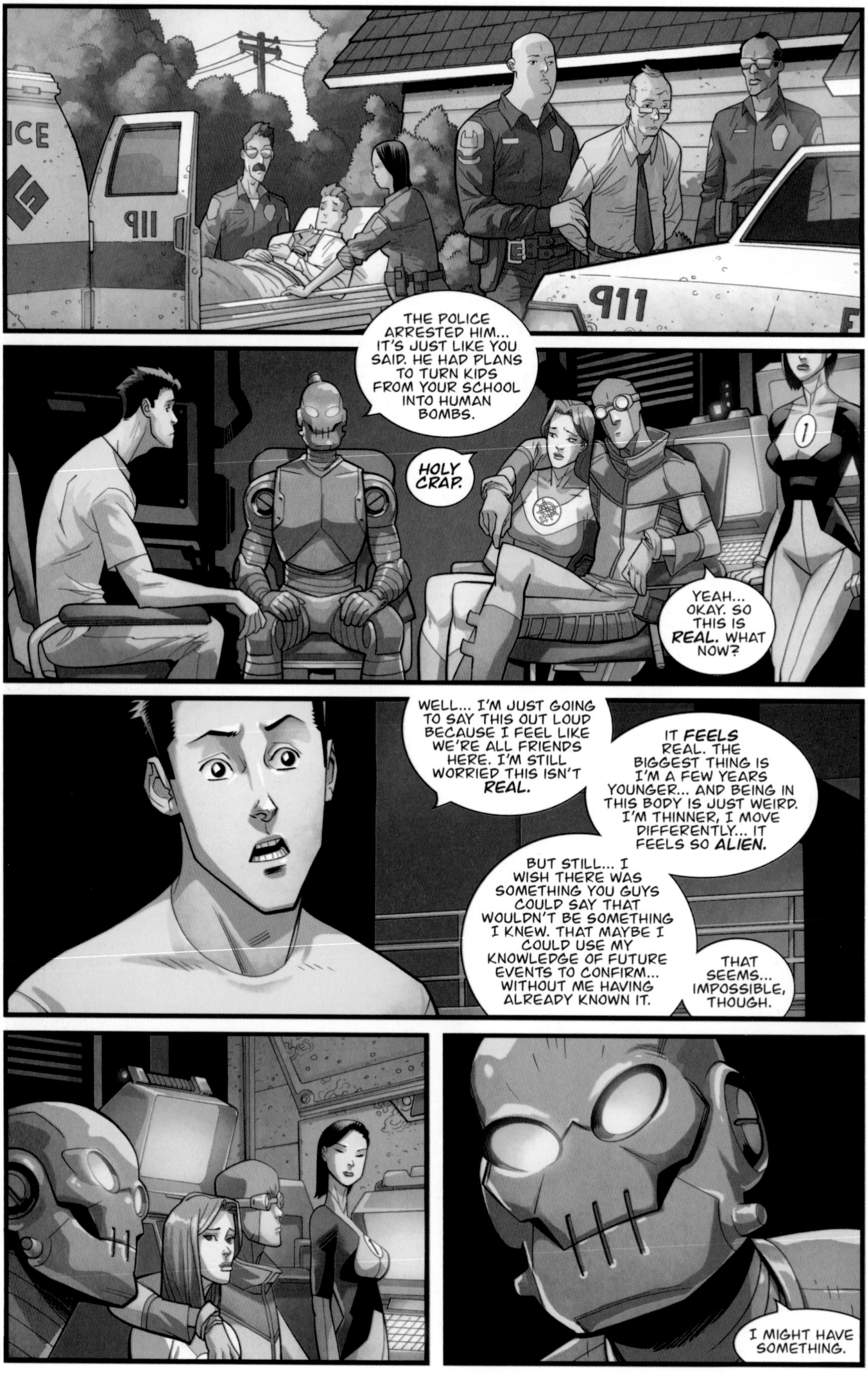

ICE
911
911
THE POLICE ARRESTED HIM... IT'S JUST LIKE YOU SAID. HE HAD PLANS TO TURN KIDS FROM YOUR SCHOOL INTO HUMAN BOMBS.
HOLY CRAP.
YEAH... OKAY. SO THIS IS REAL. WHAT NOW?
WELL... I'M JUST GOING TO SAY THIS OUT LOUD BECAUSE I FEEL LIKE WE'RE ALL FRIENDS HERE. I'M STILL WORRIED THIS ISN'T REAL.
IT FEELS REAL. THE BIGGEST THING IS I'M A FEW YEARS YOUNGER... AND BEING IN THIS BODY IS JUST WEIRD. I'M THINNER, I MOVE DIFFERENTLY... IT FEELS SO ALIEN.
BUT STILL... I WISH THERE WAS SOMETHING YOU GUYS COULD SAY THAT WOULDN'T BE SOMETHING I KNEW. THAT MAYBE I COULD USE MY KNOWLEDGE OF FUTURE EVENTS TO CONFIRM... WITHOUT ME HAVING ALREADY KNOWN IT.
THAT SEEMS... IMPOSSIBLE, THOUGH.
I MIGHT HAVE SOMETHING.

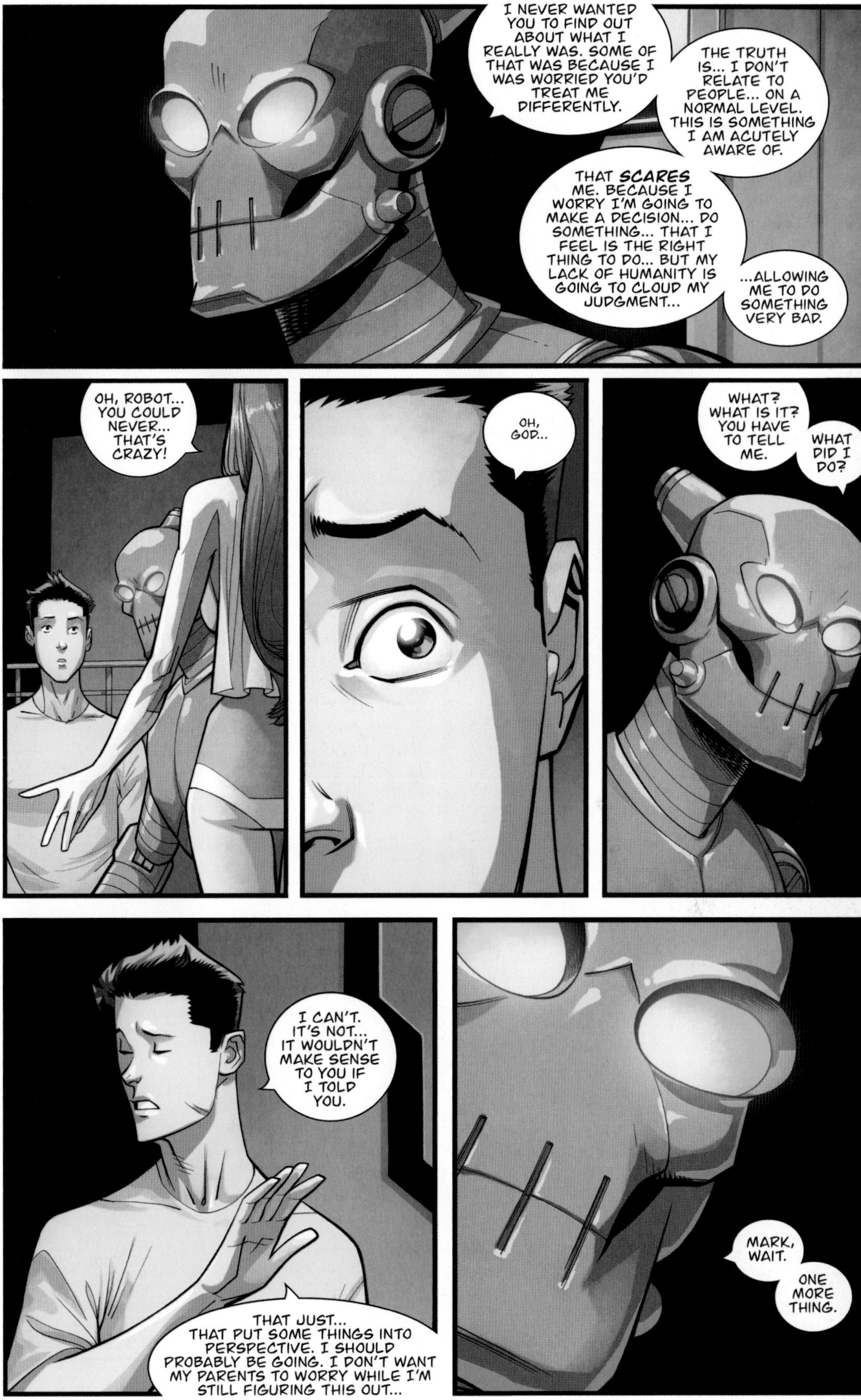
I NEVER WANTED YOU TO FIND OUT ABOUT WHAT I REALLY WAS. SOME OF THAT WAS BECAUSE I WAS WORRIED YOU'D TREAT ME DIFFERENTLY.
THE TRUTH IS... I DON'T RELATE TO PEOPLE... ON A NORMAL LEVEL. THIS IS SOMETHING I AM ACUTELY AWARE OF.
THAT **SCARES** ME. BECAUSE I WORRY I'M GOING TO MAKE A DECISION... DO SOMETHING... THAT I FEEL IS THE RIGHT THING TO DO... BUT MY LACK OF HUMANITY IS GOING TO CLOUD MY JUDGMENT...
...ALLOWING ME TO DO SOMETHING VERY BAD.
OH, ROBOT... YOU COULD NEVER... THAT'S CRAZY!
OH, GOD...
WHAT? WHAT IS IT? YOU HAVE TO TELL ME.
WHAT DID I DO?
I CAN'T. IT'S NOT... IT WOULDN'T MAKE SENSE TO YOU IF I TOLD YOU.
THAT JUST... THAT PUT SOME THINGS INTO PERSPECTIVE. I SHOULD PROBABLY BE GOING. I DON'T WANT MY PARENTS TO WORRY WHILE I'M STILL FIGURING THIS OUT...
MARK, WAIT.
ONE MORE THING.

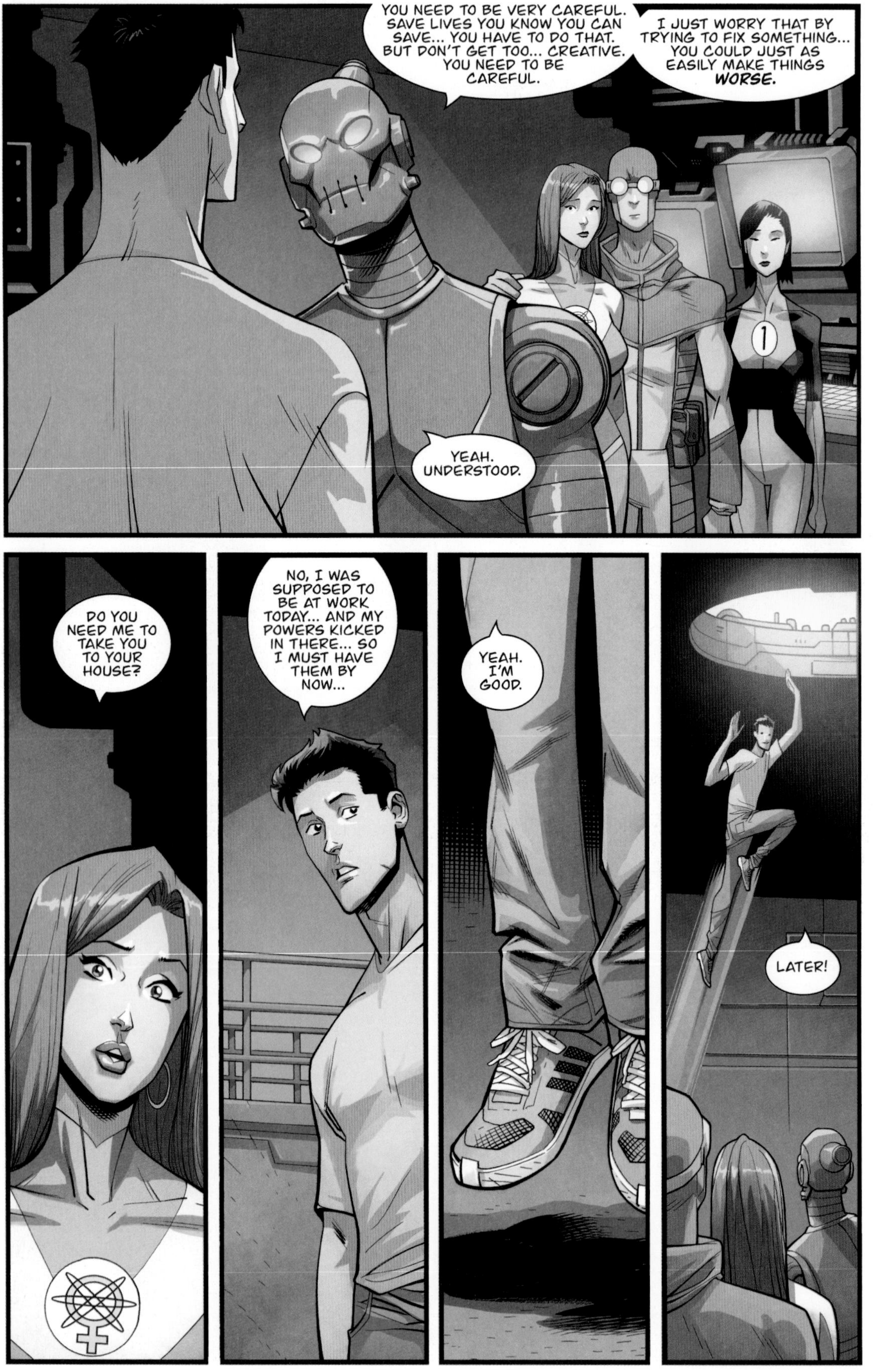
YOU NEED TO BE VERY CAREFUL. SAVE LIVES YOU KNOW YOU CAN SAVE... YOU HAVE TO DO THAT. BUT DON'T GET TOO... CREATIVE. YOU NEED TO BE CAREFUL.
I JUST WORRY THAT BY TRYING TO FIX SOMETHING... YOU COULD JUST AS EASILY MAKE THINGS **WORSE.**
YEAH. UNDERSTOOD.
DO YOU NEED ME TO TAKE YOU TO YOUR HOUSE?
NO, I WAS SUPPOSED TO BE AT WORK TODAY... AND MY POWERS KICKED IN THERE... SO I MUST HAVE THEM BY NOW...
YEAH. I'M GOOD.
LATER!

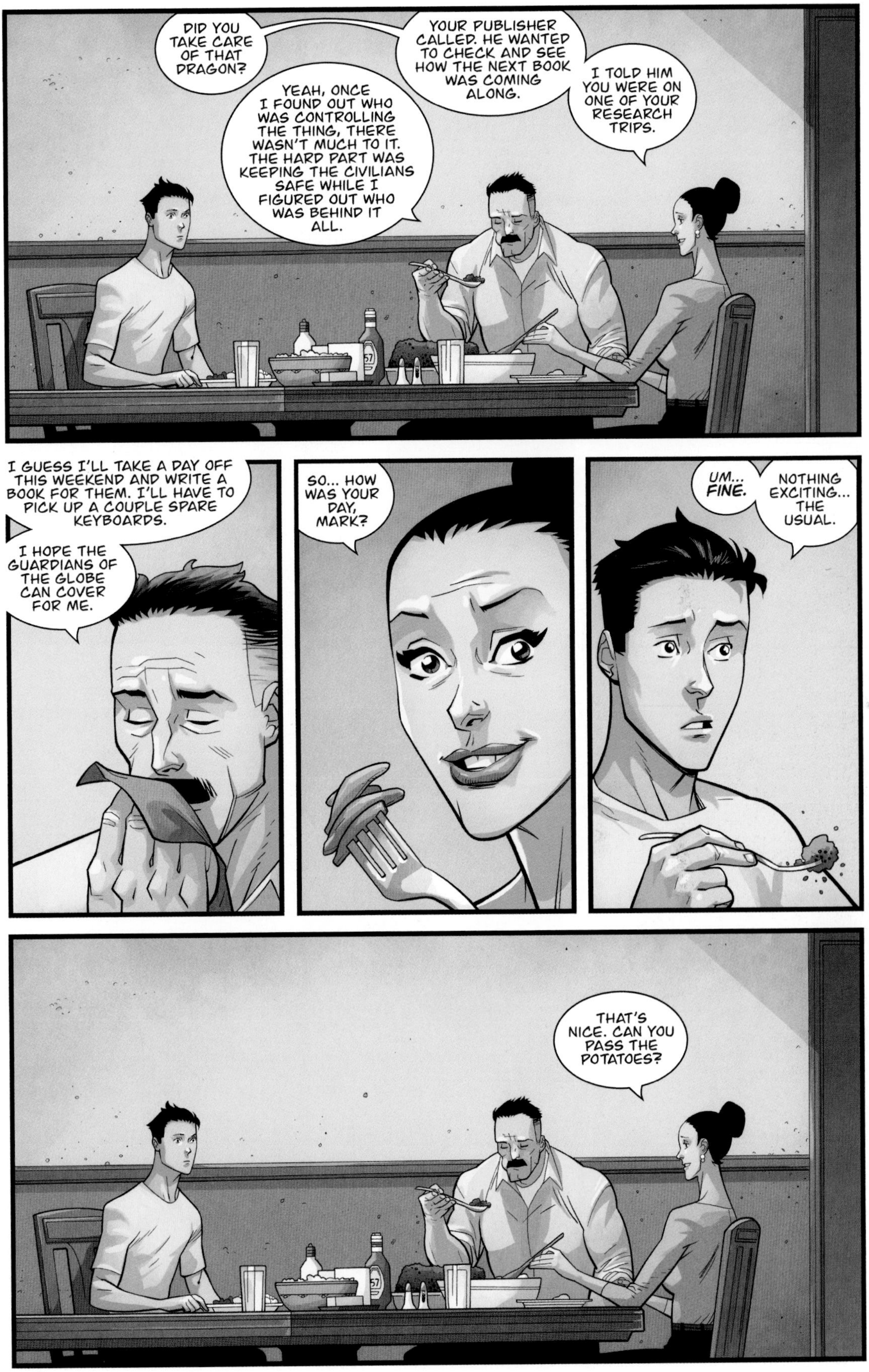
DID YOU TAKE CARE OF THAT DRAGON?
YEAH, ONCE I FOUND OUT WHO WAS CONTROLLING THE THING, THERE WASN'T MUCH TO IT. THE HARD PART WAS KEEPING THE CIVILIANS SAFE WHILE I FIGURED OUT WHO WAS BEHIND IT ALL.
YOUR PUBLISHER CALLED. HE WANTED TO CHECK AND SEE HOW THE NEXT BOOK WAS COMING ALONG.
I TOLD HIM YOU WERE ON ONE OF YOUR RESEARCH TRIPS.
I GUESS I'LL TAKE A DAY OFF THIS WEEKEND AND WRITE A BOOK FOR THEM. I'LL HAVE TO PICK UP A COUPLE SPARE KEYBOARDS.
I HOPE THE GUARDIANS OF THE GLOBE CAN COVER FOR ME.
SO... HOW WAS YOUR DAY, MARK?
UM... FINE.
NOTHING EXCITING... THE USUAL.
THAT'S NICE. CAN YOU PASS THE POTATOES?

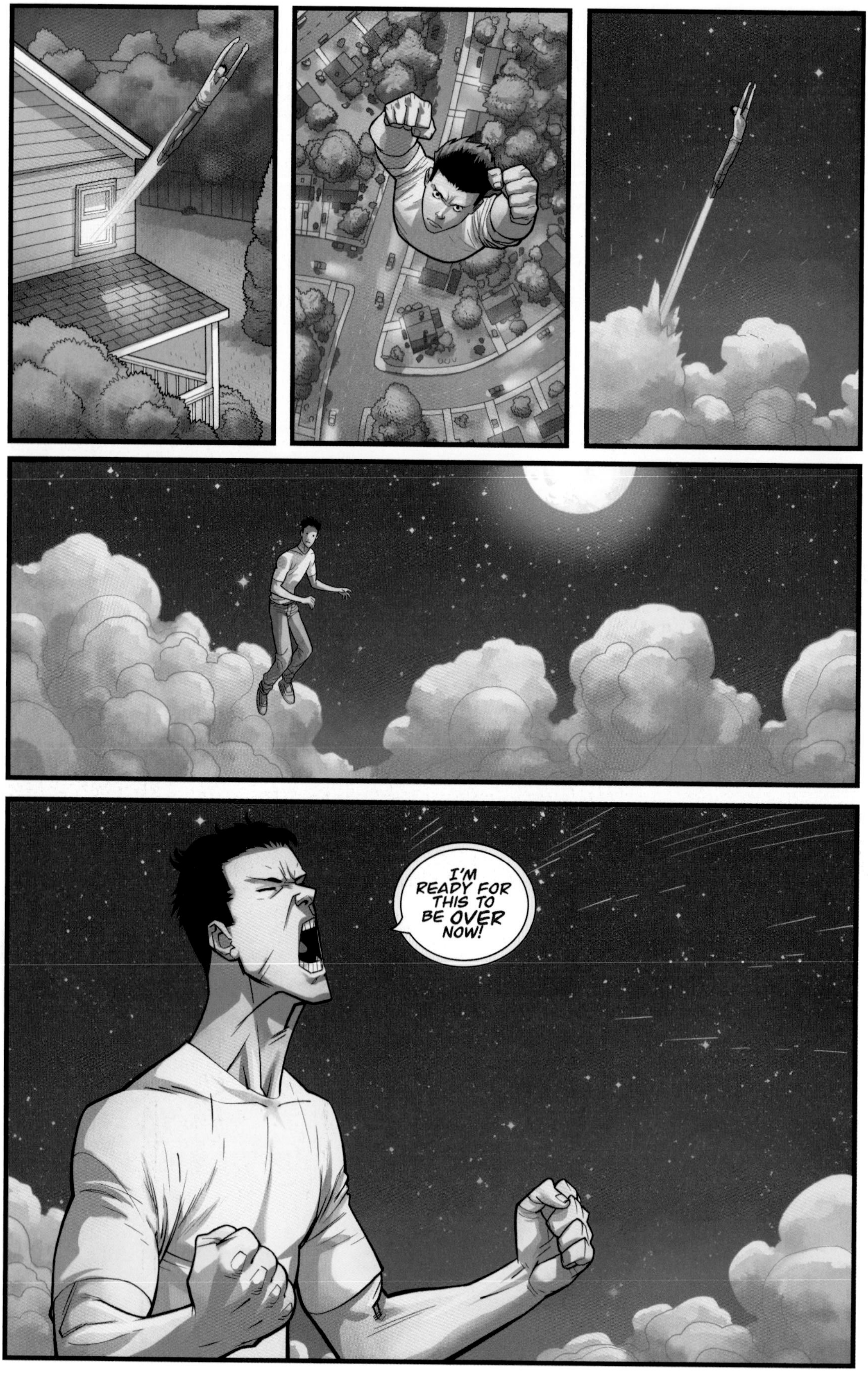
I'M READY FOR THIS TO BE OVER NOW!

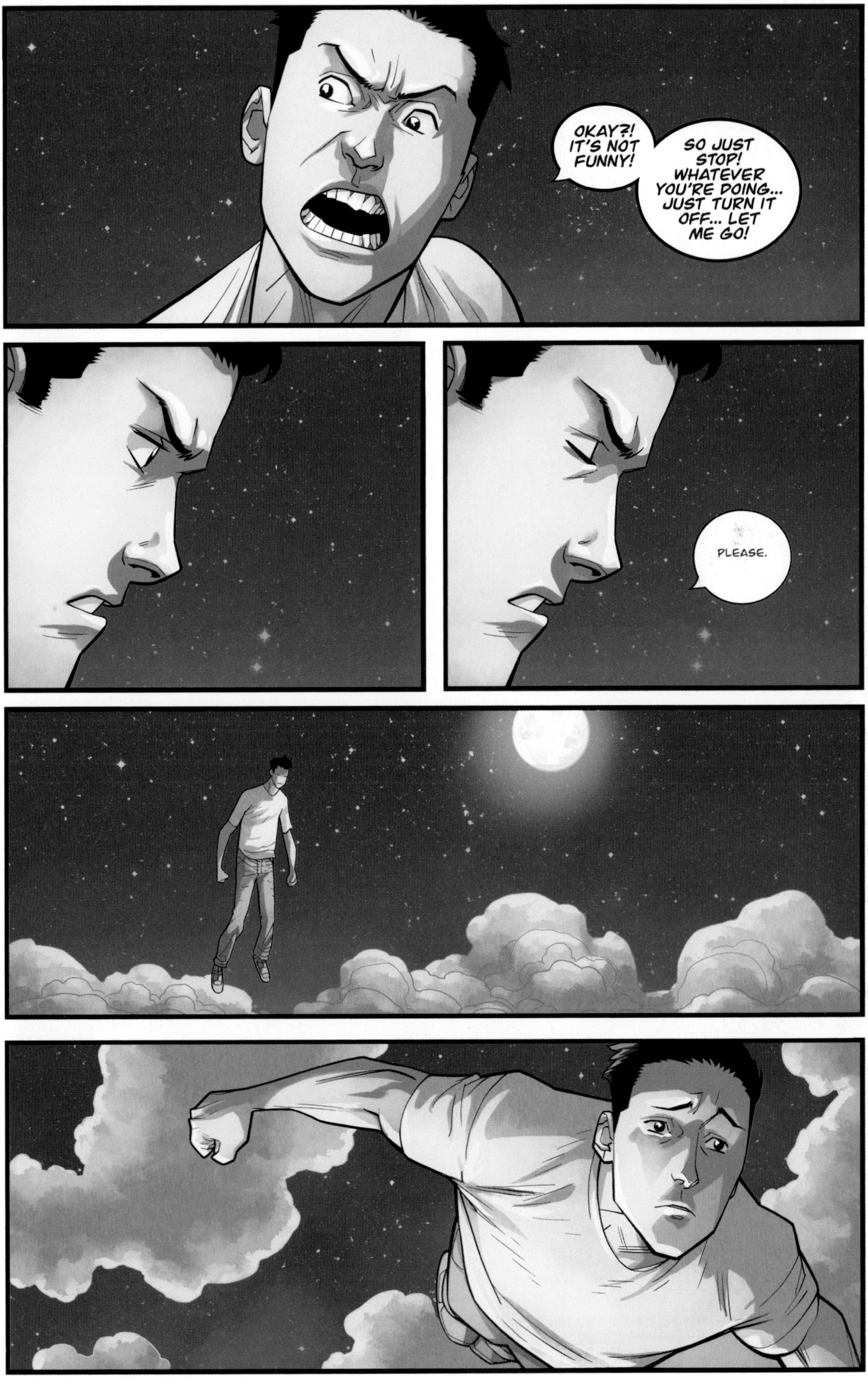
OKAY?! IT'S NOT FUNNY!
SO JUST STOP! WHATEVER YOU'RE DOING... JUST TURN IT OFF... LET ME GO!
PLEASE.

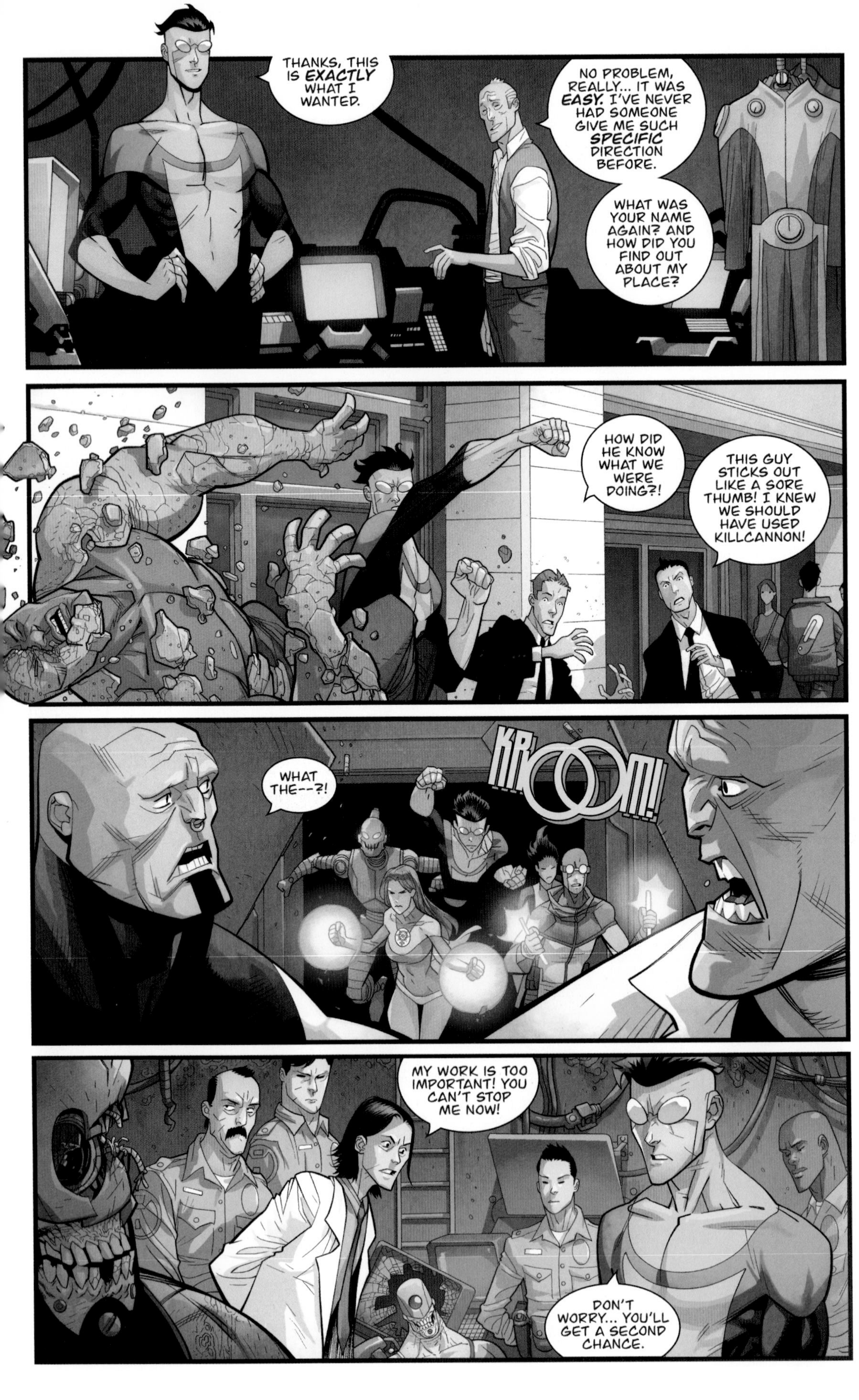
THANKS, THIS IS EXACTLY WHAT I WANTED.
NO PROBLEM, REALLY... IT WAS EASY. I'VE NEVER HAD SOMEONE GIVE ME SUCH SPECIFIC DIRECTION BEFORE.
WHAT WAS YOUR NAME AGAIN? AND HOW DID YOU FIND OUT ABOUT MY PLACE?
HOW DID HE KNOW WHAT WE WERE DOING?!
THIS GUY STICKS OUT LIKE A SORE THUMB! I KNEW WE SHOULD HAVE USED KILLCANNON!
WHAT THE--?!
KROOOM!
MY WORK IS TOO IMPORTANT! YOU CAN'T STOP ME NOW!
DON'T WORRY... YOU'LL GET A SECOND CHANCE.

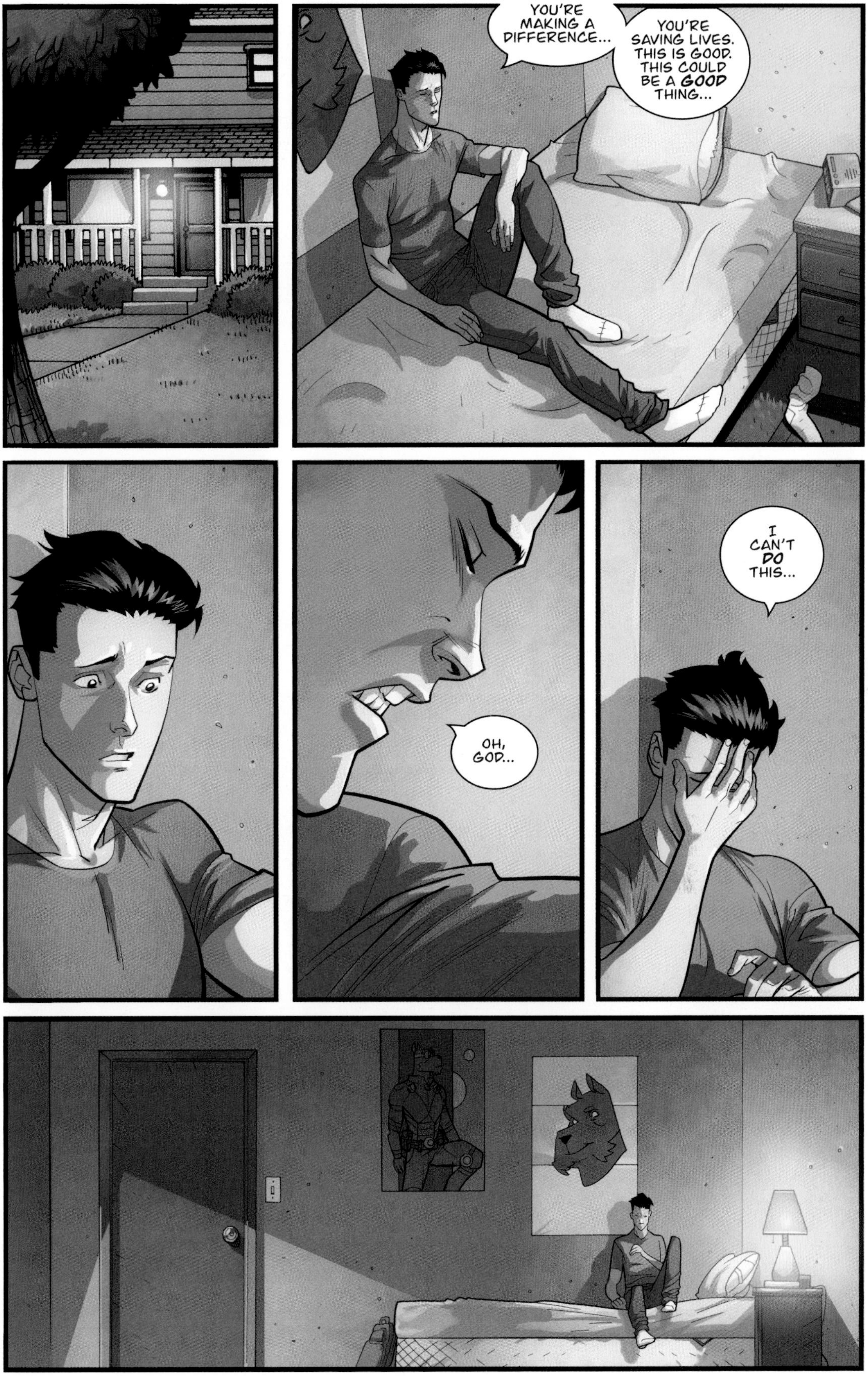
YOU'RE MAKING A DIFFERENCE...
YOU'RE SAVING LIVES. THIS IS GOOD. THIS COULD BE A GOOD THING...
OH, GOD...
I CAN'T DO THIS...

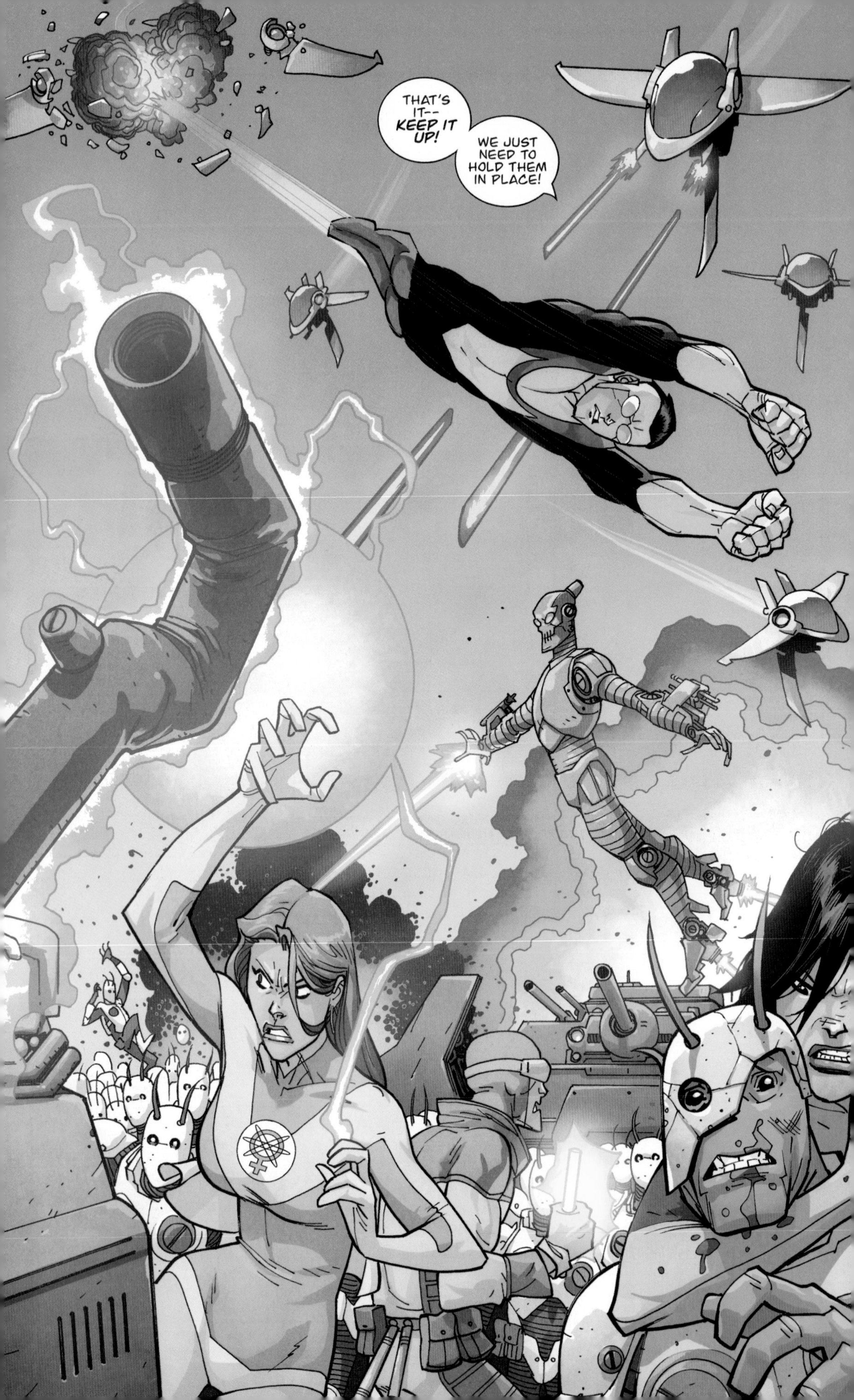
THAT'S IT-- KEEP IT UP!
WE JUST NEED TO HOLD THEM IN PLACE!

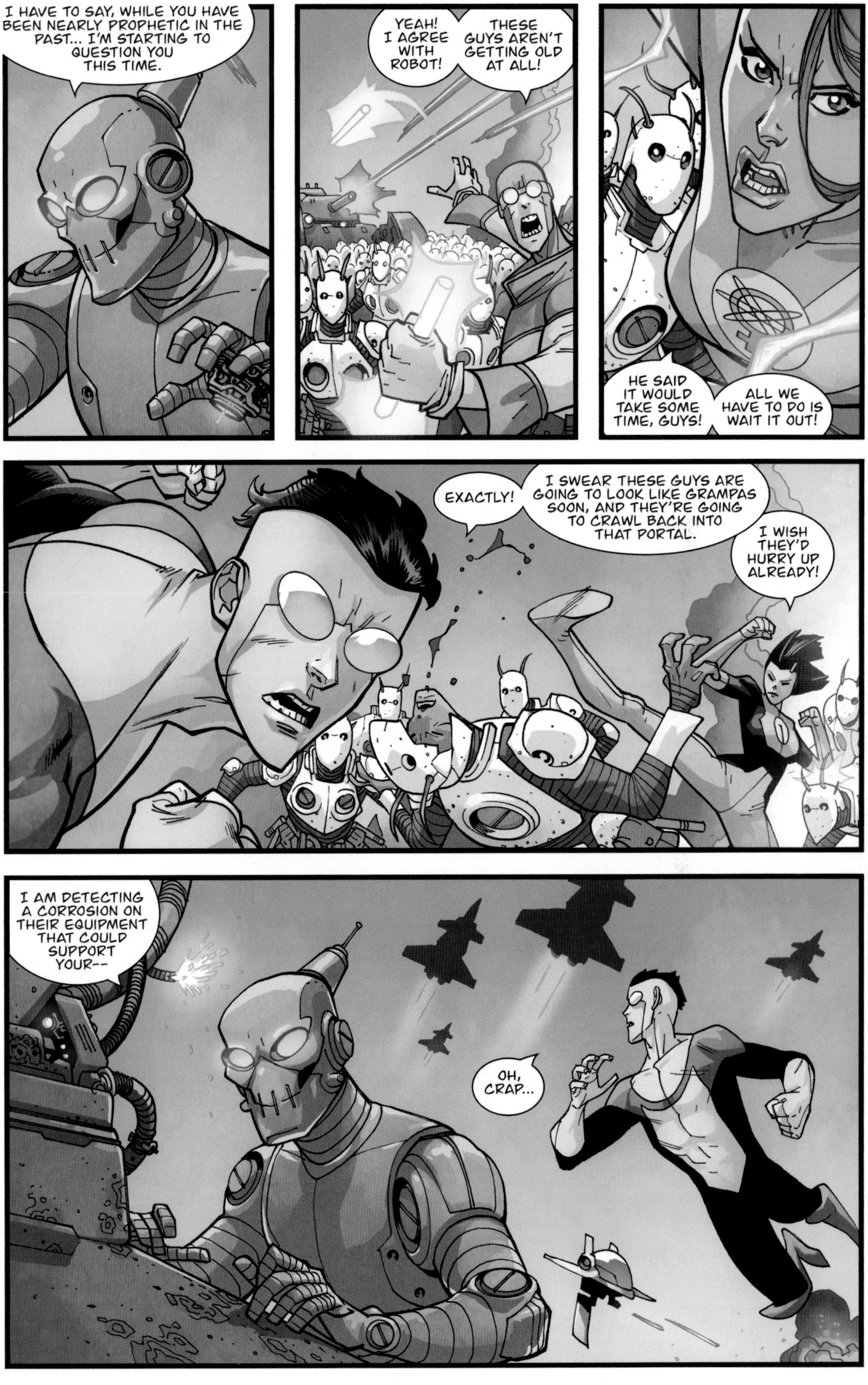
I HAVE TO SAY, WHILE YOU HAVE BEEN NEARLY PROPHETIC IN THE PAST... I'M STARTING TO QUESTION YOU THIS TIME.
YEAH! I AGREE WITH ROBOT!
THESE GUYS AREN'T GETTING OLD AT ALL!
HE SAID IT WOULD TAKE SOME TIME, GUYS!
ALL WE HAVE TO DO IS WAIT IT OUT!
EXACTLY!
I SWEAR THESE GUYS ARE GOING TO LOOK LIKE GRAMPAS SOON, AND THEY'RE GOING TO CRAWL BACK INTO THAT PORTAL.
I WISH THEY'D HURRY UP ALREADY!
I AM DETECTING A CORROSION ON THEIR EQUIPMENT THAT COULD SUPPORT YOUR--
OH, CRAP...

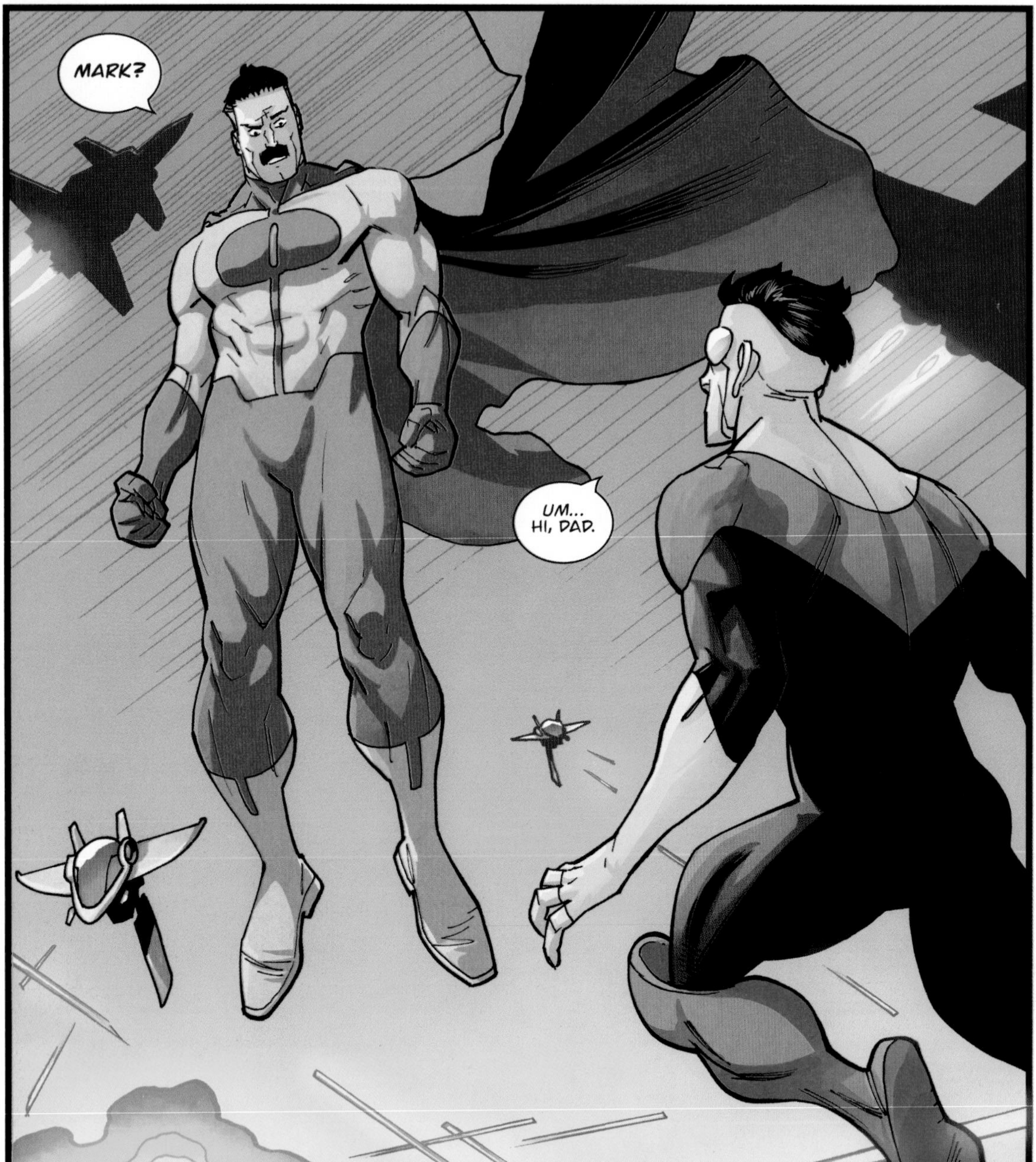
MARK?
UM... HI, DAD.

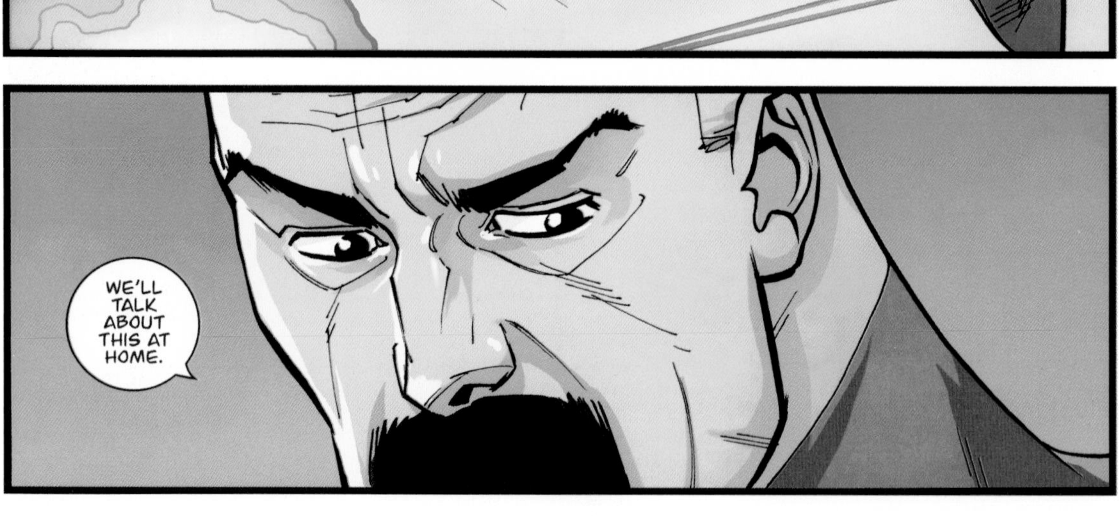
WE'LL TALK ABOUT THIS AT HOME.

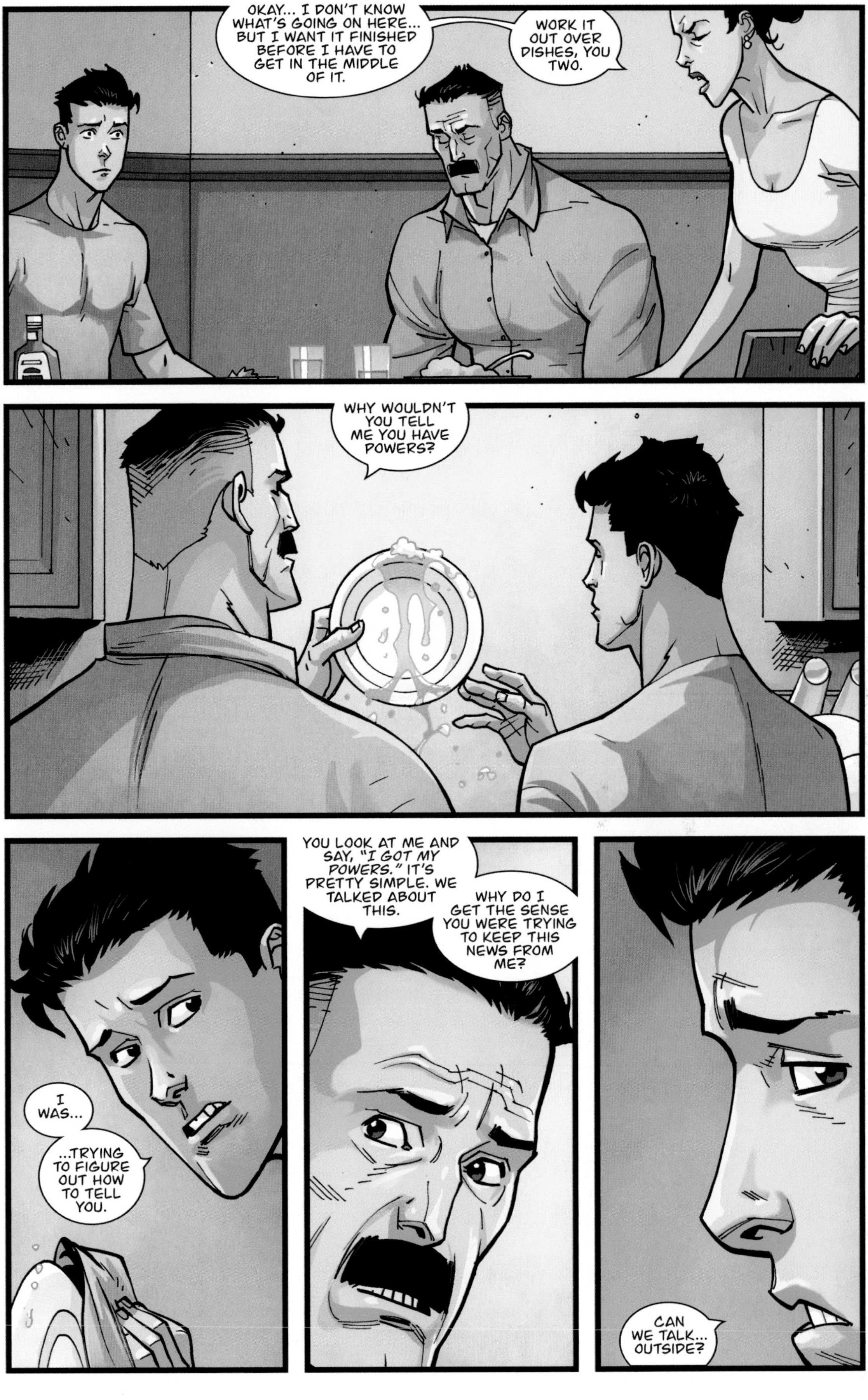
OKAY... I DON'T KNOW WHAT'S GOING ON HERE... BUT I WANT IT FINISHED BEFORE I HAVE TO GET IN THE MIDDLE OF IT.
WORK IT OUT OVER DISHES, YOU TWO.
WHY WOULDN'T YOU TELL ME YOU HAVE POWERS?
I WAS...
...TRYING TO FIGURE OUT HOW TO TELL YOU.
YOU LOOK AT ME AND SAY, "I GOT MY POWERS." IT'S PRETTY SIMPLE. WE TALKED ABOUT THIS.
WHY DO I GET THE SENSE YOU WERE TRYING TO KEEP THIS NEWS FROM ME?
CAN WE TALK... OUTSIDE?

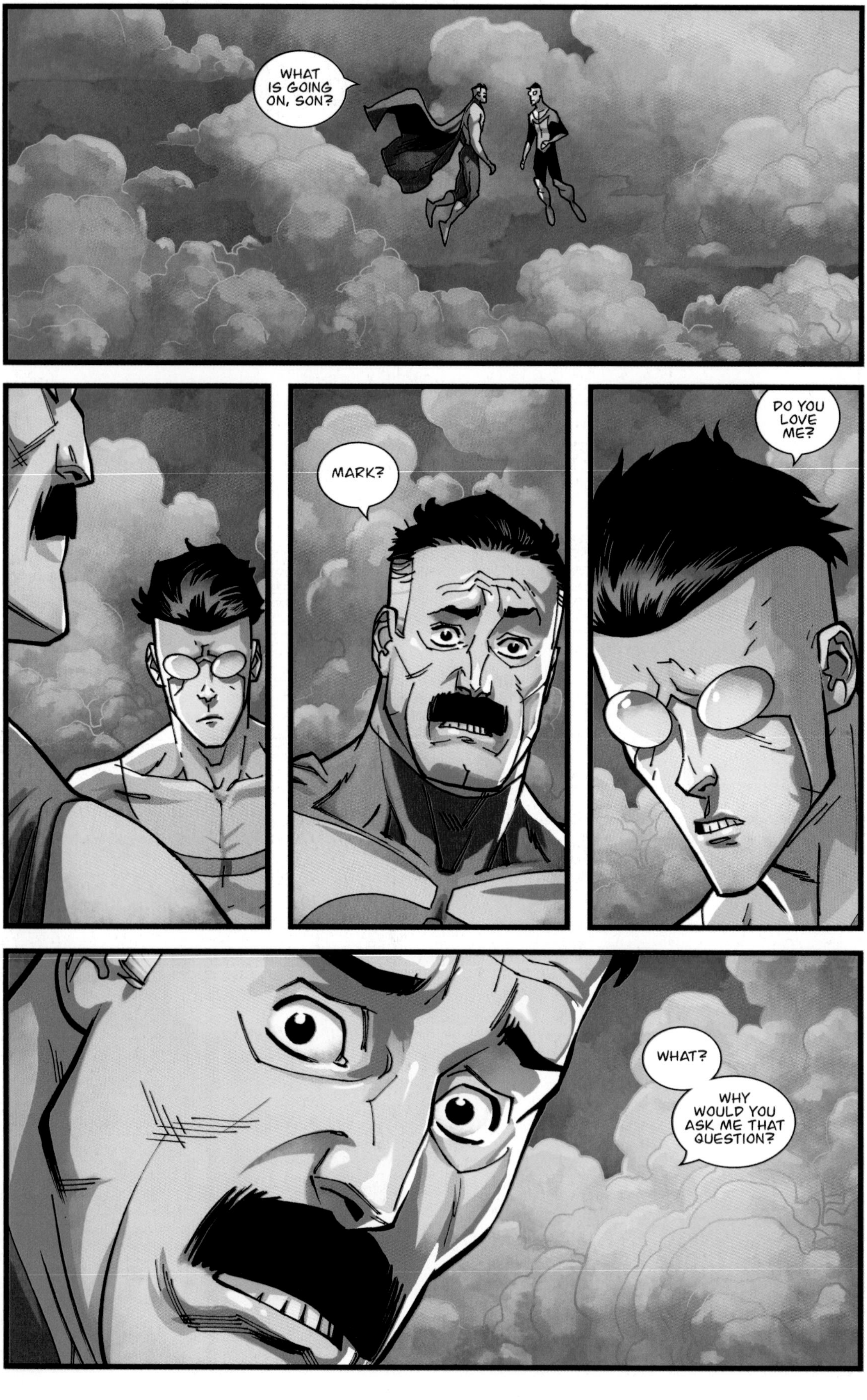
WHAT IS GOING ON, SON?
MARK?
DO YOU LOVE ME?
WHAT?
WHY WOULD YOU ASK ME THAT QUESTION?

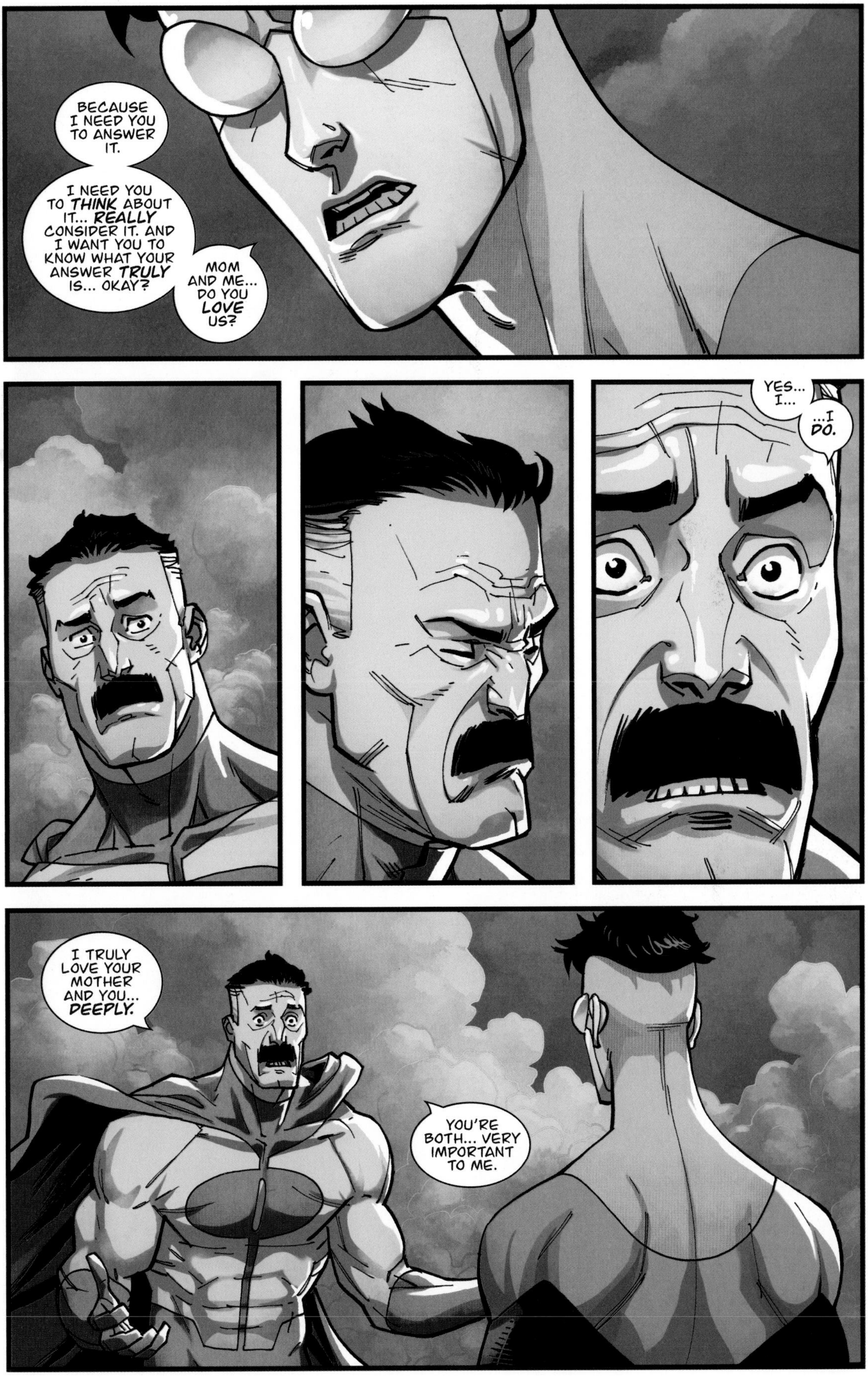
BECAUSE I NEED YOU TO ANSWER IT.
I NEED YOU TO THINK ABOUT IT... REALLY CONSIDER IT. AND I WANT YOU TO KNOW WHAT YOUR ANSWER TRULY IS... OKAY?
MOM AND ME... DO YOU LOVE US?
YES... I...
...I DO.
I TRULY LOVE YOUR MOTHER AND YOU... DEEPLY.
YOU'RE BOTH... VERY IMPORTANT TO ME.

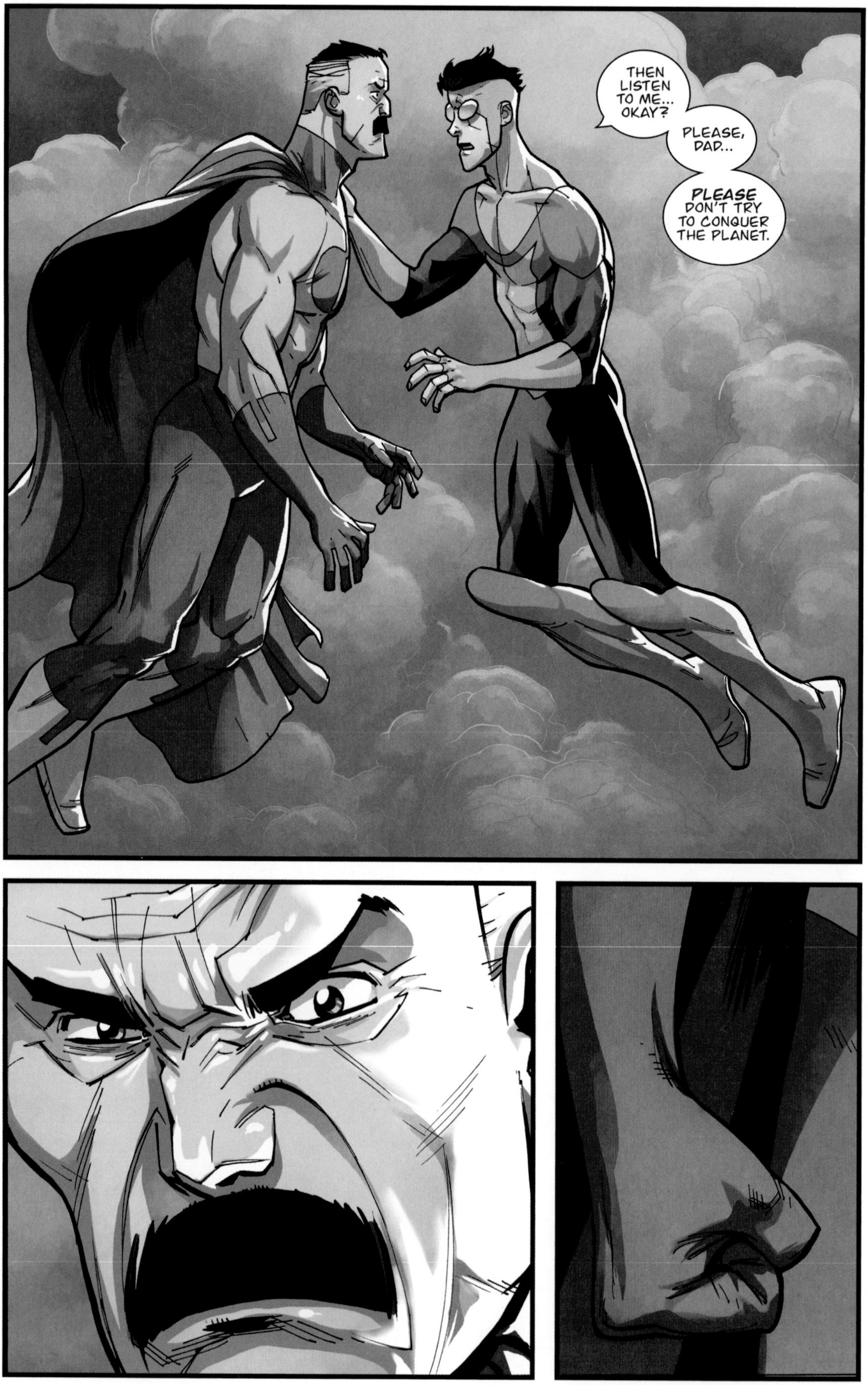
THEN LISTEN TO ME... OKAY?
PLEASE, DAD...
PLEASE DON'T TRY TO CONQUER THE PLANET.

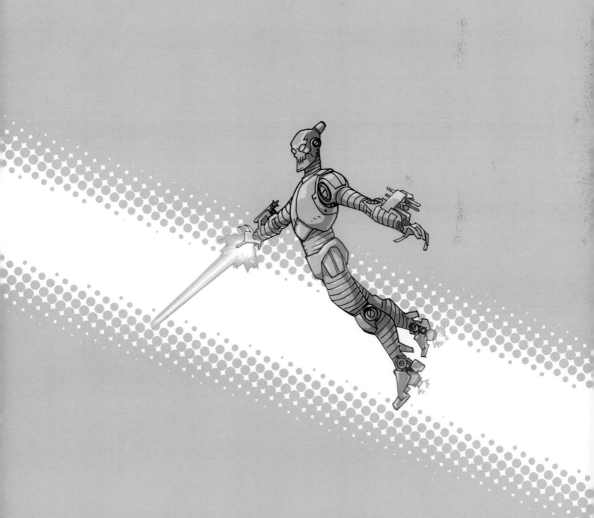

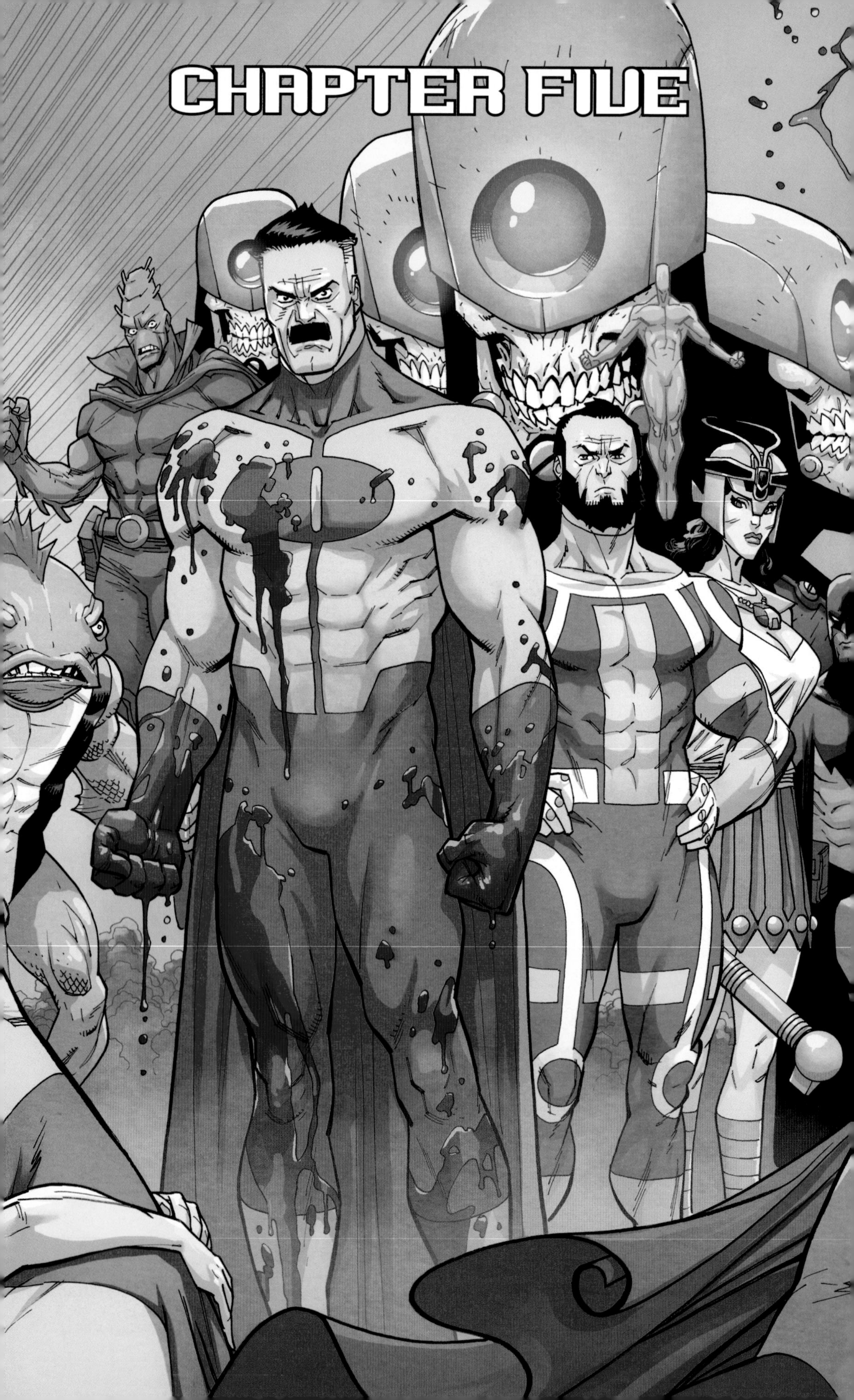
CHAPTER FIVE

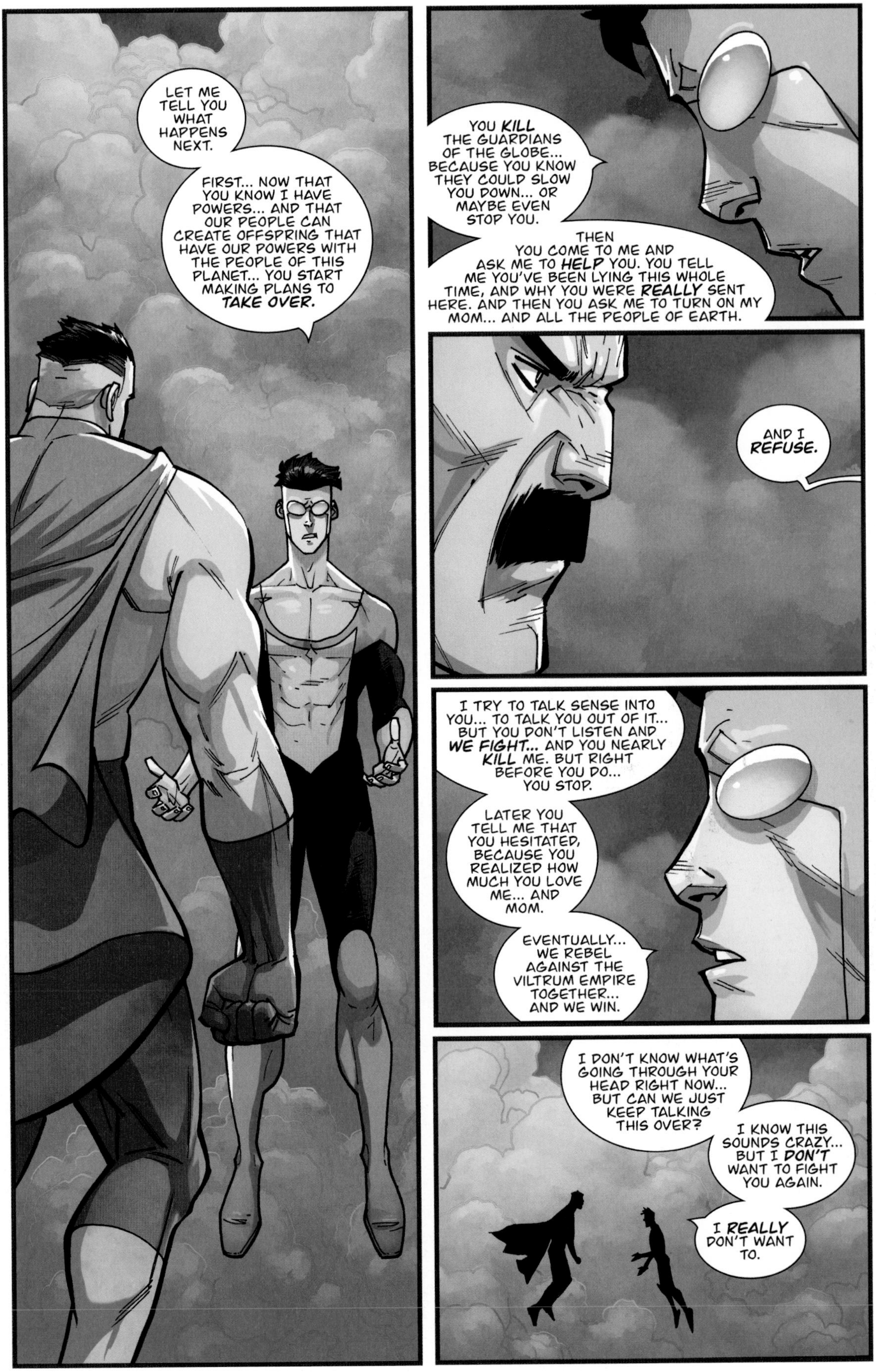
LET ME TELL YOU WHAT HAPPENS NEXT.
FIRST... NOW THAT YOU KNOW I HAVE POWERS... AND THAT OUR PEOPLE CAN CREATE OFFSPRING THAT HAVE OUR POWERS WITH THE PEOPLE OF THIS PLANET... YOU START MAKING PLANS TO TAKE OVER.
YOU KILL THE GUARDIANS OF THE GLOBE... BECAUSE YOU KNOW THEY COULD SLOW YOU DOWN... OR MAYBE EVEN STOP YOU.
THEN YOU COME TO ME AND ASK ME TO HELP YOU. YOU TELL ME YOU'VE BEEN LYING THIS WHOLE TIME, AND WHY YOU WERE REALLY SENT HERE. AND THEN YOU ASK ME TO TURN ON MY MOM... AND ALL THE PEOPLE OF EARTH.
AND I REFUSE.
I TRY TO TALK SENSE INTO YOU... TO TALK YOU OUT OF IT... BUT YOU DON'T LISTEN AND WE FIGHT... AND YOU NEARLY KILL ME. BUT RIGHT BEFORE YOU DO... YOU STOP.
LATER YOU TELL ME THAT YOU HESITATED, BECAUSE YOU REALIZED HOW MUCH YOU LOVE ME... AND MOM.
EVENTUALLY... WE REBEL AGAINST THE VILTRUM EMPIRE TOGETHER... AND WE WIN.
I DON'T KNOW WHAT'S GOING THROUGH YOUR HEAD RIGHT NOW... BUT CAN WE JUST KEEP TALKING THIS OVER?
I KNOW THIS SOUNDS CRAZY... BUT I DON'T WANT TO FIGHT YOU AGAIN.
I REALLY DON'T WANT TO.

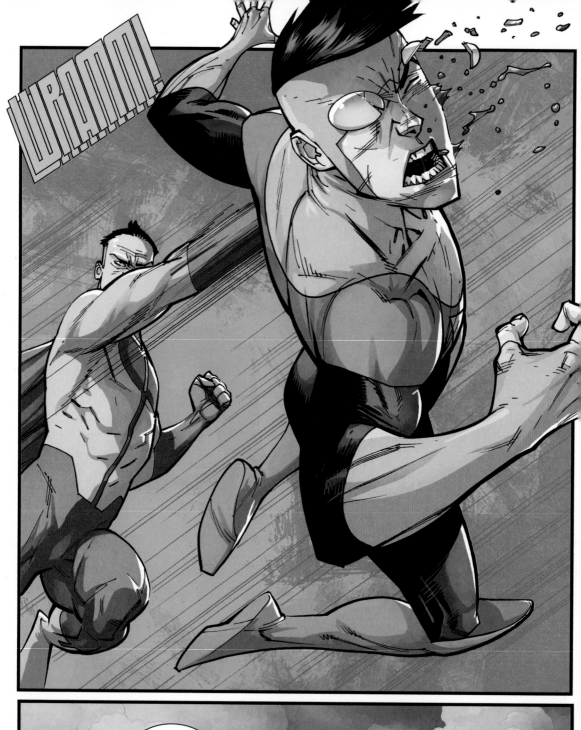

YOU CAN'T DEFY THE VILTRUM EMPIRE.

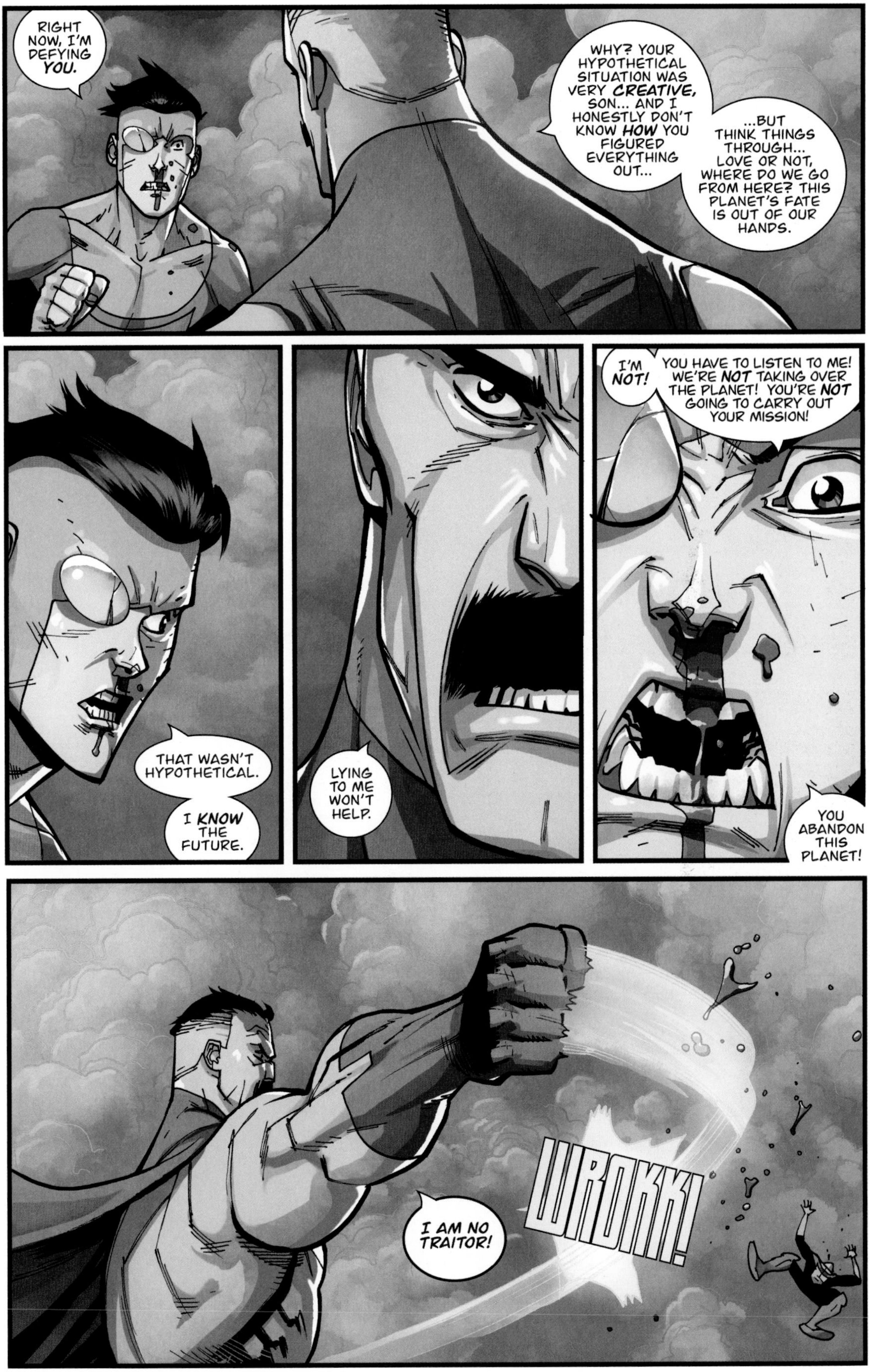
RIGHT NOW, I'M DEFYING *YOU.*
WHY? YOUR HYPOTHETICAL SITUATION WAS VERY *CREATIVE,* SON... AND I HONESTLY DON'T KNOW *HOW* YOU FIGURED EVERYTHING OUT...
...BUT THINK THINGS THROUGH... LOVE OR NOT, WHERE DO WE GO FROM HERE? THIS PLANET'S FATE IS OUT OF OUR HANDS.
THAT WASN'T HYPOTHETICAL.
I *KNOW* THE FUTURE.
LYING TO ME WON'T HELP.
I'M *NOT!*
YOU HAVE TO LISTEN TO ME! WE'RE *NOT* TAKING OVER THE PLANET! YOU'RE *NOT* GOING TO CARRY OUT YOUR MISSION!
YOU ABANDON THIS PLANET!
I AM NO TRAITOR!
WROKK!

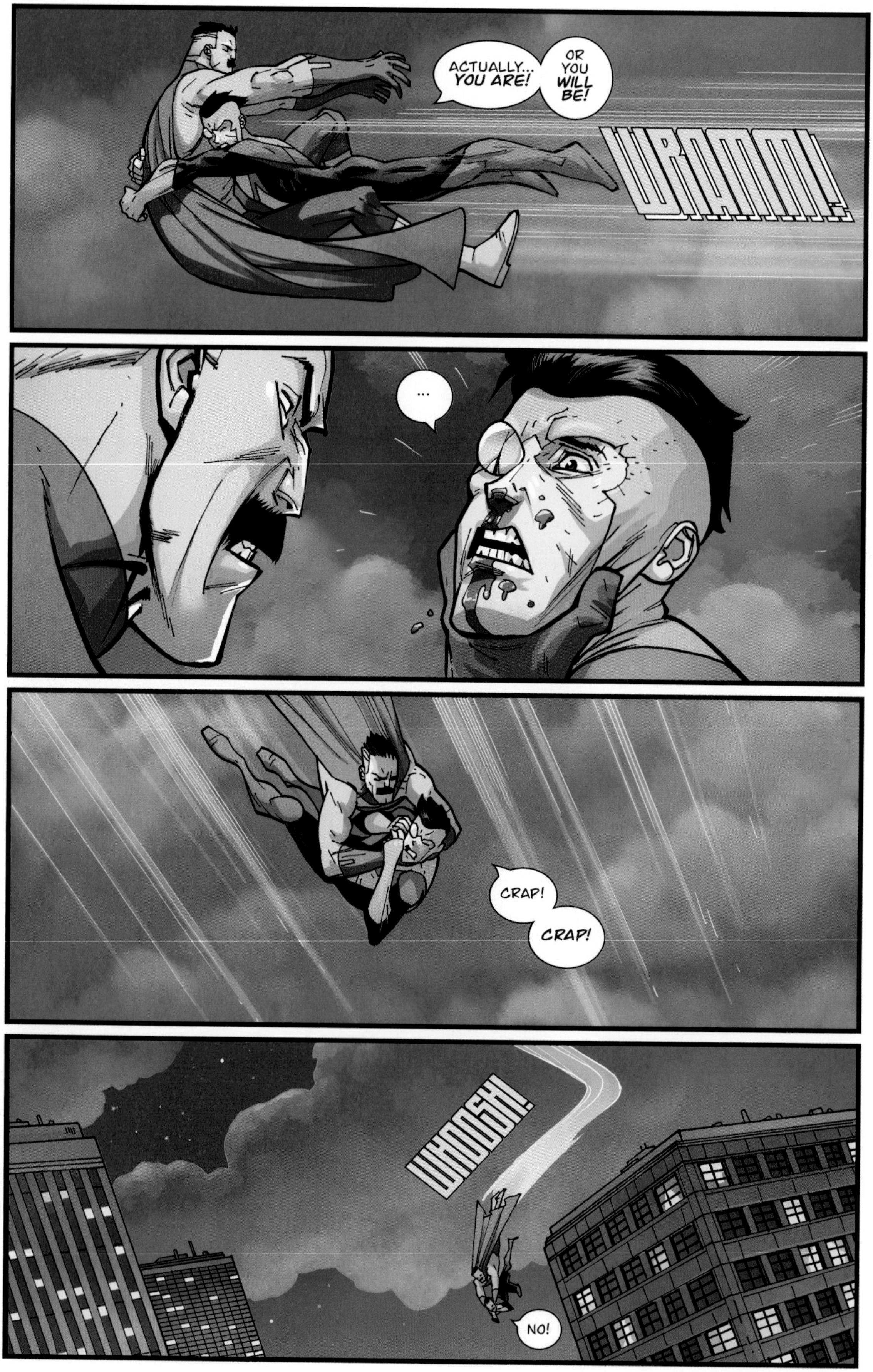
ACTUALLY... YOU ARE!
OR YOU WILL BE!
WHAMM!
...
CRAP!
CRAP!
WHOOSH!
NO!

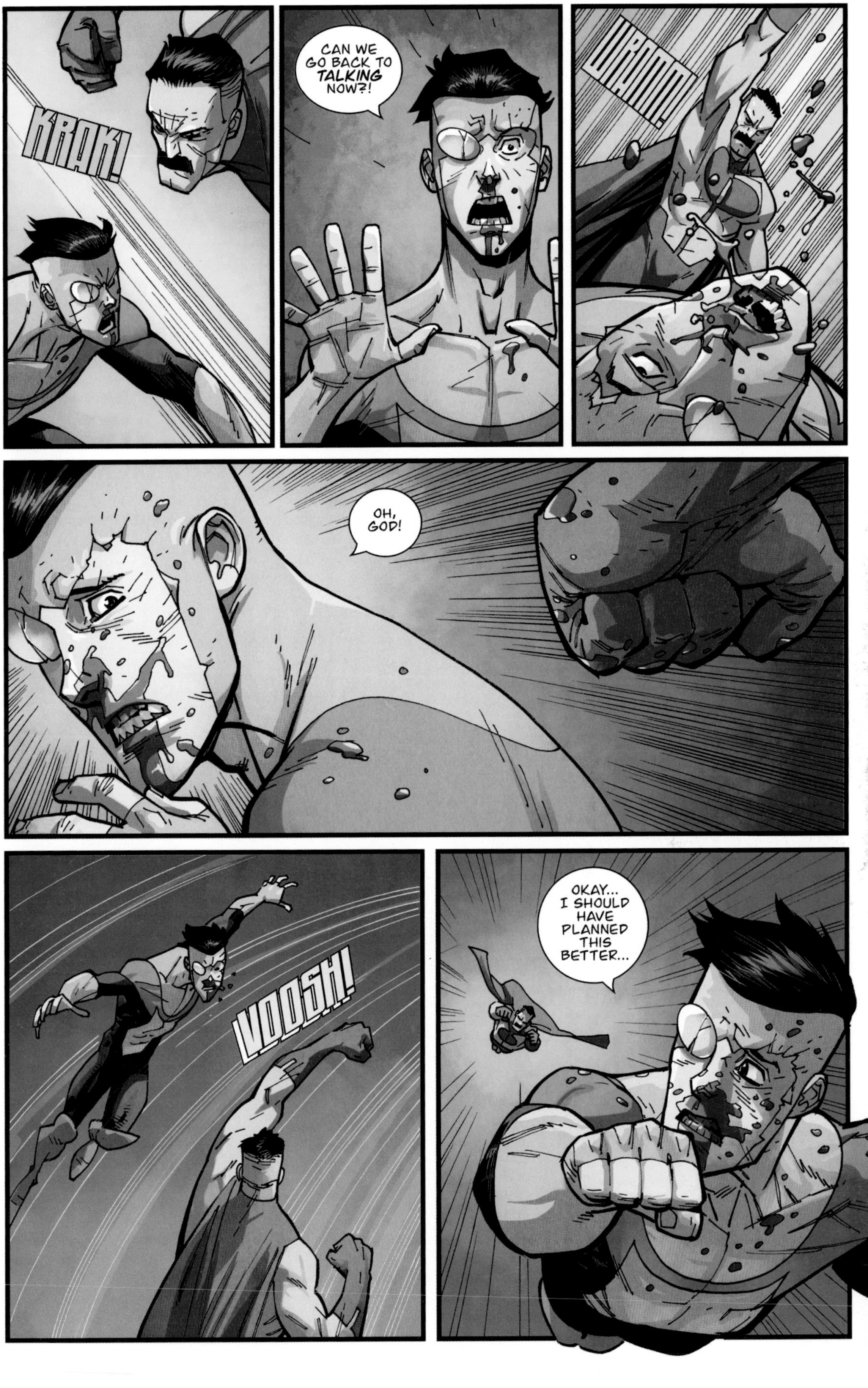
KRAK!
CAN WE GO BACK TO TALKING NOW?!
OH, GOD!
VOOSH!
OKAY... I SHOULD HAVE PLANNED THIS BETTER...

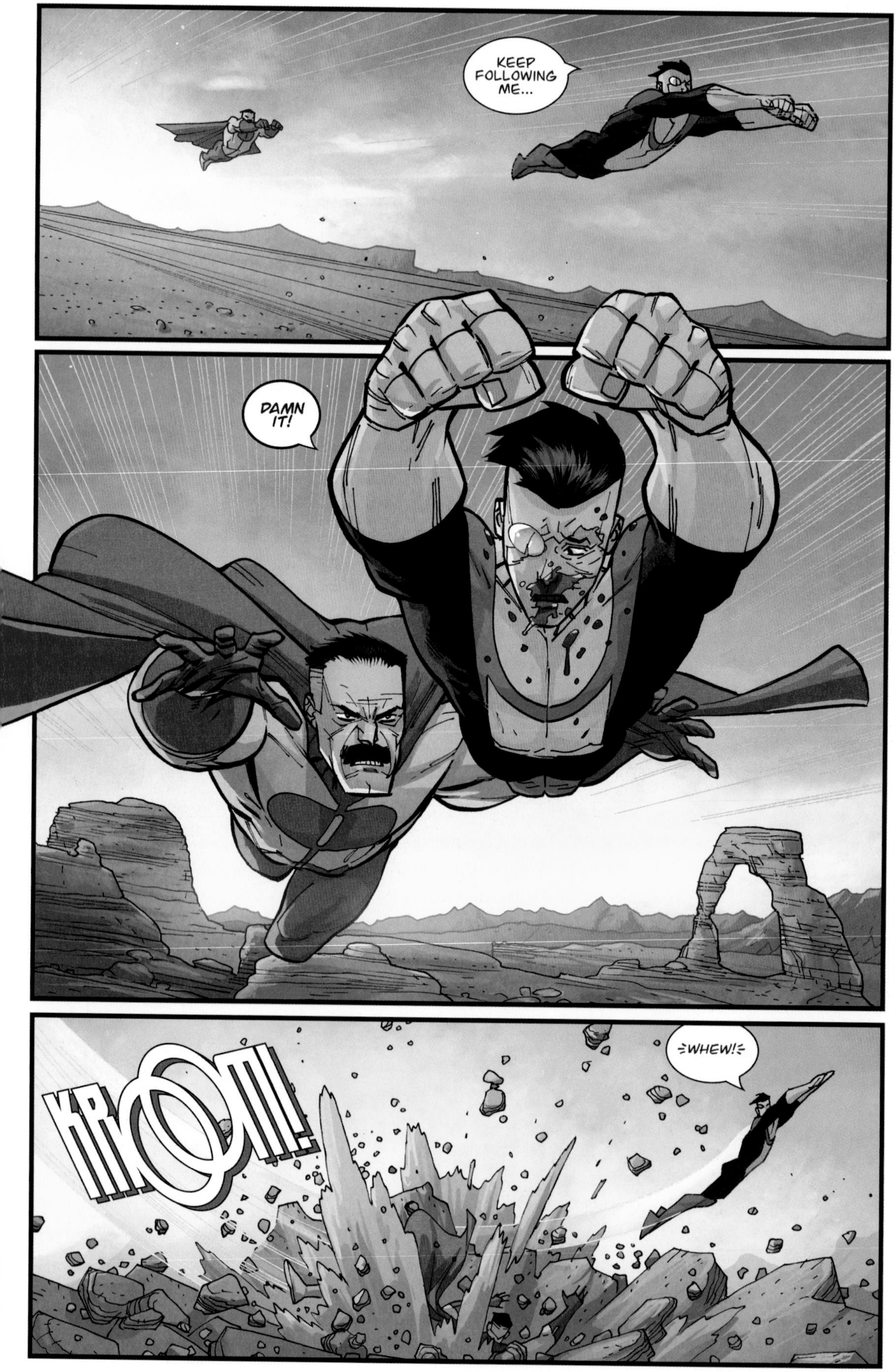
KEEP FOLLOWING ME...
DAMN IT!
KRROOM!!
WHEW!

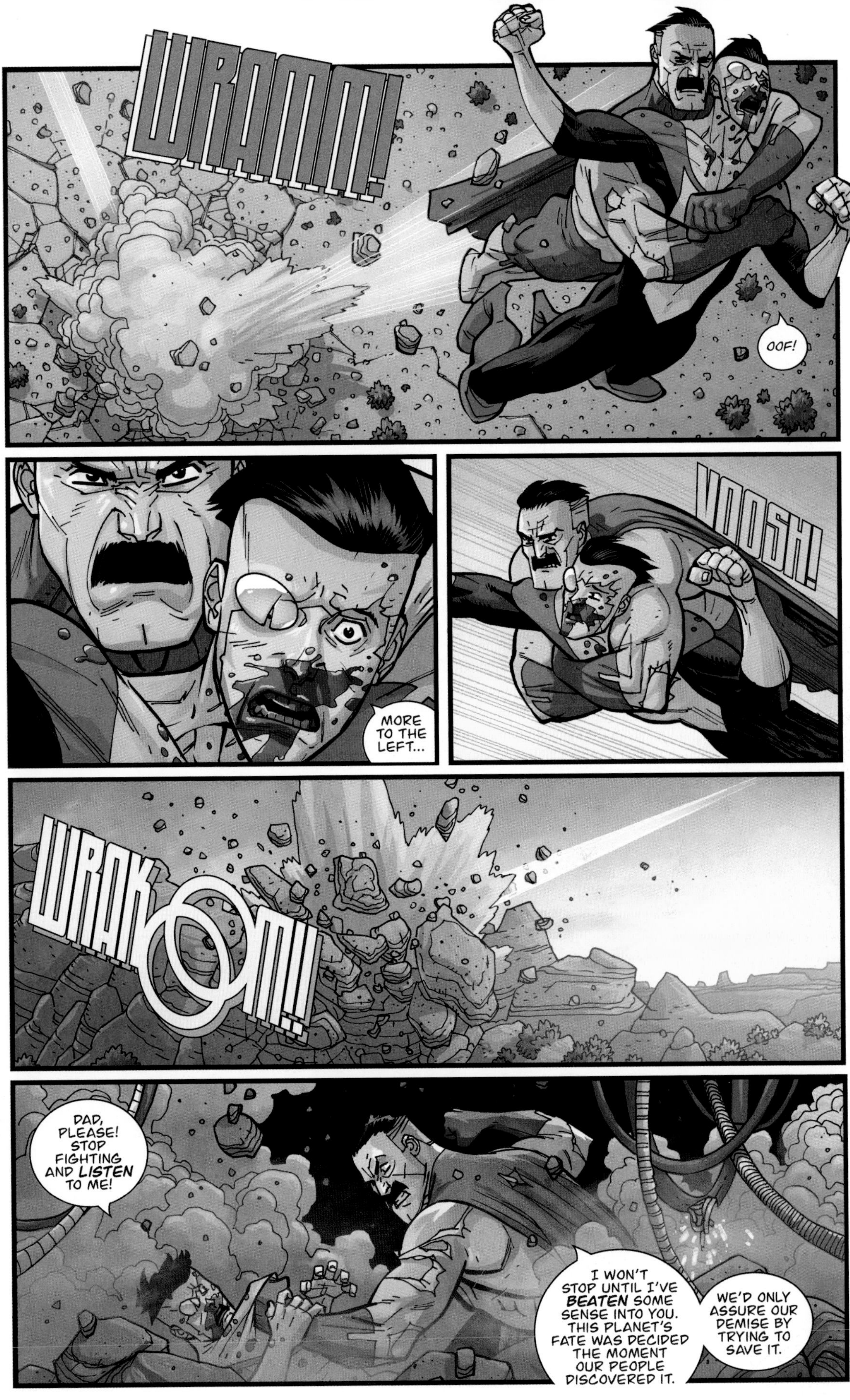
WRAMM!
OOF!
MORE TO THE LEFT...
VOOSH!
WRAKOOM!!
DAD, PLEASE! STOP FIGHTING AND *LISTEN* TO ME!
I WON'T STOP UNTIL I'VE *BEATEN* SOME SENSE INTO YOU. THIS PLANET'S FATE WAS DECIDED THE MOMENT OUR PEOPLE DISCOVERED IT.
WE'D ONLY ASSURE OUR DEMISE BY TRYING TO SAVE IT.

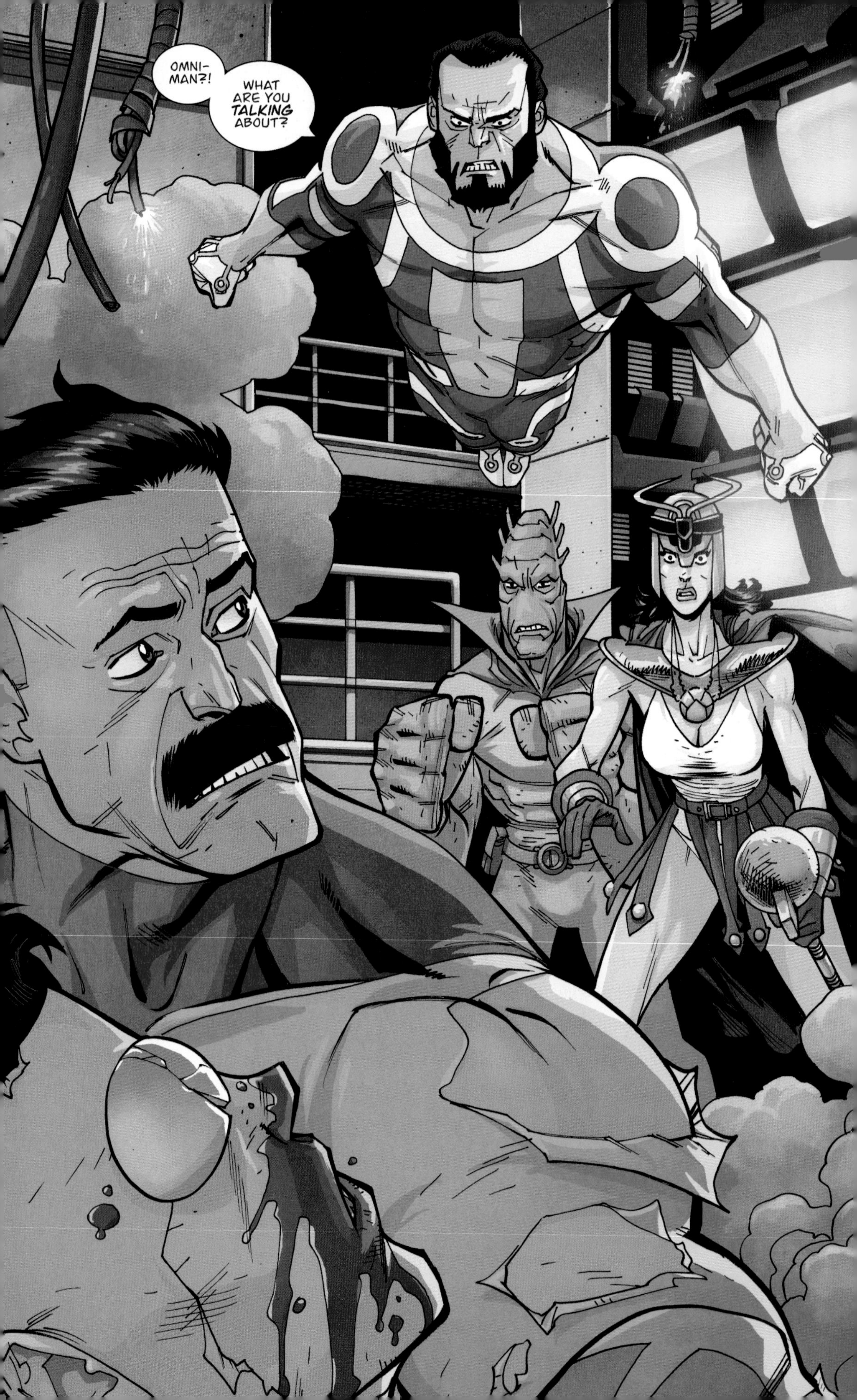
OMNI-MAN?!
WHAT ARE YOU TALKING ABOUT?

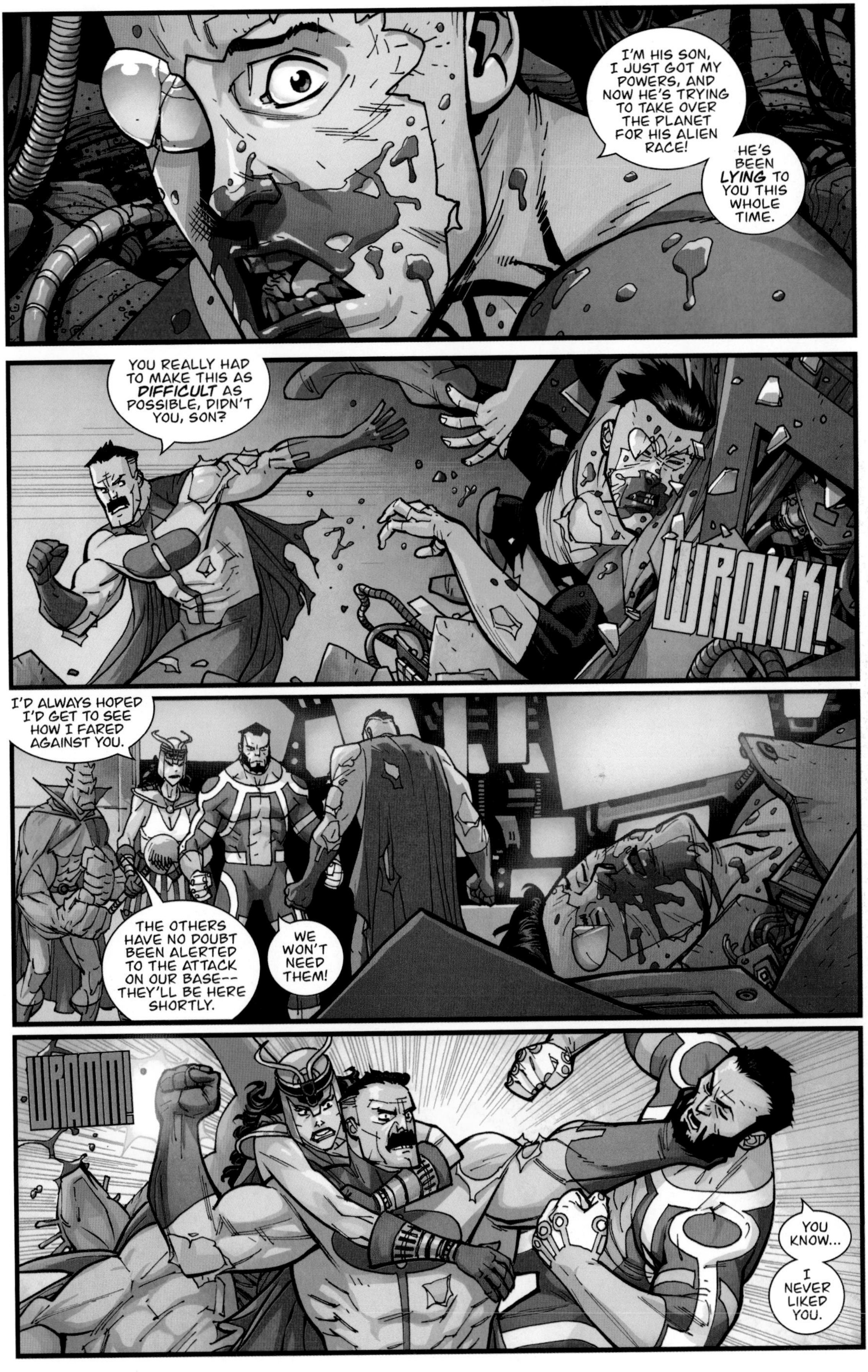
I'M HIS SON, I JUST GOT MY POWERS, AND NOW HE'S TRYING TO TAKE OVER THE PLANET FOR HIS ALIEN RACE!
HE'S BEEN LYING TO YOU THIS WHOLE TIME.
YOU REALLY HAD TO MAKE THIS AS DIFFICULT AS POSSIBLE, DIDN'T YOU, SON?
WRAKK!
I'D ALWAYS HOPED I'D GET TO SEE HOW I FARED AGAINST YOU.
THE OTHERS HAVE NO DOUBT BEEN ALERTED TO THE ATTACK ON OUR BASE-- THEY'LL BE HERE SHORTLY.
WE WON'T NEED THEM!
WRAMM!
YOU KNOW...
I NEVER LIKED YOU.

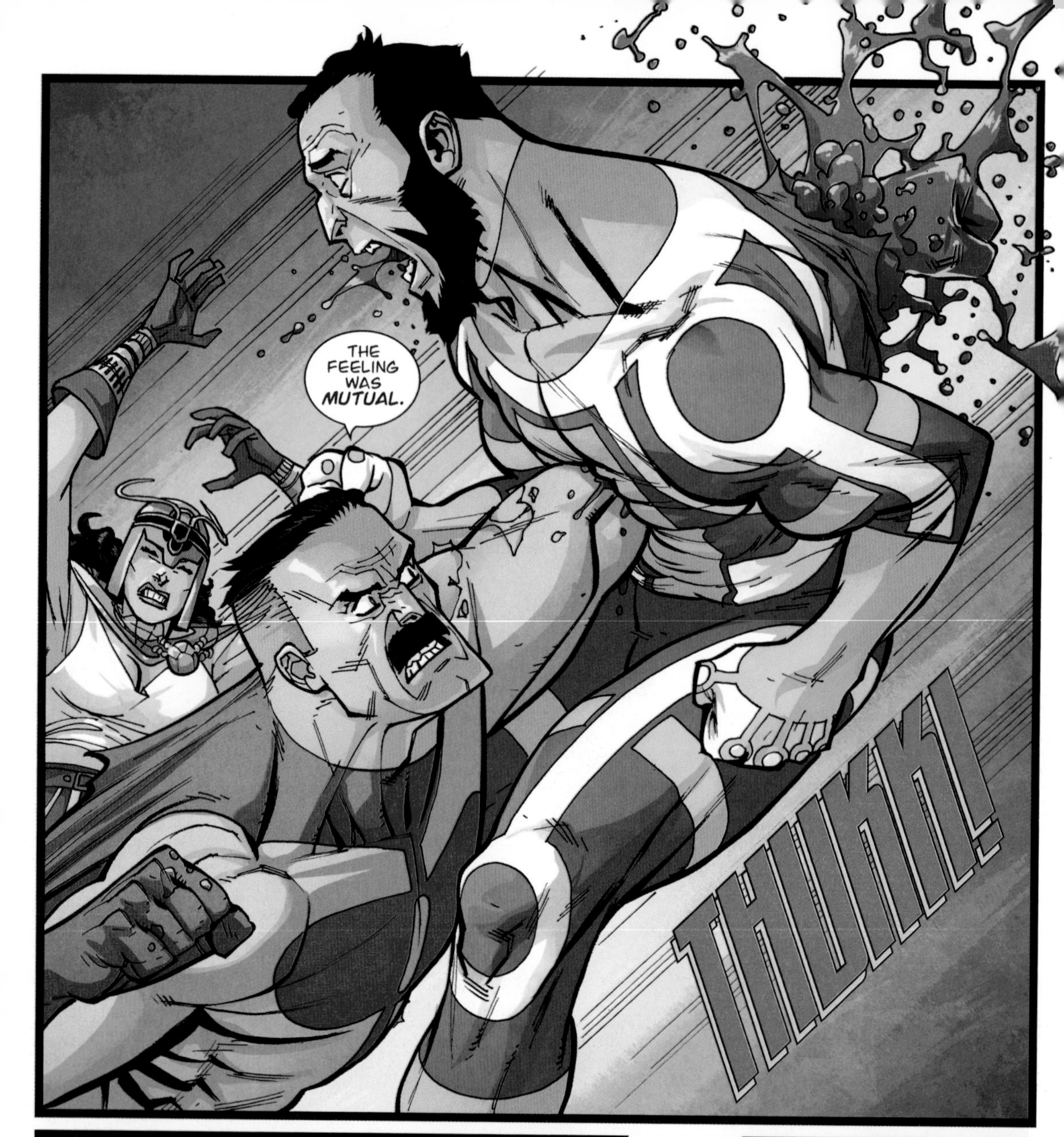
THE FEELING WAS MUTUAL.
THUKK!

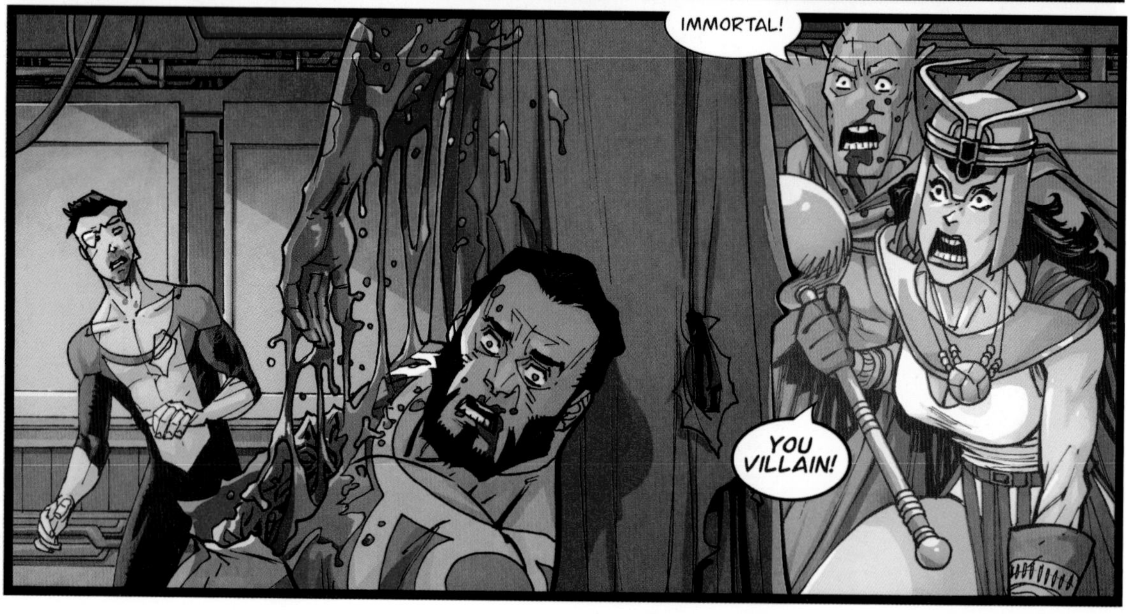
IMMORTAL!
YOU VILLAIN!

STOP FIGHTING THIS!

THIS ISN'T YOU. I KNOW YOU!

YOU DON'T WANT TO DO THIS! YOU JUST FEEL LIKE YOU *HAVE* NO CHOICE!

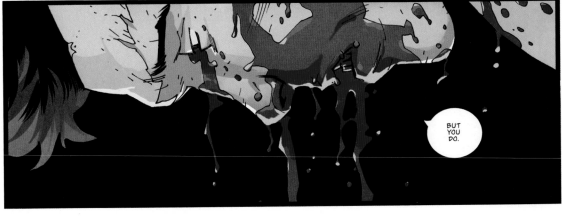

BUT YOU DO.

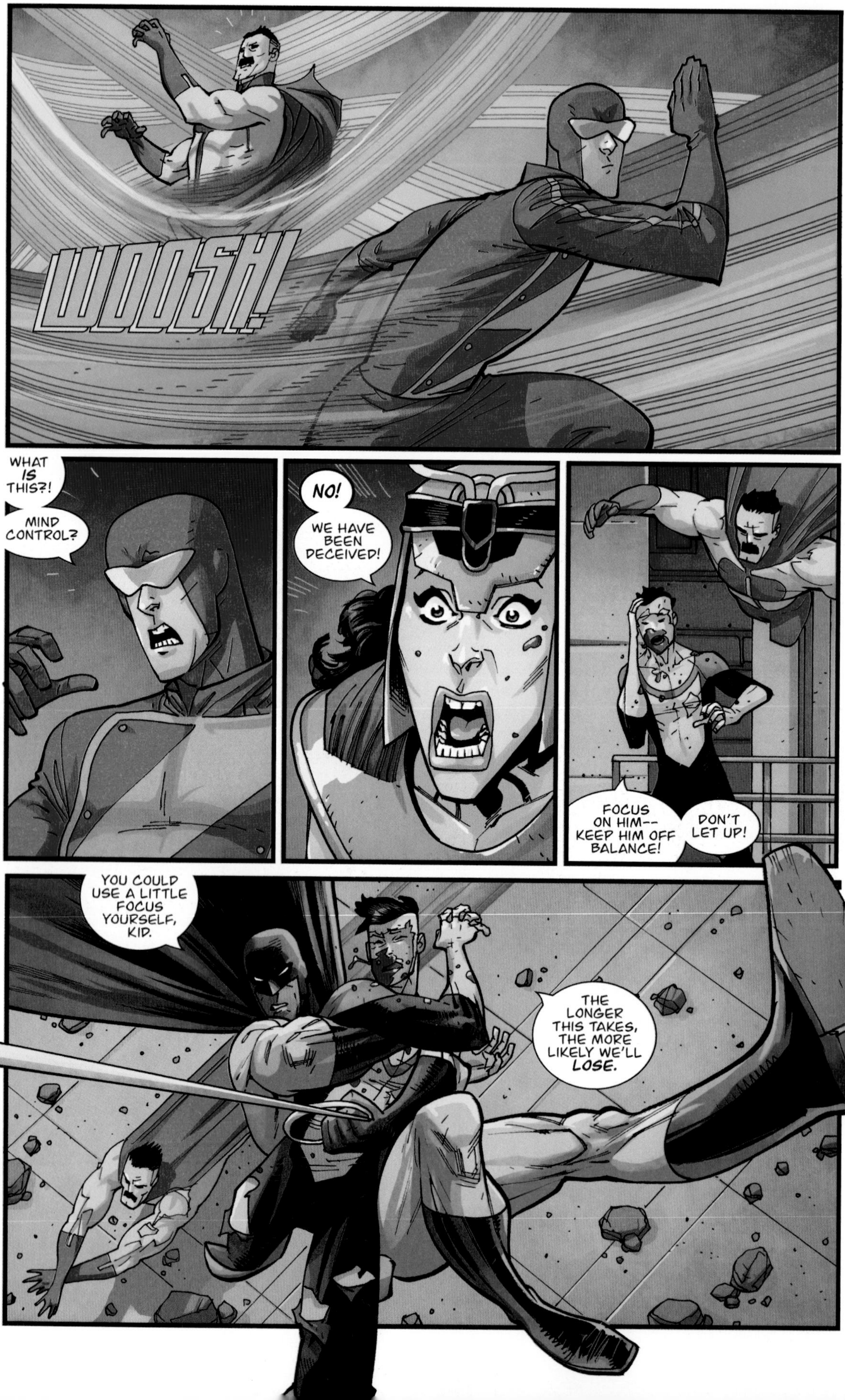
WOOSH!
WHAT IS THIS?!
MIND CONTROL?
NO!
WE HAVE BEEN DECEIVED!
FOCUS ON HIM-- KEEP HIM OFF BALANCE!
DON'T LET UP!
YOU COULD USE A LITTLE FOCUS YOURSELF, KID.
THE LONGER THIS TAKES, THE MORE LIKELY WE'LL LOSE.

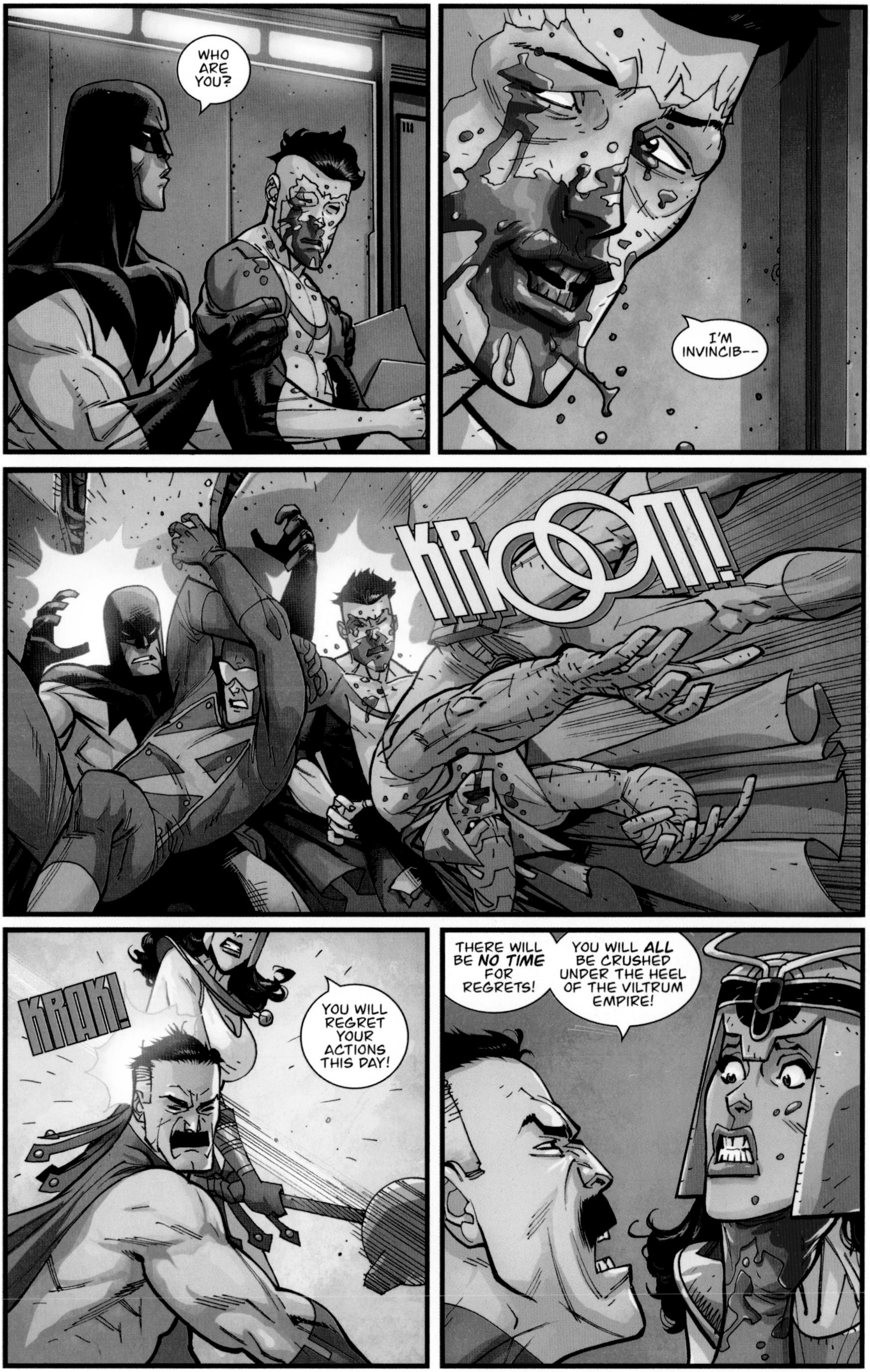
WHO ARE YOU?
I'M INVINCIB--
KROOM!
KRAK!
YOU WILL REGRET YOUR ACTIONS THIS DAY!
THERE WILL BE NO TIME FOR REGRETS!
YOU WILL ALL BE CRUSHED UNDER THE HEEL OF THE VILTRUM EMPIRE!

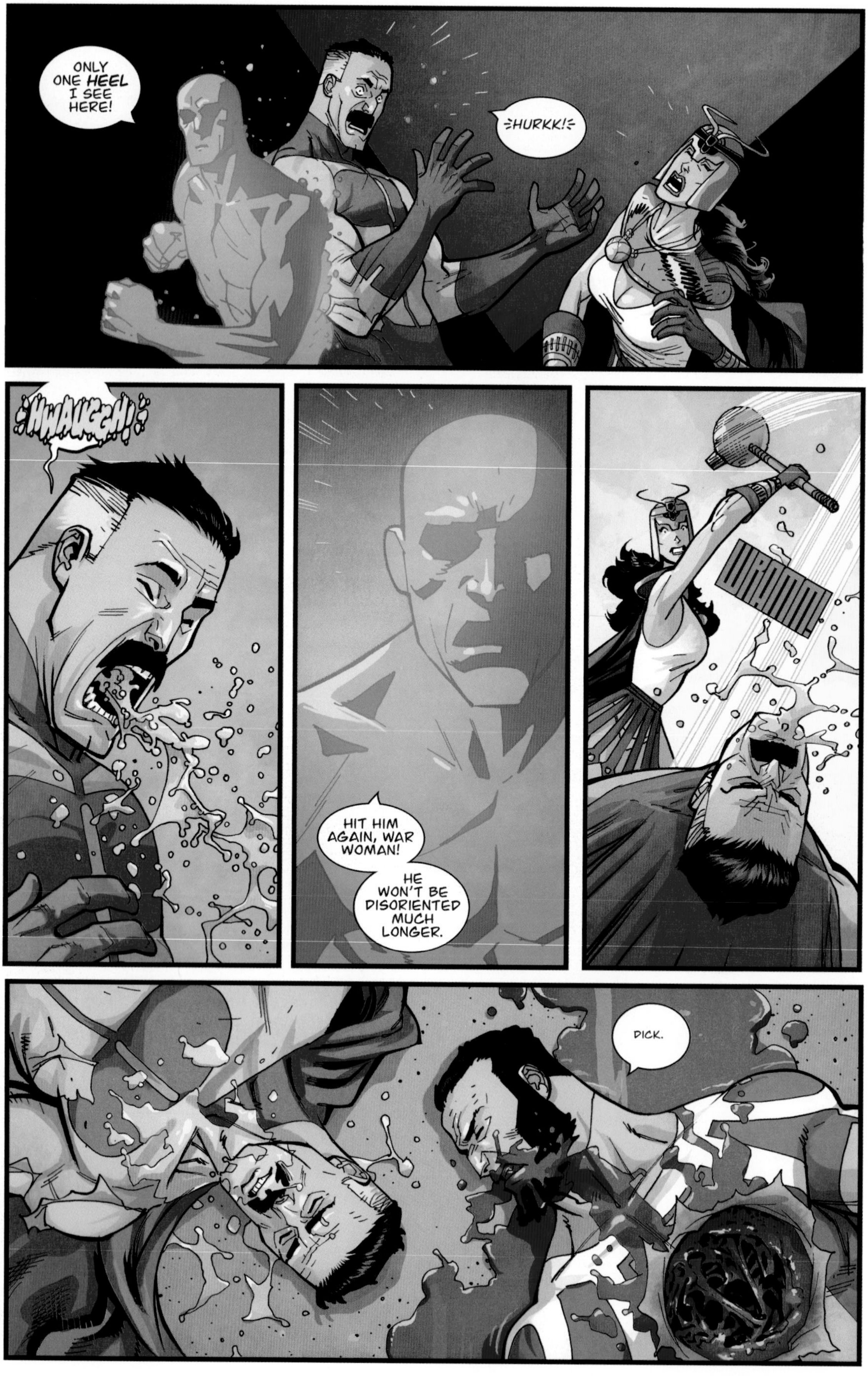
ONLY ONE HEEL I SEE HERE!
HURKK!
HWAUGGH!
HIT HIM AGAIN, WAR WOMAN!
HE WON'T BE DISORIENTED MUCH LONGER.
DICK.

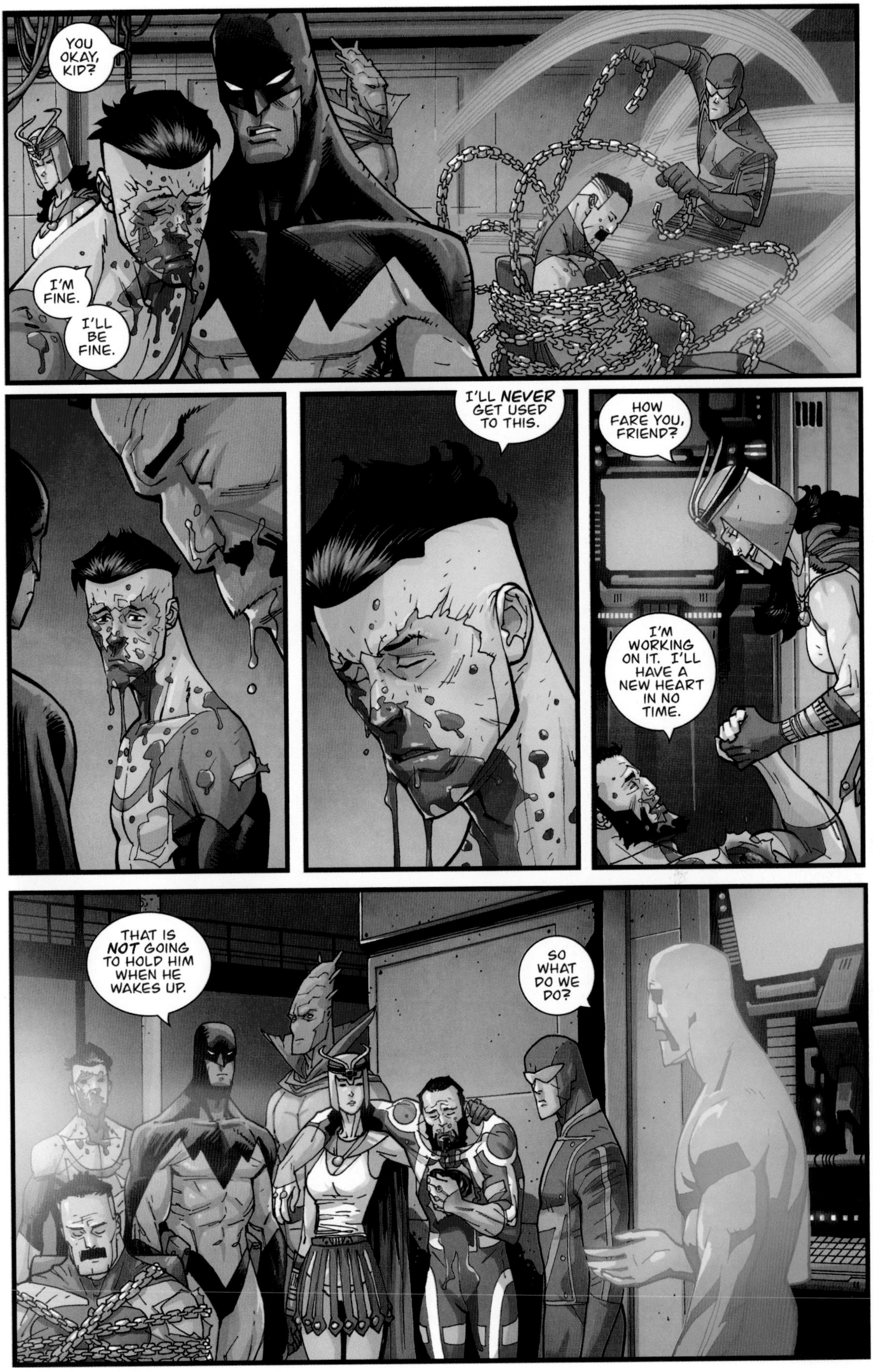
YOU OKAY, KID?
I'M FINE.
I'LL BE FINE.
I'LL **NEVER** GET USED TO THIS.
HOW FARE YOU, FRIEND?
I'M WORKING ON IT. I'LL HAVE A NEW HEART IN NO TIME.
THAT IS **NOT** GOING TO HOLD HIM WHEN HE WAKES UP.
SO WHAT DO WE DO?

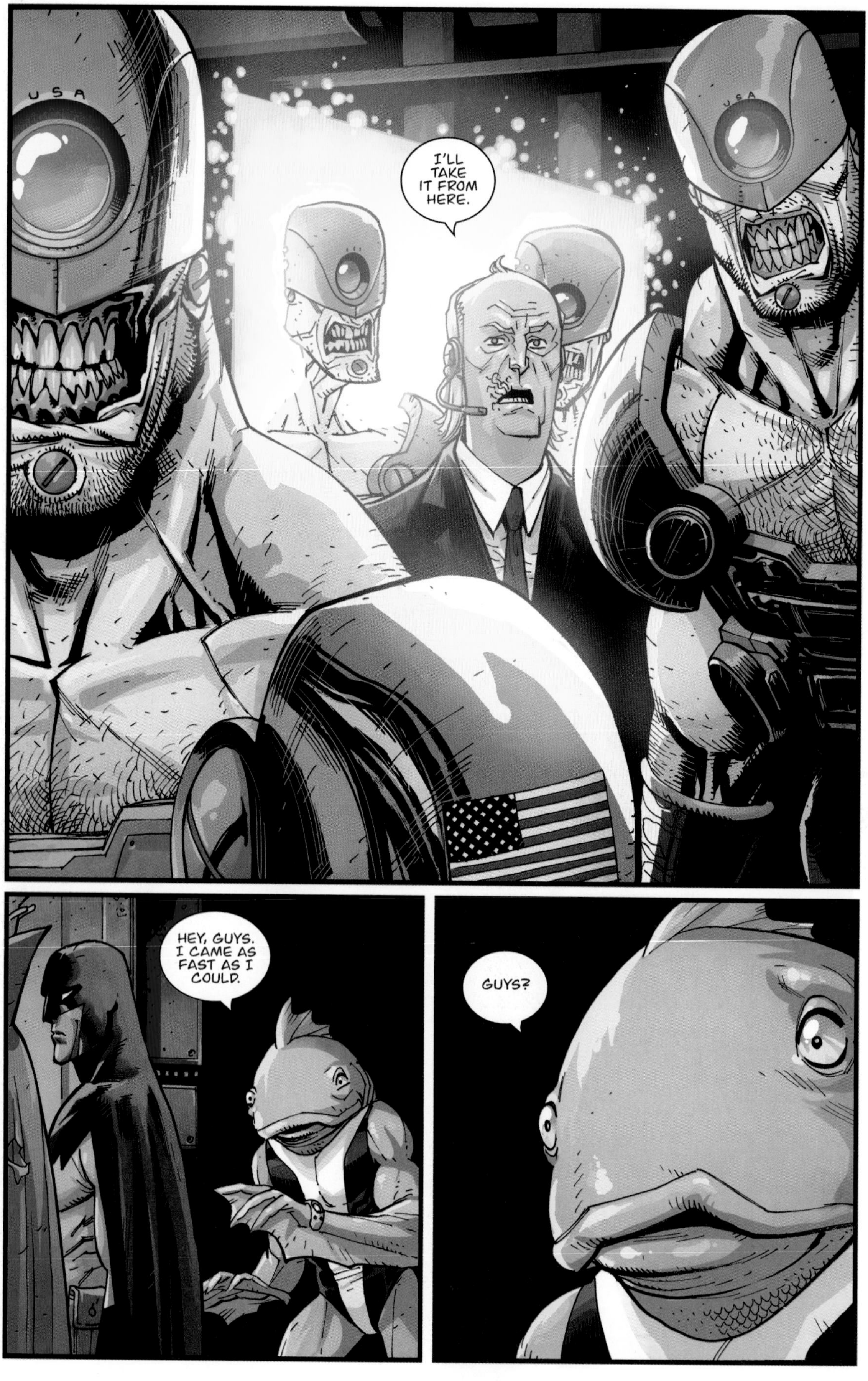
I'LL TAKE IT FROM HERE.
HEY, GUYS. I CAME AS FAST AS I COULD.
GUYS?

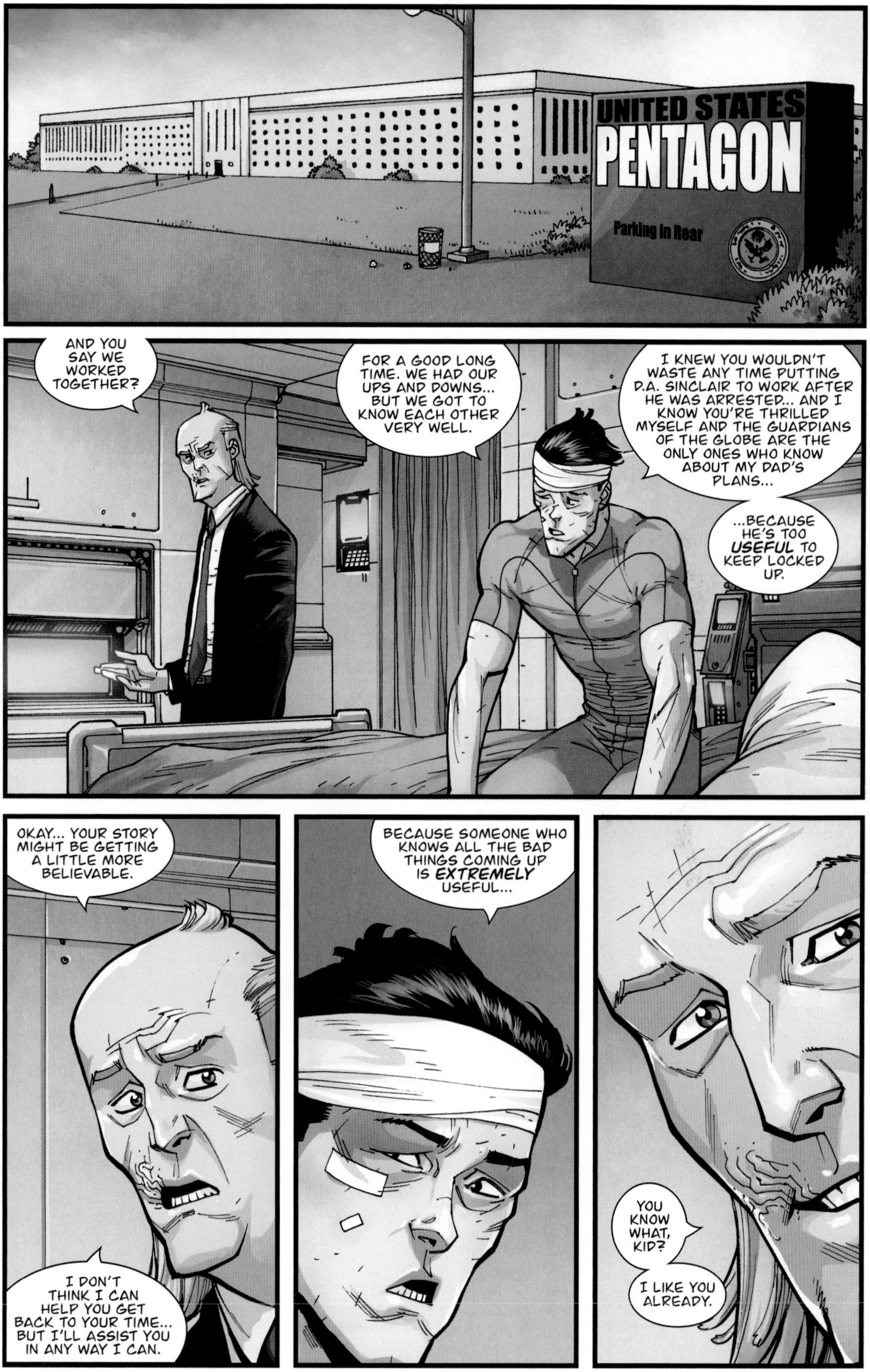
UNITED STATES
PENTAGON
Parking in Rear
AND YOU SAY WE WORKED TOGETHER?
FOR A GOOD LONG TIME. WE HAD OUR UPS AND DOWNS... BUT WE GOT TO KNOW EACH OTHER VERY WELL.
I KNEW YOU WOULDN'T WASTE ANY TIME PUTTING D.A. SINCLAIR TO WORK AFTER HE WAS ARRESTED... AND I KNOW YOU'RE THRILLED MYSELF AND THE GUARDIANS OF THE GLOBE ARE THE ONLY ONES WHO KNOW ABOUT MY DAD'S PLANS...
...BECAUSE HE'S TOO USEFUL TO KEEP LOCKED UP.
OKAY... YOUR STORY MIGHT BE GETTING A LITTLE MORE BELIEVABLE.
I DON'T THINK I CAN HELP YOU GET BACK TO YOUR TIME... BUT I'LL ASSIST YOU IN ANY WAY I CAN.
BECAUSE SOMEONE WHO KNOWS ALL THE BAD THINGS COMING UP IS EXTREMELY USEFUL...
YOU KNOW WHAT, KID?
I LIKE YOU ALREADY.

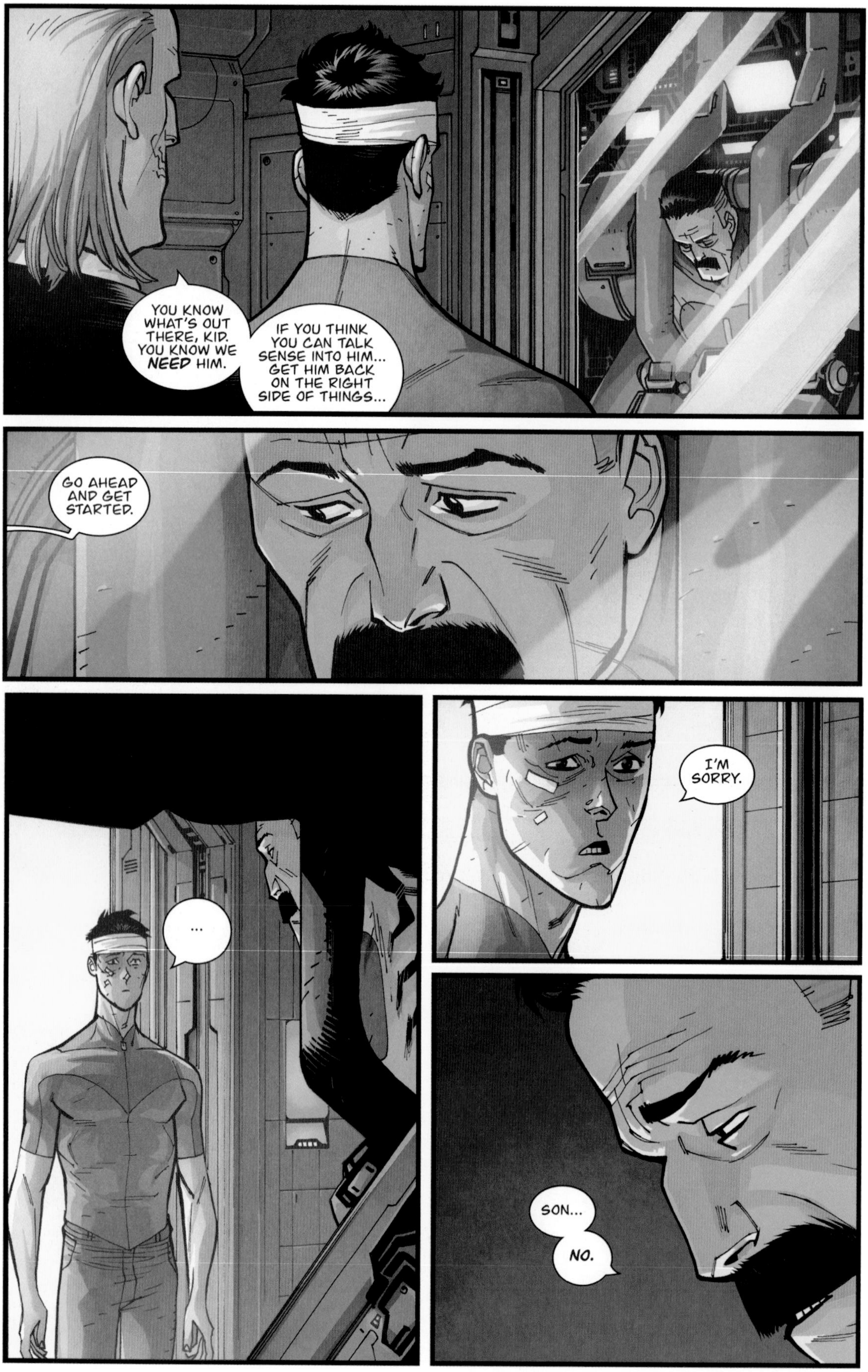
YOU KNOW WHAT'S OUT THERE, KID. YOU KNOW WE NEED HIM.
IF YOU THINK YOU CAN TALK SENSE INTO HIM... GET HIM BACK ON THE RIGHT SIDE OF THINGS...
GO AHEAD AND GET STARTED.
...
I'M SORRY.
SON...
NO.

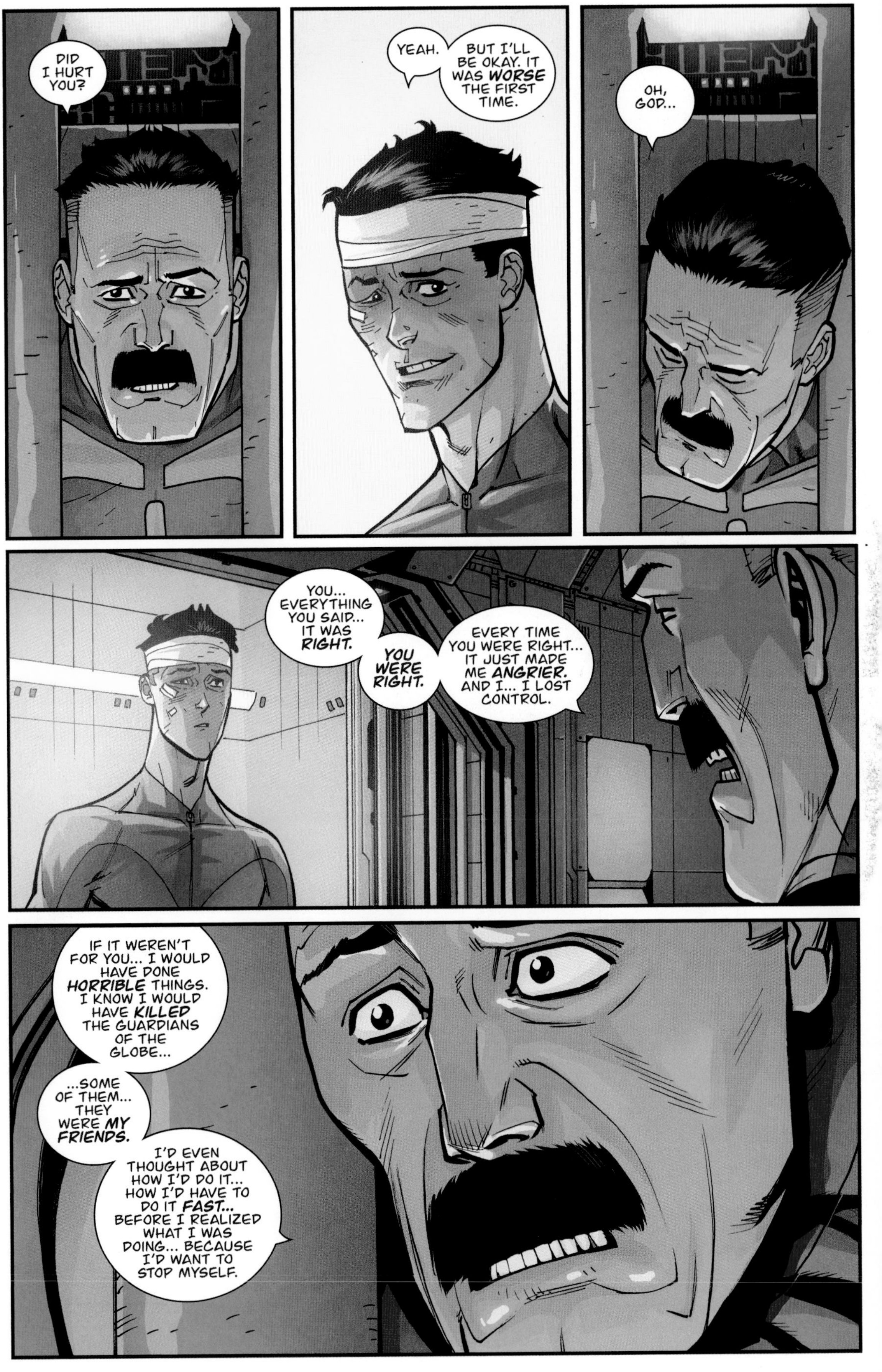
DID I HURT YOU?
YEAH.
BUT I'LL BE OKAY. IT WAS WORSE THE FIRST TIME.
OH, GOD...
YOU... EVERYTHING YOU SAID... IT WAS RIGHT.
YOU WERE RIGHT.
EVERY TIME YOU WERE RIGHT... IT JUST MADE ME ANGRIER. AND I... I LOST CONTROL.
IF IT WEREN'T FOR YOU... I WOULD HAVE DONE HORRIBLE THINGS. I KNOW I WOULD HAVE KILLED THE GUARDIANS OF THE GLOBE...
...SOME OF THEM... THEY WERE MY FRIENDS.
I'D EVEN THOUGHT ABOUT HOW I'D DO IT... HOW I'D HAVE TO DO IT FAST... BEFORE I REALIZED WHAT I WAS DOING... BECAUSE I'D WANT TO STOP MYSELF.

I WOULD HAVE KILLED **SO MANY**... AND I WOULD HAVE LIVED WITH THAT GUILT FOR THE **REST OF MY LIFE**.

THIS PLANET HAS... **CHANGED** ME. AND THERE'S NO GOING BACK FROM THAT, SON. WITHOUT YOU... I DON'T KNOW WHAT IT WOULD HAVE TAKEN... WHAT I WOULD HAVE DONE... TO MAKE ME REALIZE THAT.

THANK YOU.

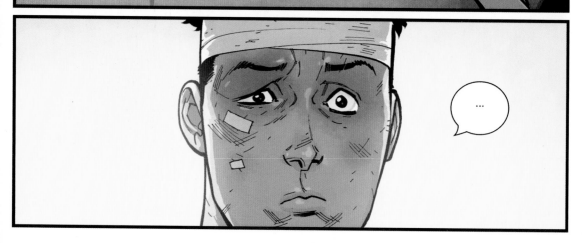

...

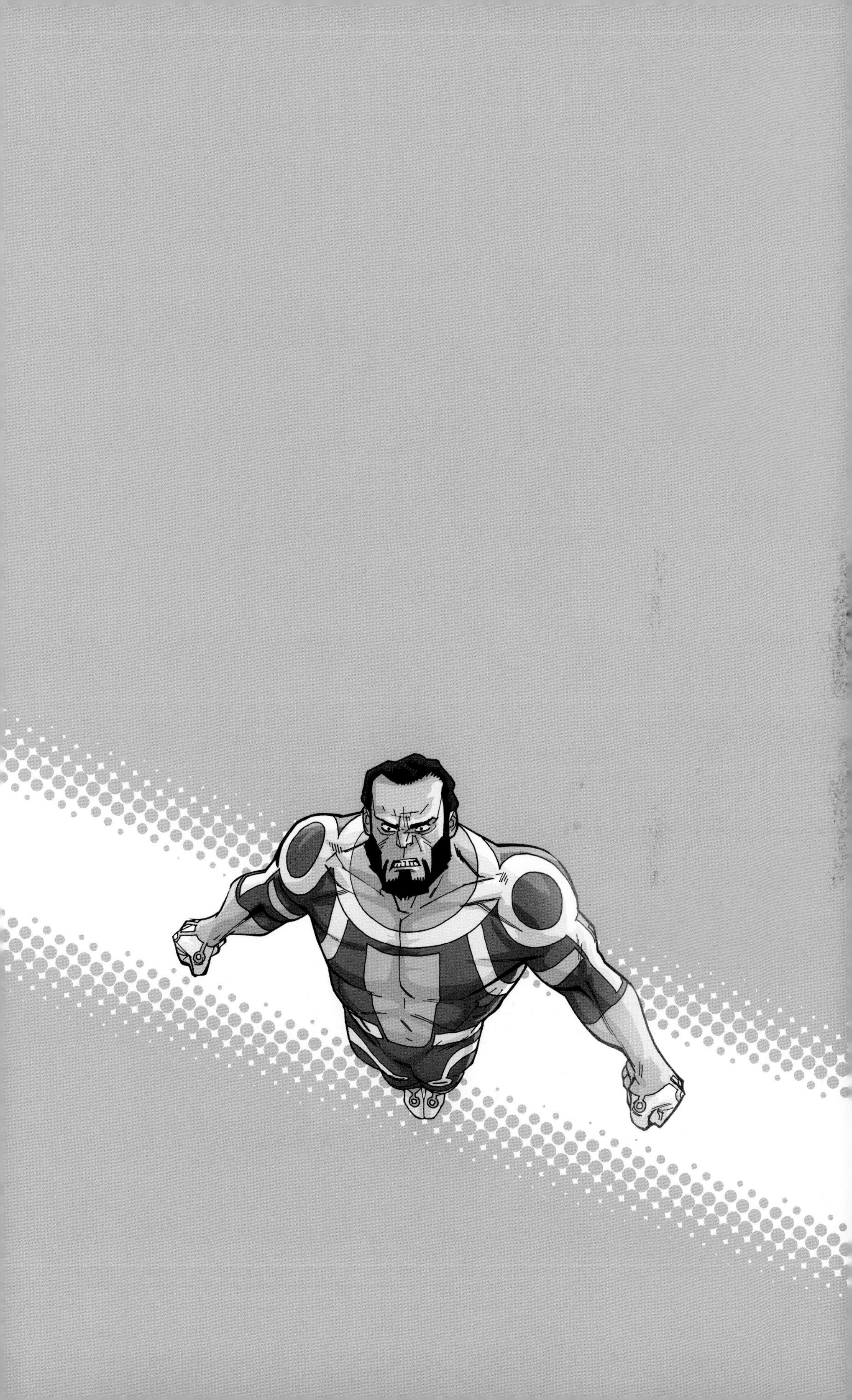

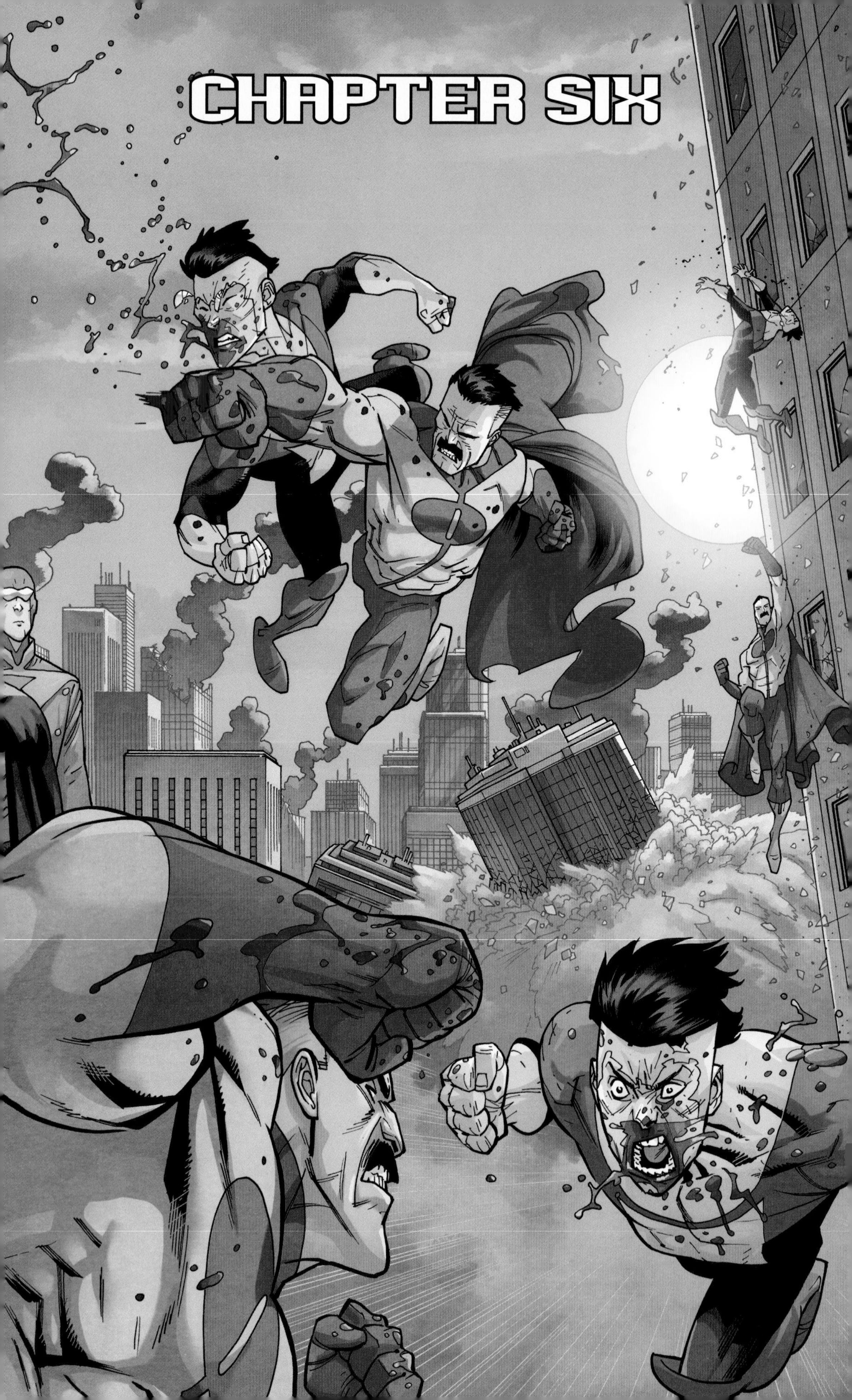
CHAPTER SIX

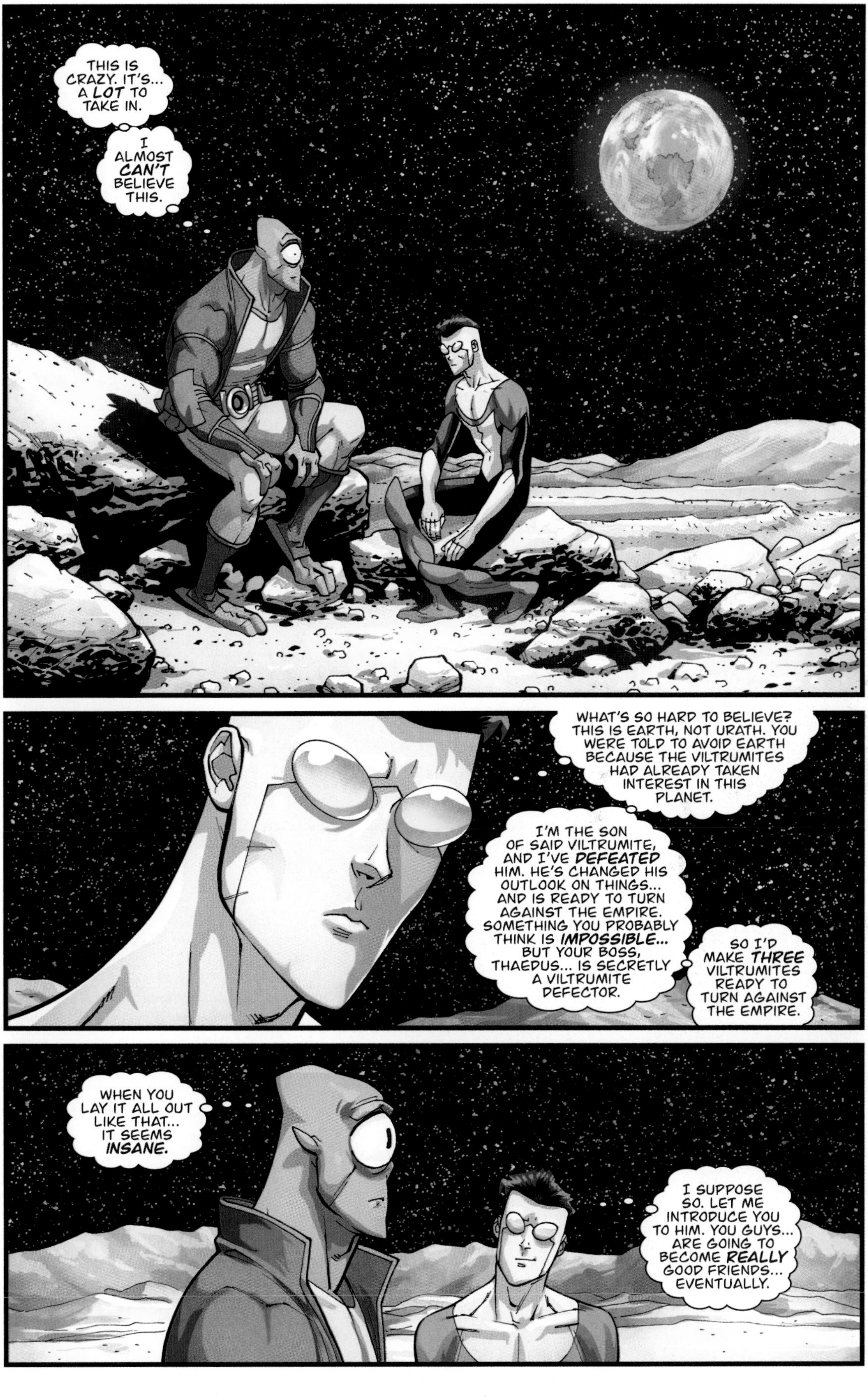
THIS IS CRAZY. IT'S... A LOT TO TAKE IN.
I ALMOST CAN'T BELIEVE THIS.
WHAT'S SO HARD TO BELIEVE? THIS IS EARTH, NOT URATH. YOU WERE TOLD TO AVOID EARTH BECAUSE THE VILTRUMITES HAD ALREADY TAKEN INTEREST IN THIS PLANET.
I'M THE SON OF SAID VILTRUMITE, AND I'VE DEFEATED HIM. HE'S CHANGED HIS OUTLOOK ON THINGS... AND IS READY TO TURN AGAINST THE EMPIRE. SOMETHING YOU PROBABLY THINK IS IMPOSSIBLE... BUT YOUR BOSS, THAEDUS... IS SECRETLY A VILTRUMITE DEFECTOR.
SO I'D MAKE THREE VILTRUMITES READY TO TURN AGAINST THE EMPIRE.
WHEN YOU LAY IT ALL OUT LIKE THAT... IT SEEMS INSANE.
I SUPPOSE SO. LET ME INTRODUCE YOU TO HIM. YOU GUYS... ARE GOING TO BECOME REALLY GOOD FRIENDS... EVENTUALLY.

UNITED STATES
PENTAGON

Parking in Rear

LOOKING AT YOU NOW... I HONESTLY HAVE NO *IDEA* HOW I DIDN'T REALIZE YOU WERE A VILTRUMITE.

I HATE TO SAY IT, BUT YOU BI-CLOPS REALLY DO ALL LOOK SIMILAR TO ME.

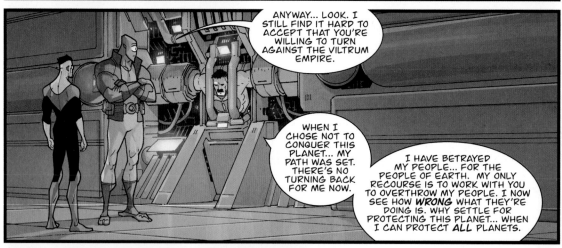

ANYWAY... LOOK. I STILL FIND IT HARD TO ACCEPT THAT YOU'RE WILLING TO TURN AGAINST THE VILTRUM EMPIRE.

WHEN I CHOSE NOT TO CONQUER THIS PLANET... MY PATH WAS SET. THERE'S NO TURNING BACK FOR ME NOW.

I HAVE BETRAYED MY PEOPLE... FOR THE PEOPLE OF EARTH. MY ONLY RECOURSE IS TO WORK WITH YOU TO OVERTHROW MY PEOPLE. I NOW SEE HOW *WRONG* WHAT THEY'RE DOING IS. WHY SETTLE FOR PROTECTING THIS PLANET... WHEN I CAN PROTECT *ALL* PLANETS.

IS THIS GUY FOR REAL?

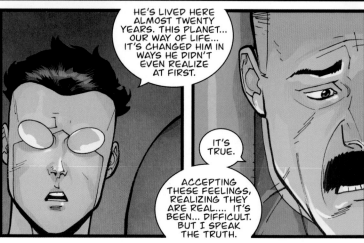

HE'S LIVED HERE ALMOST TWENTY YEARS. THIS PLANET... OUR WAY OF LIFE... IT'S CHANGED HIM IN WAYS HE DIDN'T EVEN REALIZE AT FIRST.

IT'S TRUE.

ACCEPTING THESE FEELINGS, REALIZING THEY ARE REAL..... IT'S BEEN... DIFFICULT. BUT I SPEAK THE TRUTH.

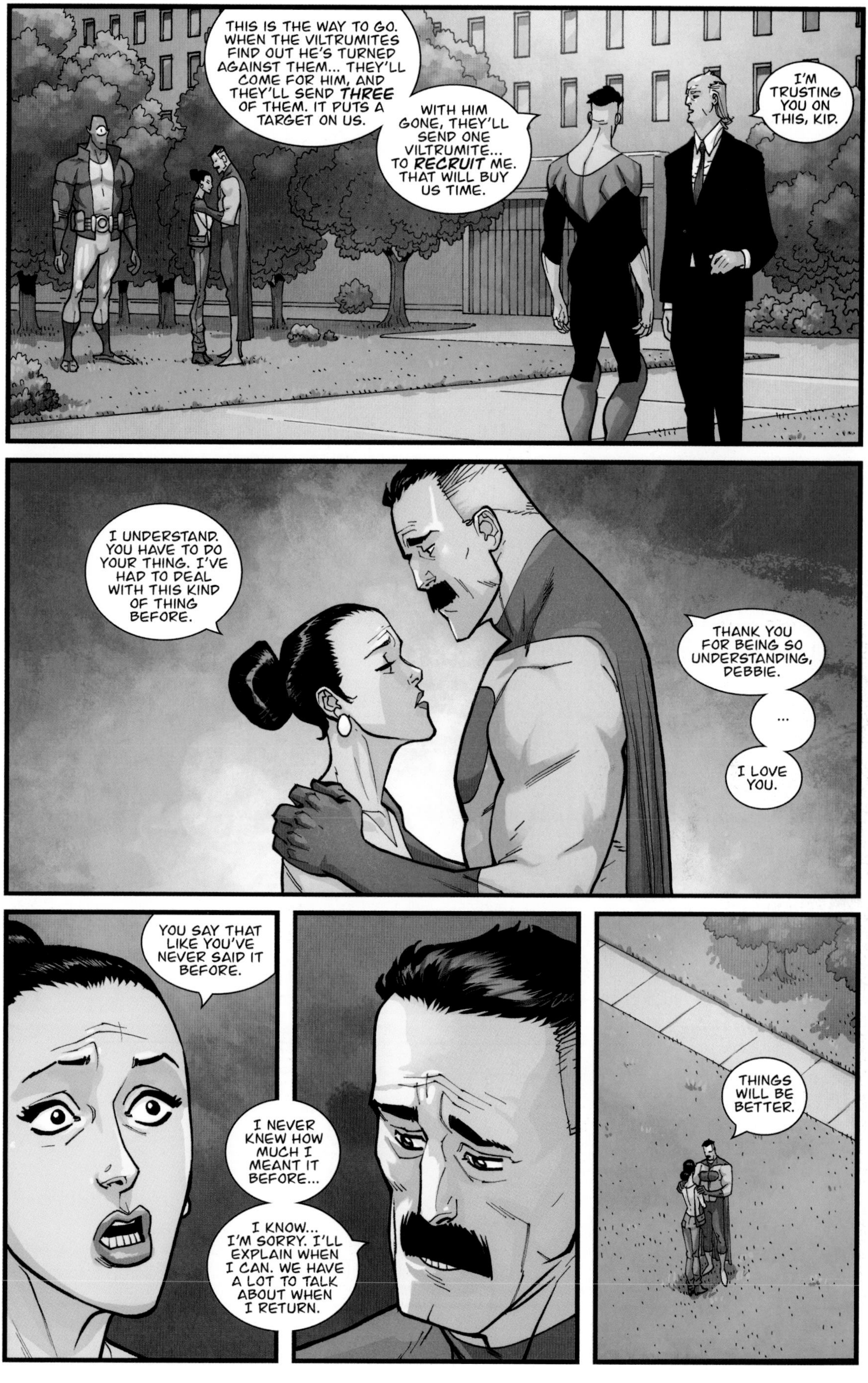
THIS IS THE WAY TO GO. WHEN THE VILTRUMITES FIND OUT HE'S TURNED AGAINST THEM... THEY'LL COME FOR HIM, AND THEY'LL SEND THREE OF THEM. IT PUTS A TARGET ON US.
WITH HIM GONE, THEY'LL SEND ONE VILTRUMITE... TO RECRUIT ME. THAT WILL BUY US TIME.
I'M TRUSTING YOU ON THIS, KID.
I UNDERSTAND. YOU HAVE TO DO YOUR THING. I'VE HAD TO DEAL WITH THIS KIND OF THING BEFORE.
THANK YOU FOR BEING SO UNDERSTANDING, DEBBIE.
...
I LOVE YOU.
YOU SAY THAT LIKE YOU'VE NEVER SAID IT BEFORE.
I NEVER KNEW HOW MUCH I MEANT IT BEFORE...
I KNOW... I'M SORRY. I'LL EXPLAIN WHEN I CAN. WE HAVE A LOT TO TALK ABOUT WHEN I RETURN.
THINGS WILL BE BETTER.

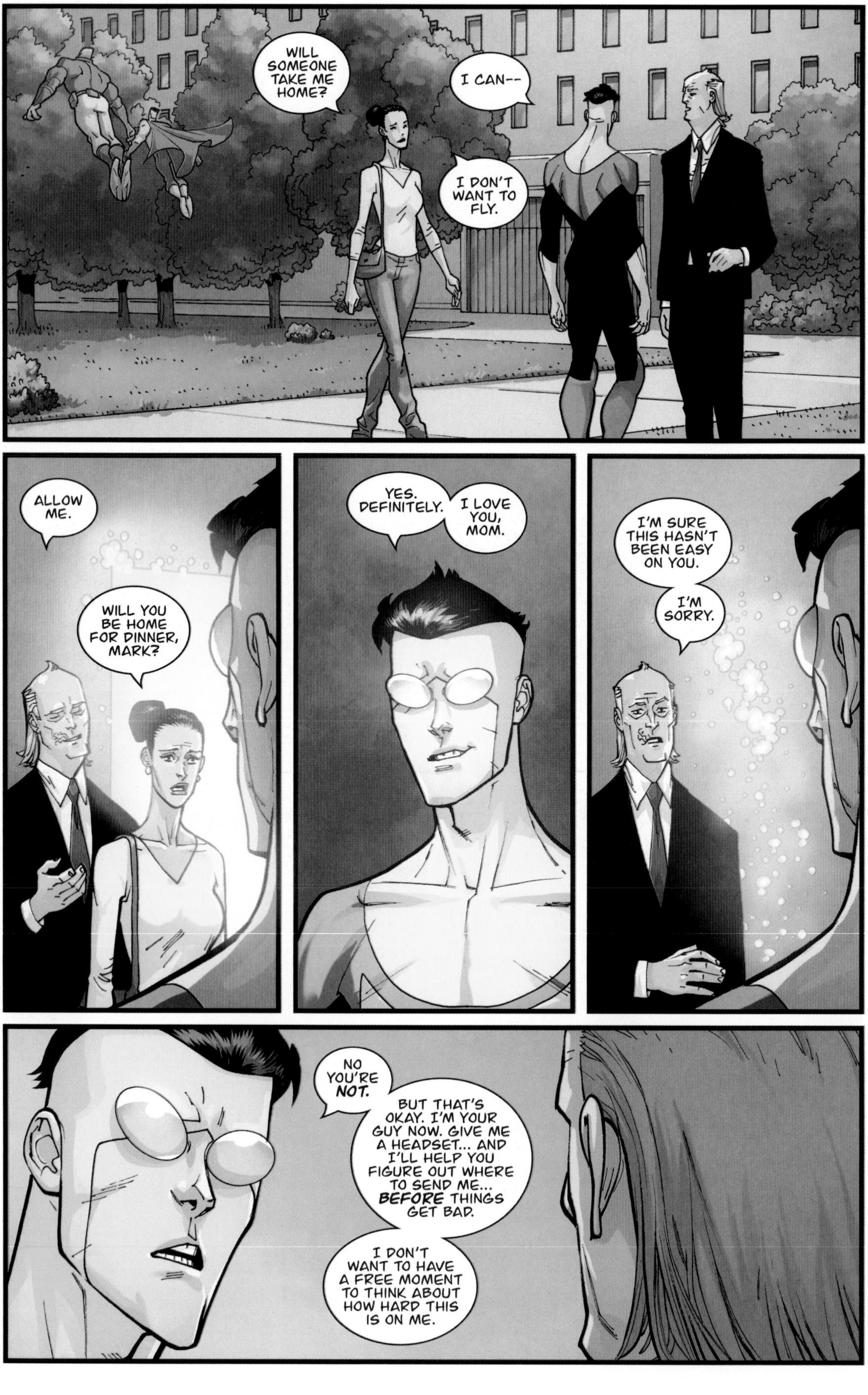
WILL SOMEONE TAKE ME HOME?
I CAN--
I DON'T WANT TO FLY.
ALLOW ME.
WILL YOU BE HOME FOR DINNER, MARK?
YES. DEFINITELY.
I LOVE YOU, MOM.
I'M SURE THIS HASN'T BEEN EASY ON YOU.
I'M SORRY.
NO YOU'RE ***NOT.***
BUT THAT'S OKAY. I'M YOUR GUY NOW. GIVE ME A HEADSET... AND I'LL HELP YOU FIGURE OUT WHERE TO SEND ME... ***BEFORE*** THINGS GET BAD.
I DON'T WANT TO HAVE A FREE MOMENT TO THINK ABOUT HOW HARD THIS IS ON ME.

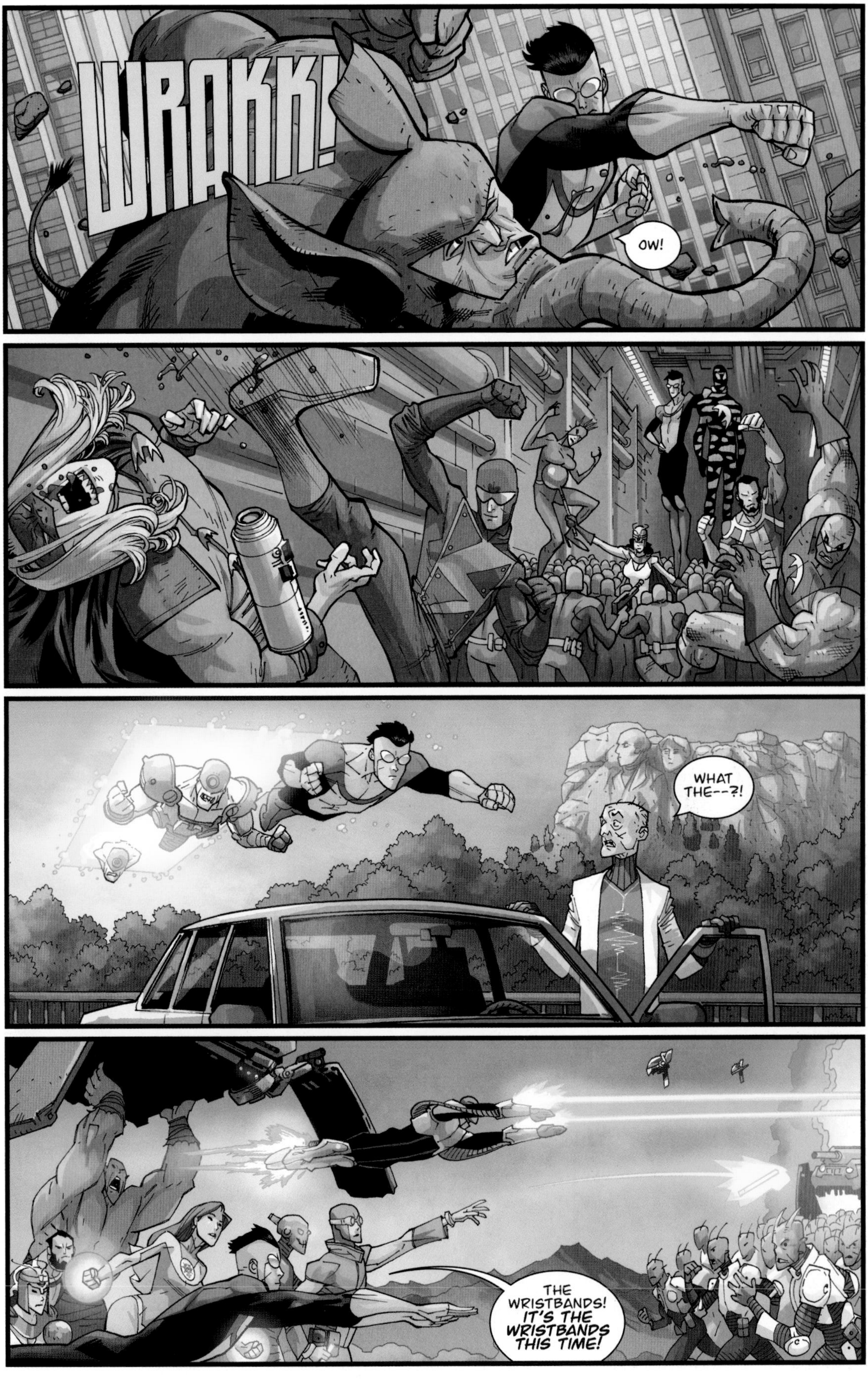
WRAKK!
OW!
WHAT THE--?!
THE WRISTBANDS! IT'S THE WRISTBANDS THIS TIME!

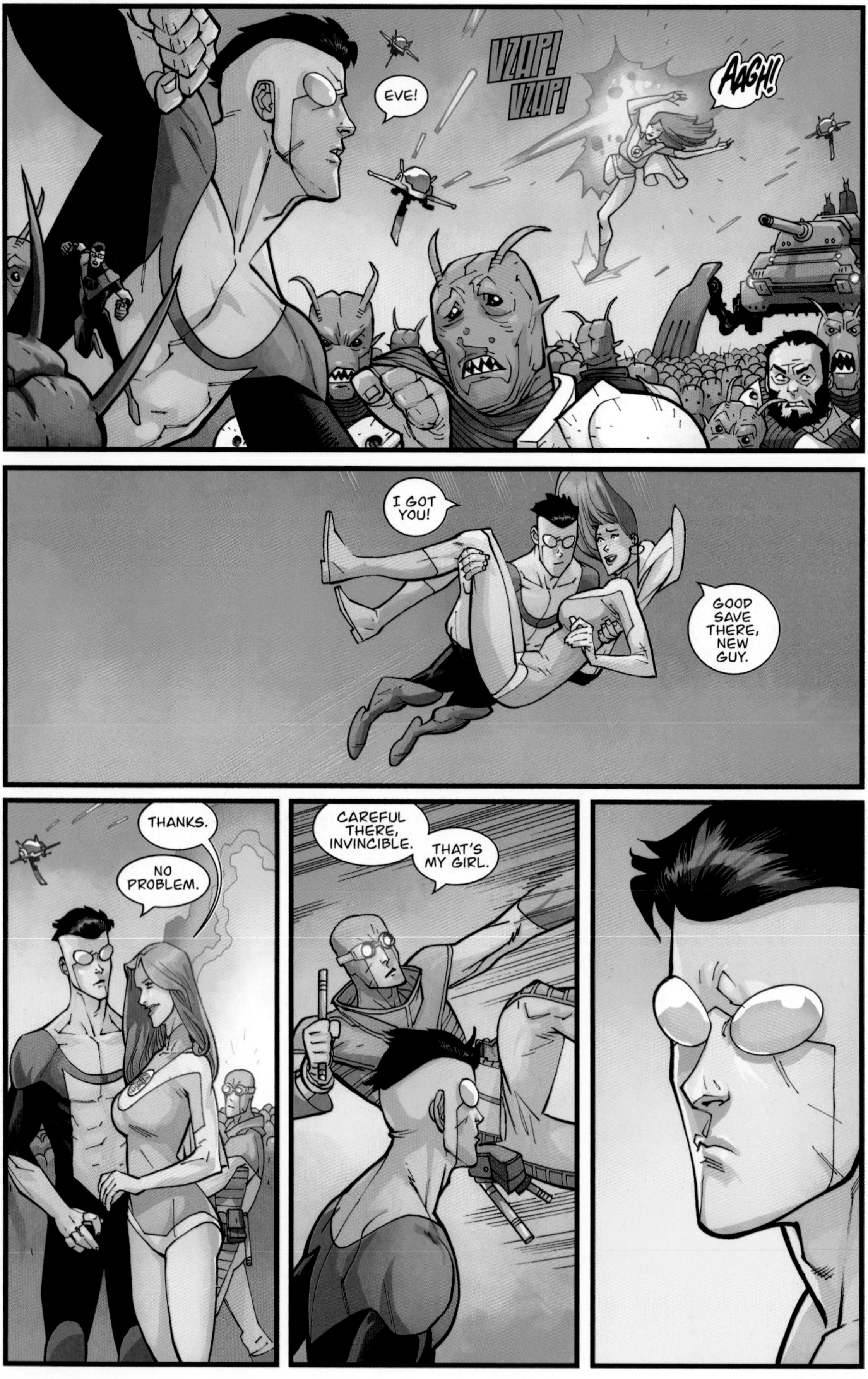

VZAP!
VZAP!
EVE!
AAGH!
I GOT YOU!
GOOD SAVE THERE, NEW GUY.
THANKS.
NO PROBLEM.
CAREFUL THERE, INVINCIBLE.
THAT'S MY GIRL.

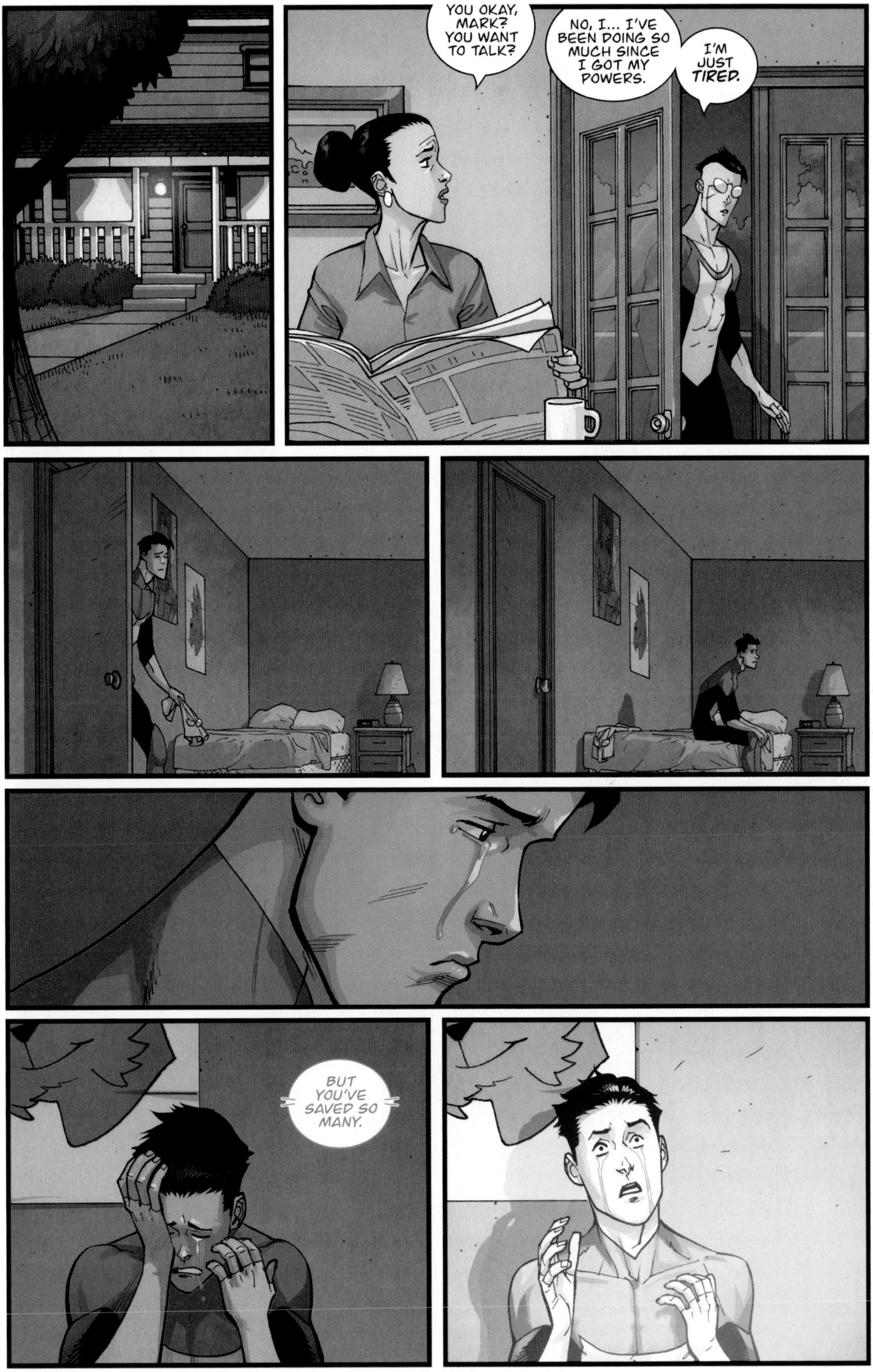
YOU OKAY, MARK? YOU WANT TO TALK?
NO, I... I'VE BEEN DOING SO MUCH SINCE I GOT MY POWERS.
I'M JUST TIRED.
BUT YOU'VE SAVED SO MANY.

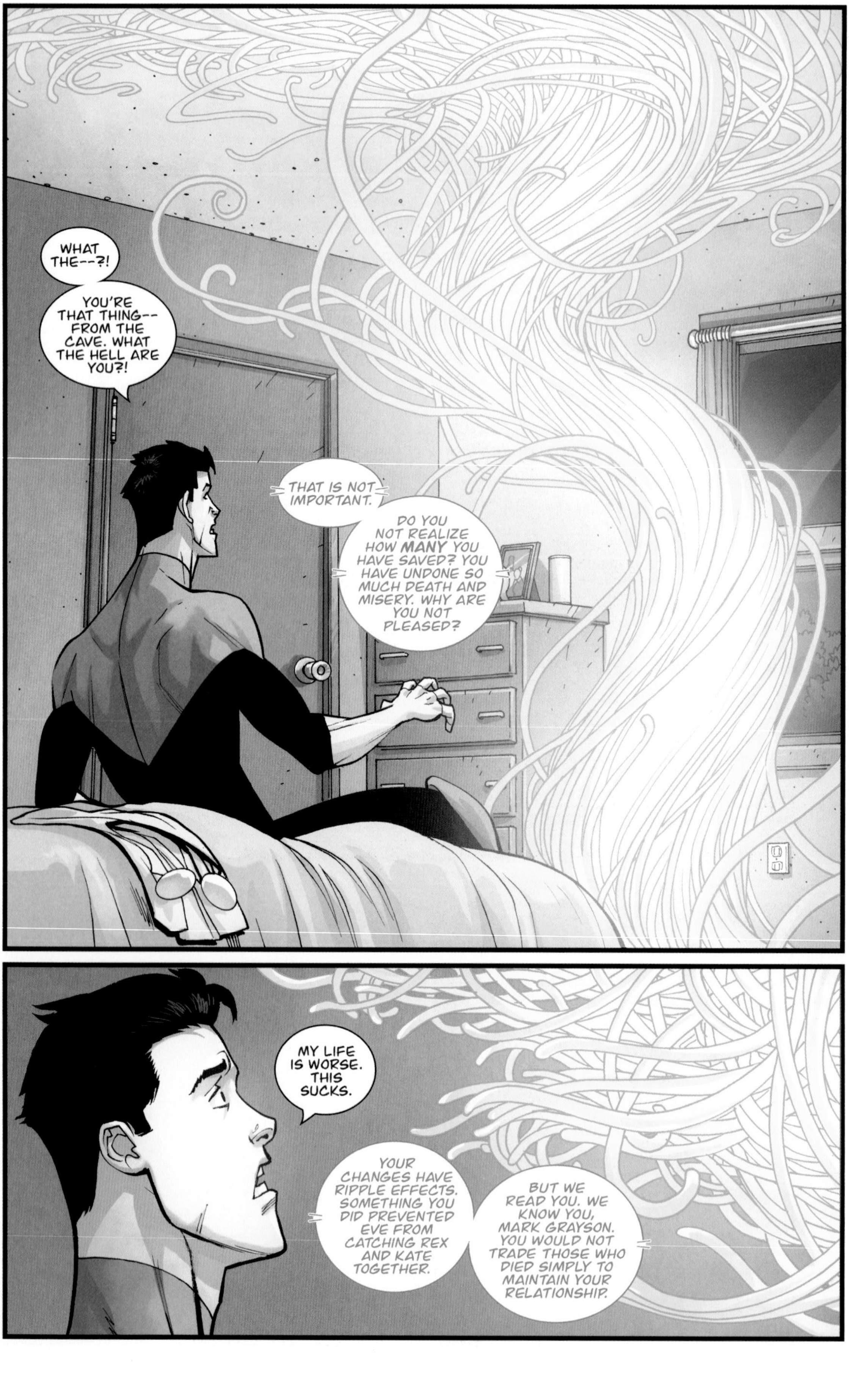
WHAT THE--?!
YOU'RE THAT THING-- FROM THE CAVE. WHAT THE HELL ARE YOU?!
THAT IS NOT IMPORTANT.
DO YOU NOT REALIZE HOW MANY YOU HAVE SAVED? YOU HAVE UNDONE SO MUCH DEATH AND MISERY. WHY ARE YOU NOT PLEASED?
MY LIFE IS WORSE. THIS SUCKS.
YOUR CHANGES HAVE RIPPLE EFFECTS. SOMETHING YOU DID PREVENTED EVE FROM CATCHING REX AND KATE TOGETHER.
BUT WE READ YOU. WE KNOW YOU, MARK GRAYSON. YOU WOULD NOT TRADE THOSE WHO DIED SIMPLY TO MAINTAIN YOUR RELATIONSHIP.

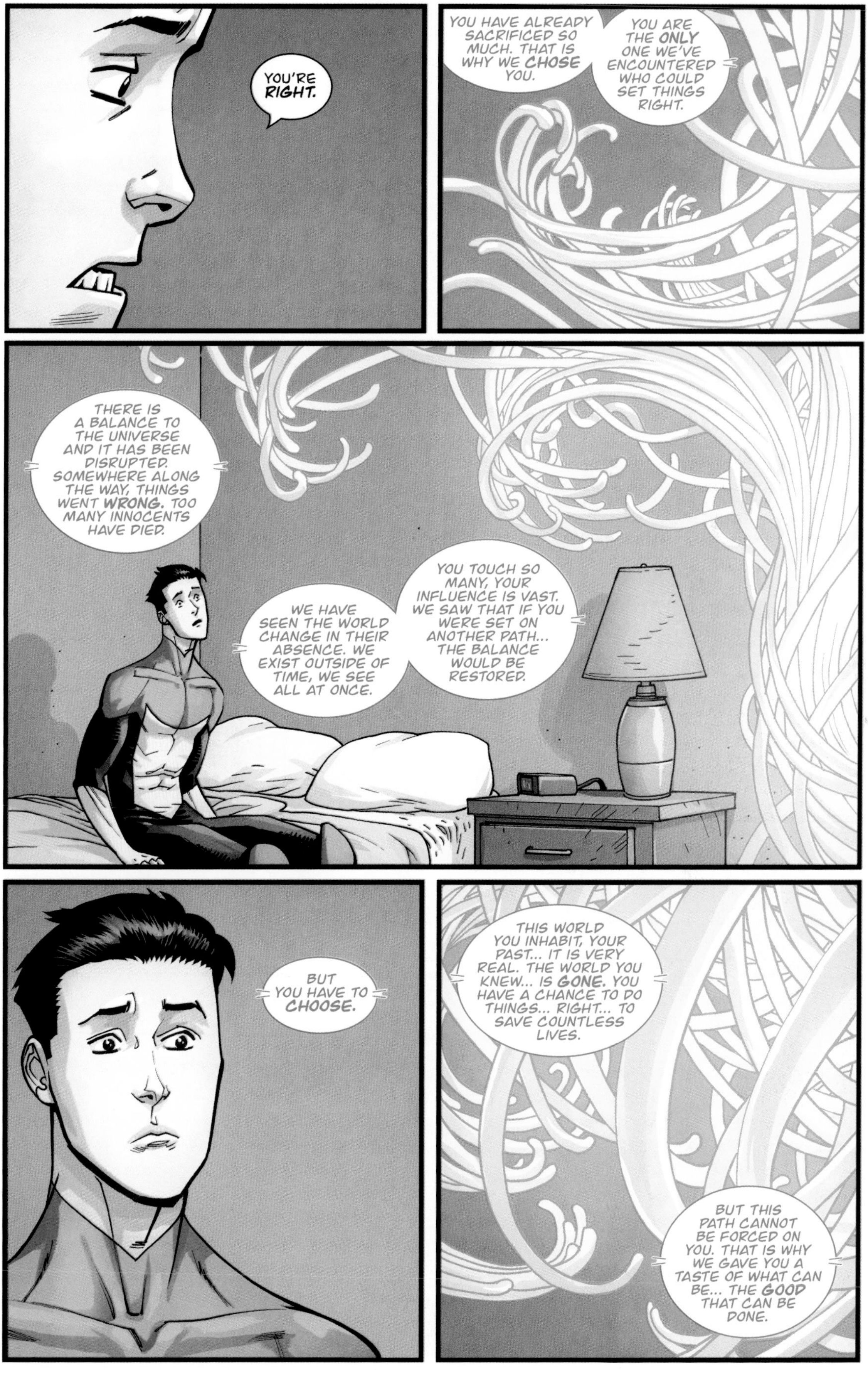
YOU'RE RIGHT.
YOU HAVE ALREADY SACRIFICED SO MUCH. THAT IS WHY WE CHOSE YOU.
YOU ARE THE ONLY ONE WE'VE ENCOUNTERED WHO COULD SET THINGS RIGHT.
THERE IS A BALANCE TO THE UNIVERSE AND IT HAS BEEN DISRUPTED. SOMEWHERE ALONG THE WAY, THINGS WENT WRONG. TOO MANY INNOCENTS HAVE DIED.
WE HAVE SEEN THE WORLD CHANGE IN THEIR ABSENCE. WE EXIST OUTSIDE OF TIME, WE SEE ALL AT ONCE.
YOU TOUCH SO MANY, YOUR INFLUENCE IS VAST. WE SAW THAT IF YOU WERE SET ON ANOTHER PATH... THE BALANCE WOULD BE RESTORED.
BUT YOU HAVE TO CHOOSE.
THIS WORLD YOU INHABIT, YOUR PAST... IT IS VERY REAL. THE WORLD YOU KNEW... IS GONE. YOU HAVE A CHANCE TO DO THINGS... RIGHT... TO SAVE COUNTLESS LIVES.
BUT THIS PATH CANNOT BE FORCED ON YOU. THAT IS WHY WE GAVE YOU A TASTE OF WHAT CAN BE... THE GOOD THAT CAN BE DONE.

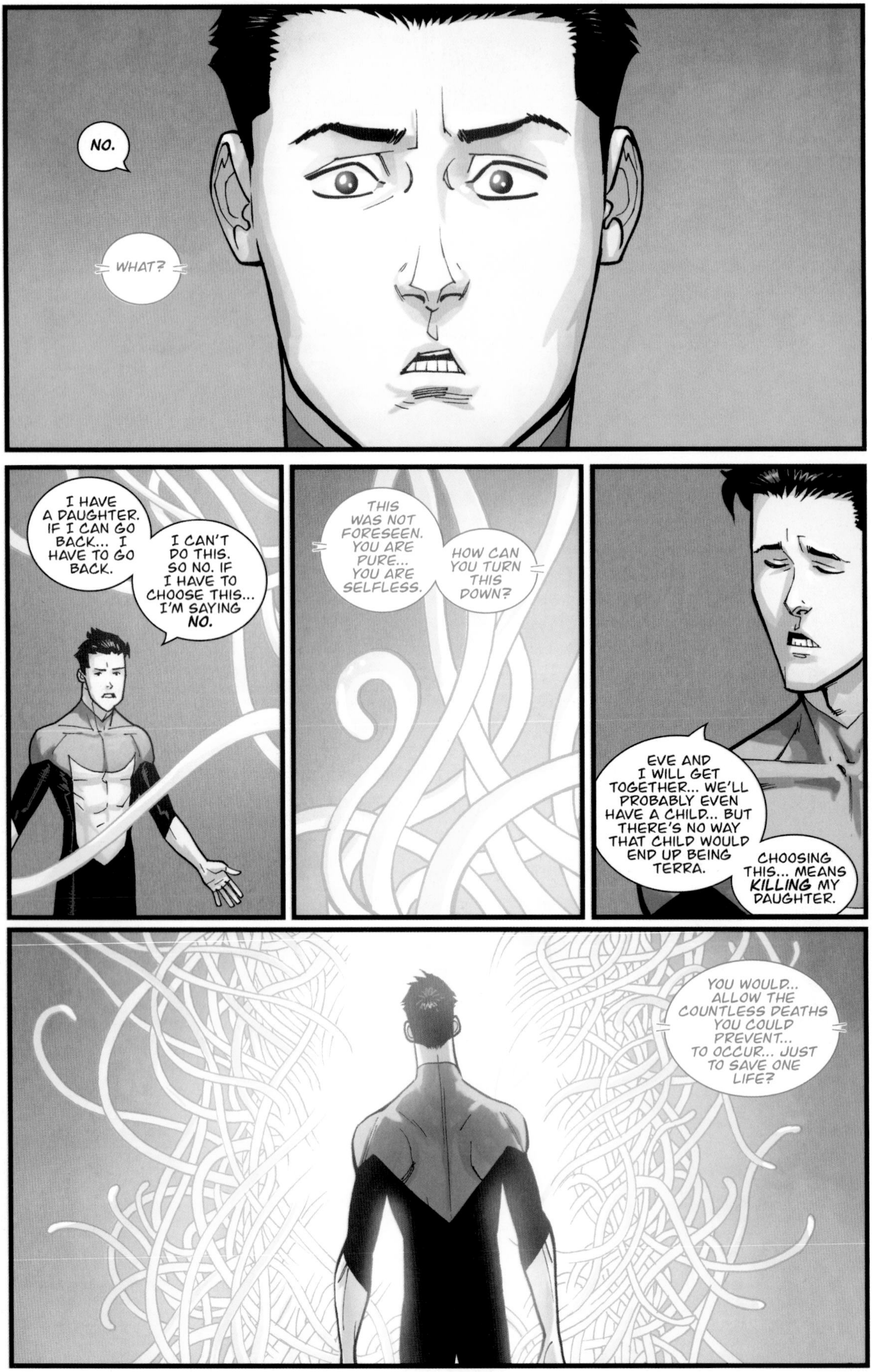
NO.
WHAT?
I HAVE A DAUGHTER. IF I CAN GO BACK... I HAVE TO GO BACK.
I CAN'T DO THIS. SO NO. IF I HAVE TO CHOOSE THIS... I'M SAYING NO.
THIS WAS NOT FORESEEN. YOU ARE PURE... YOU ARE SELFLESS.
HOW CAN YOU TURN THIS DOWN?
EVE AND I WILL GET TOGETHER... WE'LL PROBABLY EVEN HAVE A CHILD... BUT THERE'S NO WAY THAT CHILD WOULD END UP BEING TERRA.
CHOOSING THIS... MEANS KILLING MY DAUGHTER.
YOU WOULD... ALLOW THE COUNTLESS DEATHS YOU COULD PREVENT... TO OCCUR... JUST TO SAVE ONE LIFE?

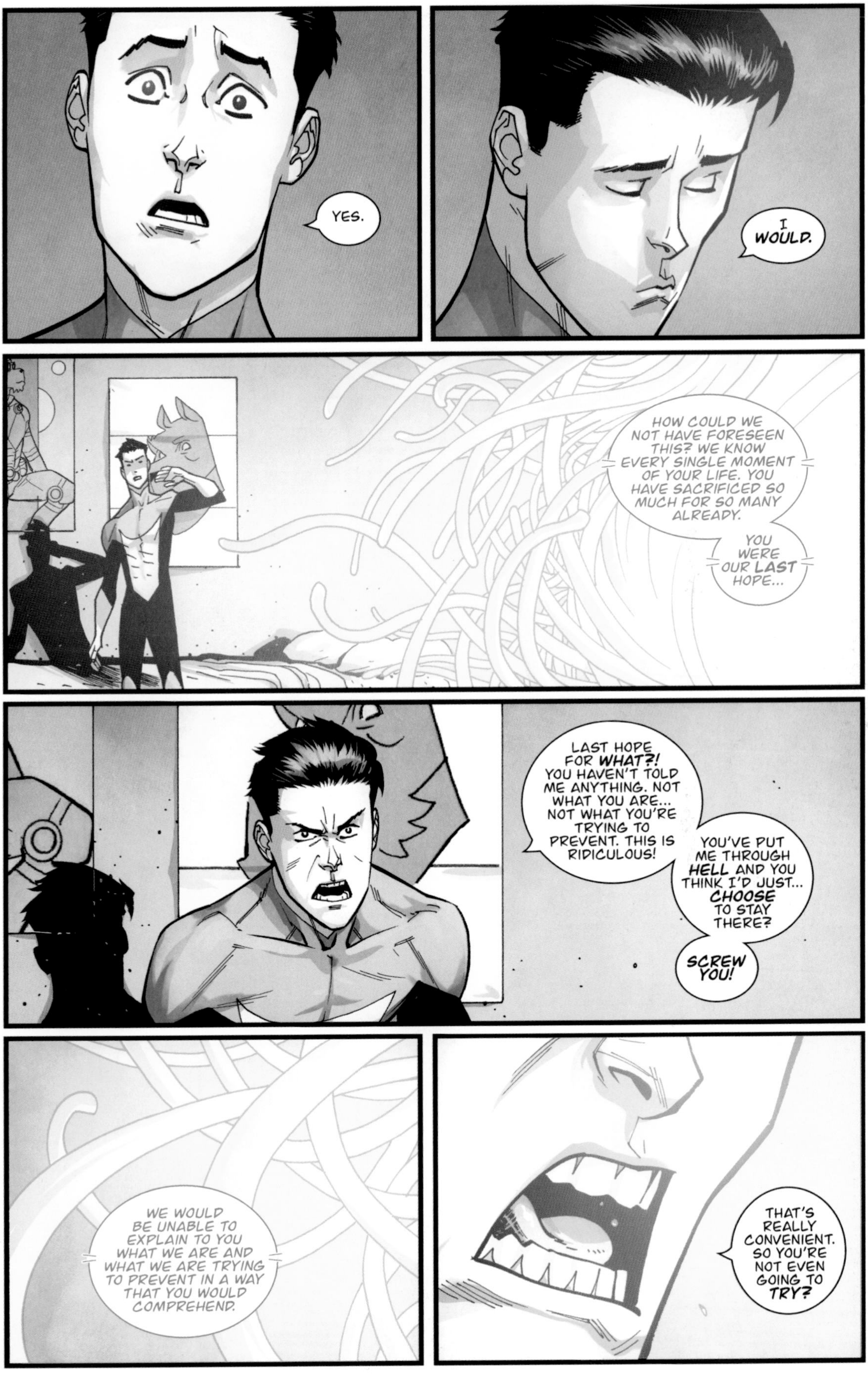
YES.
I WOULD.
HOW COULD WE NOT HAVE FORESEEN THIS? WE KNOW EVERY SINGLE MOMENT OF YOUR LIFE. YOU HAVE SACRIFICED SO MUCH FOR SO MANY ALREADY.
YOU WERE OUR LAST HOPE...
LAST HOPE FOR WHAT?! YOU HAVEN'T TOLD ME ANYTHING. NOT WHAT YOU ARE... NOT WHAT YOU'RE TRYING TO PREVENT. THIS IS RIDICULOUS!
YOU'VE PUT ME THROUGH HELL AND YOU THINK I'D JUST... CHOOSE TO STAY THERE?
SCREW YOU!
WE WOULD BE UNABLE TO EXPLAIN TO YOU WHAT WE ARE AND WHAT WE ARE TRYING TO PREVENT IN A WAY THAT YOU WOULD COMPREHEND.
THAT'S REALLY CONVENIENT. SO YOU'RE NOT EVEN GOING TO TRY?

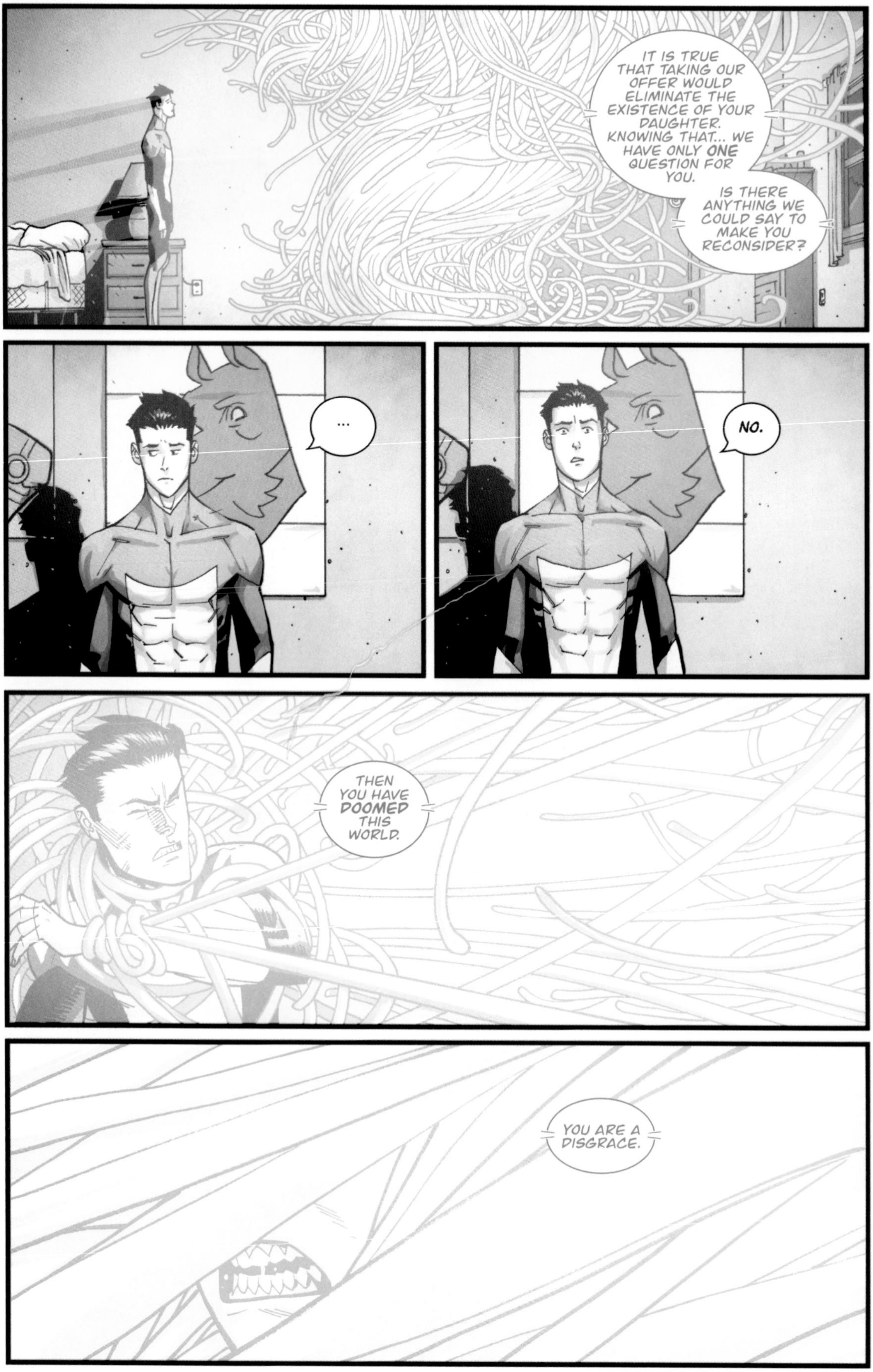
IT IS TRUE THAT TAKING OUR OFFER WOULD ELIMINATE THE EXISTENCE OF YOUR DAUGHTER. KNOWING THAT... WE HAVE ONLY **ONE** QUESTION FOR YOU.
IS THERE ANYTHING WE COULD SAY TO MAKE YOU RECONSIDER?
...
NO.
THEN YOU HAVE **DOOMED** THIS WORLD.
YOU ARE A DISGRACE.

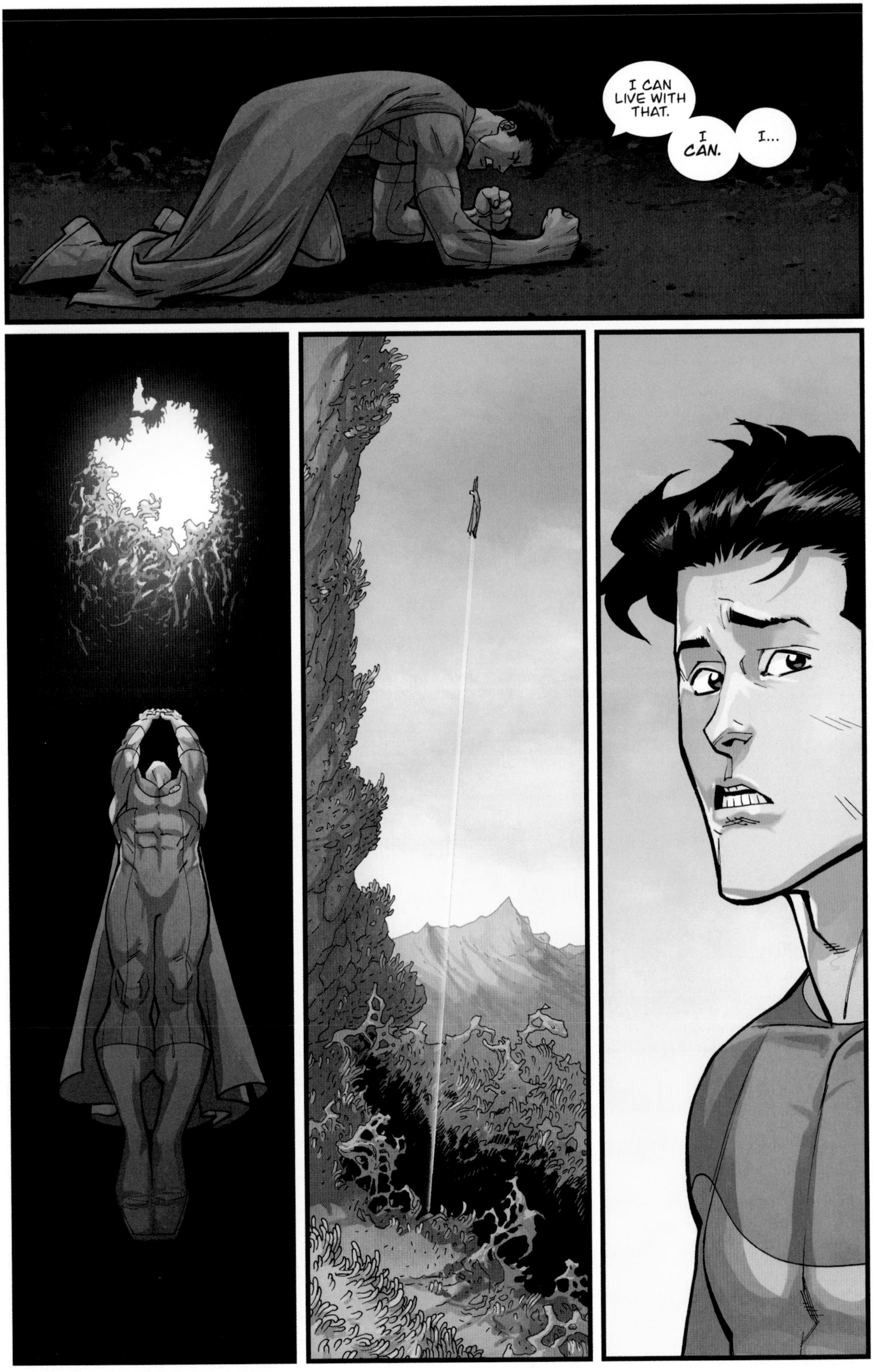
I CAN LIVE WITH THAT.
I CAN.
I...

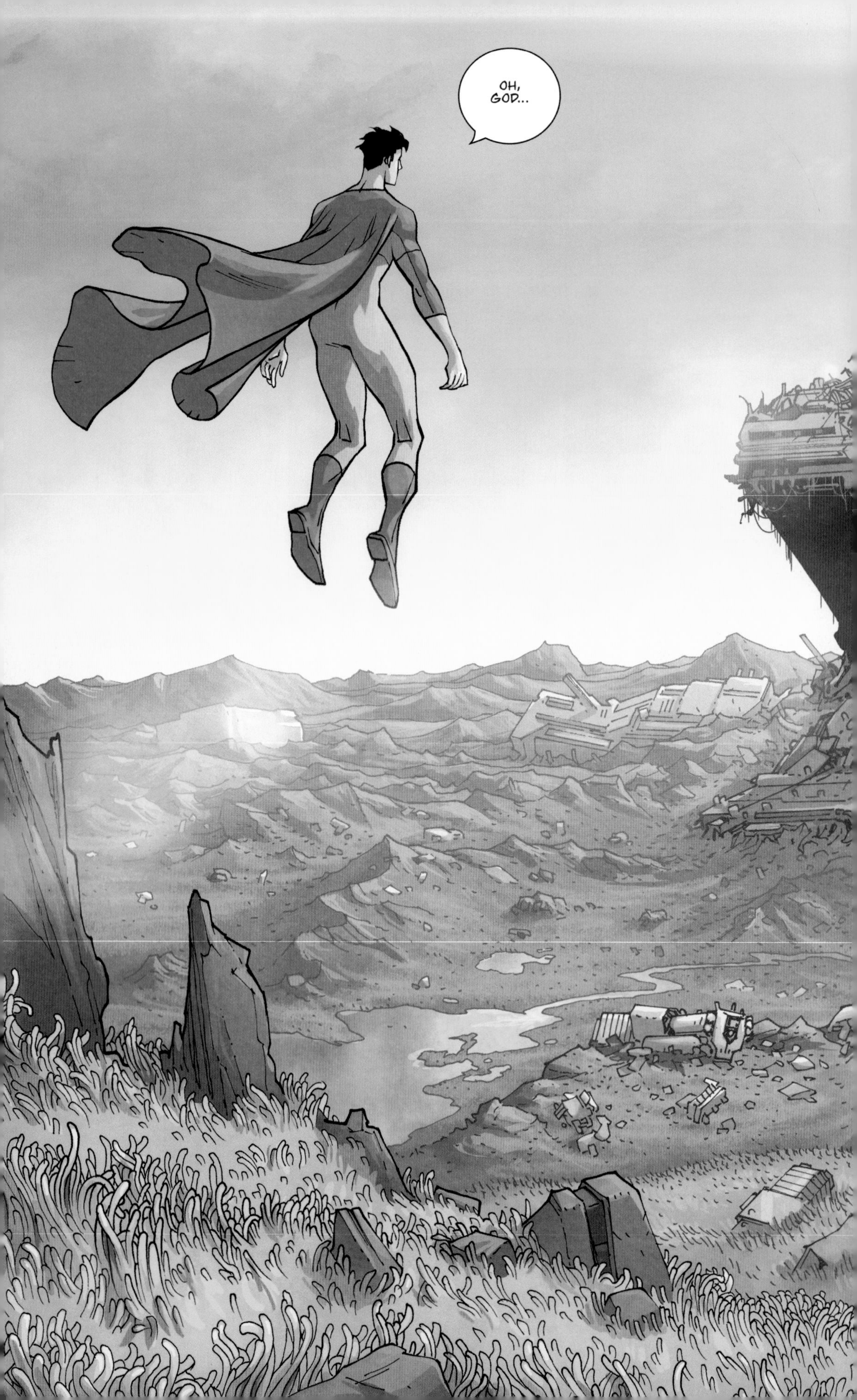
OH, GOD...

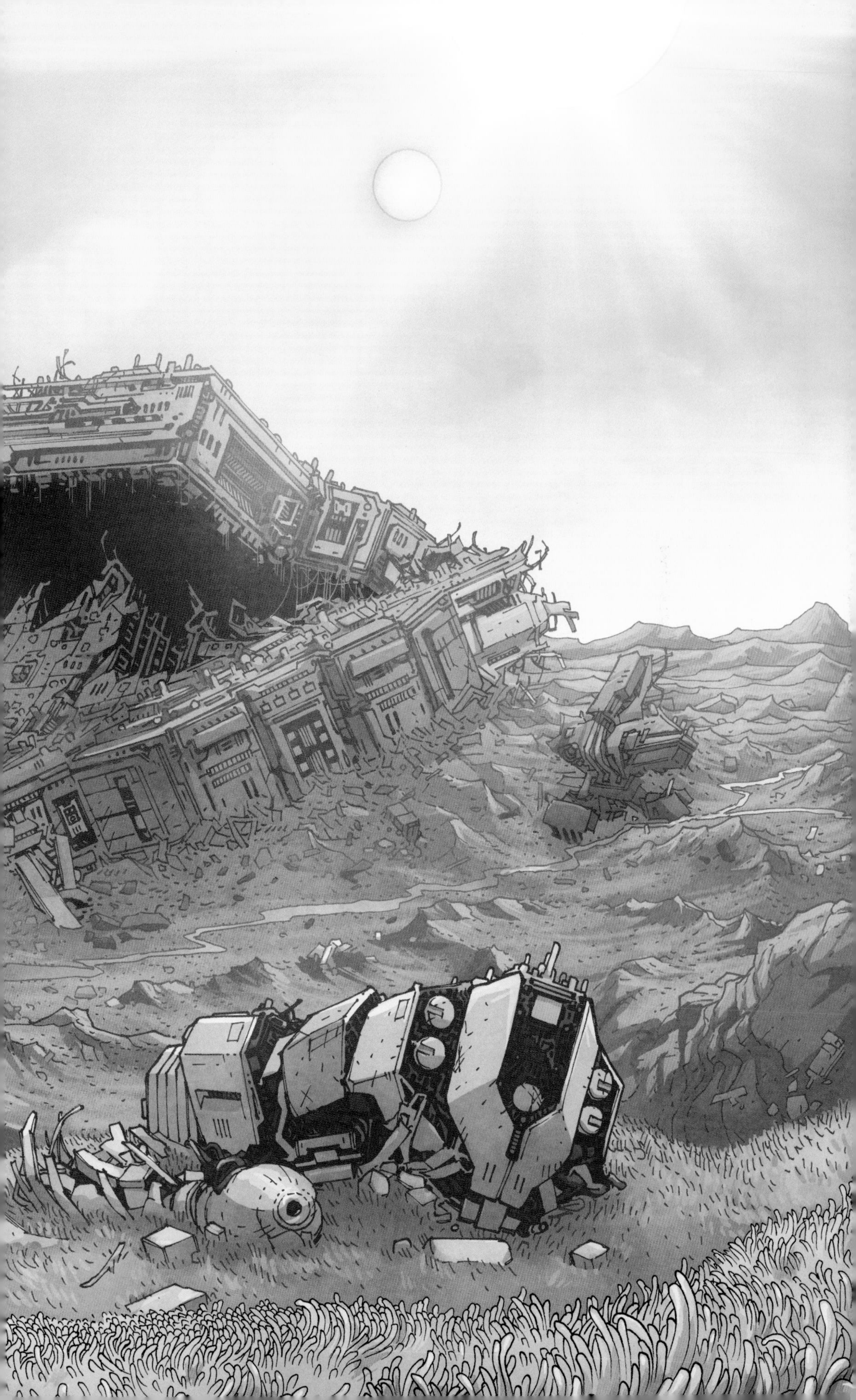

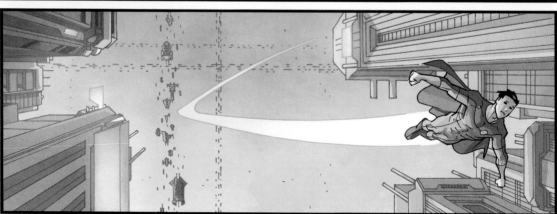

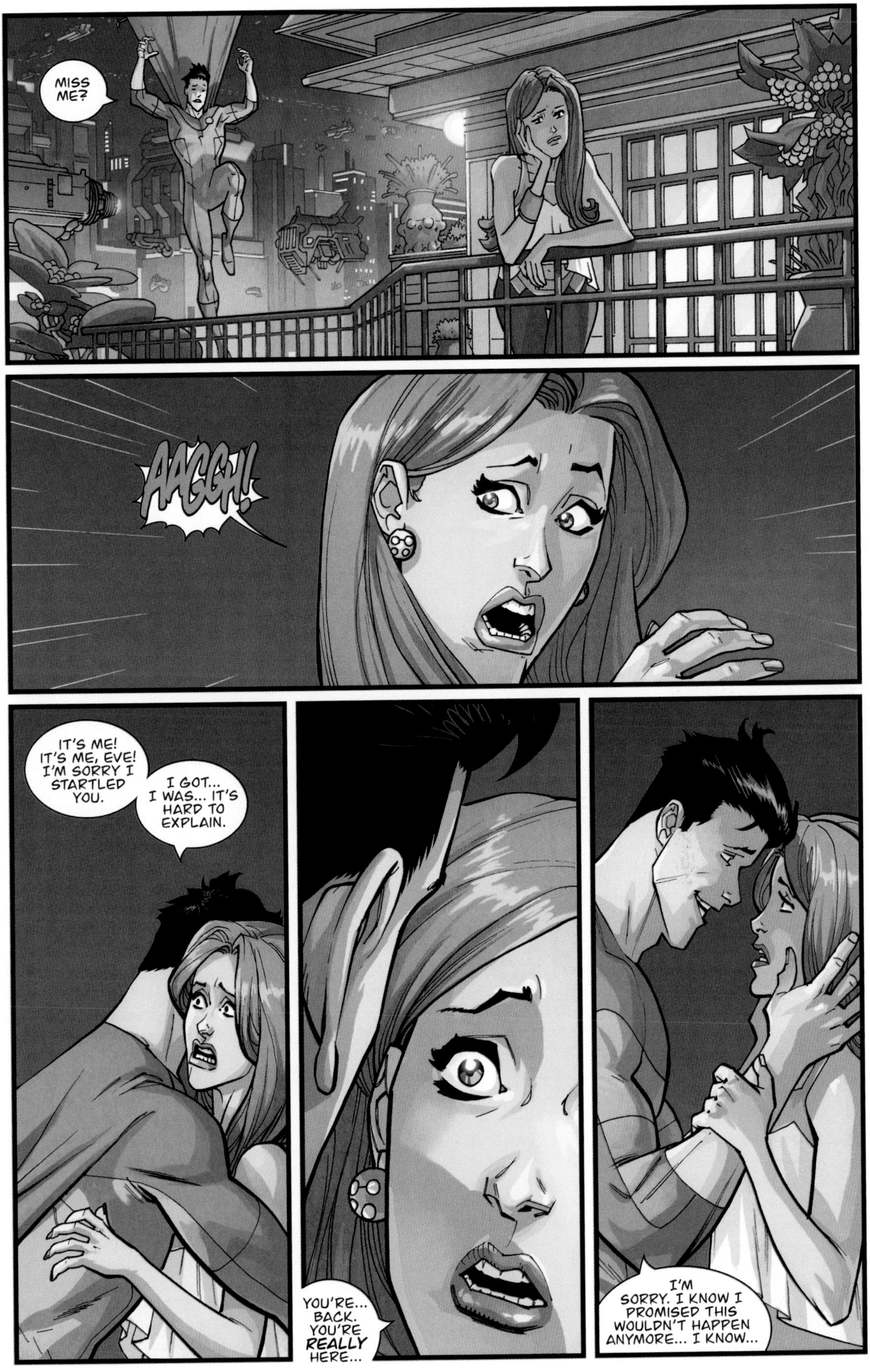
MISS ME?
AAGGH!
IT'S ME! IT'S ME, EVE! I'M SORRY I STARTLED YOU.
I GOT... I WAS... IT'S HARD TO EXPLAIN.
YOU'RE... BACK. YOU'RE REALLY HERE...
I'M SORRY. I KNOW I PROMISED THIS WOULDN'T HAPPEN ANYMORE... I KNOW...

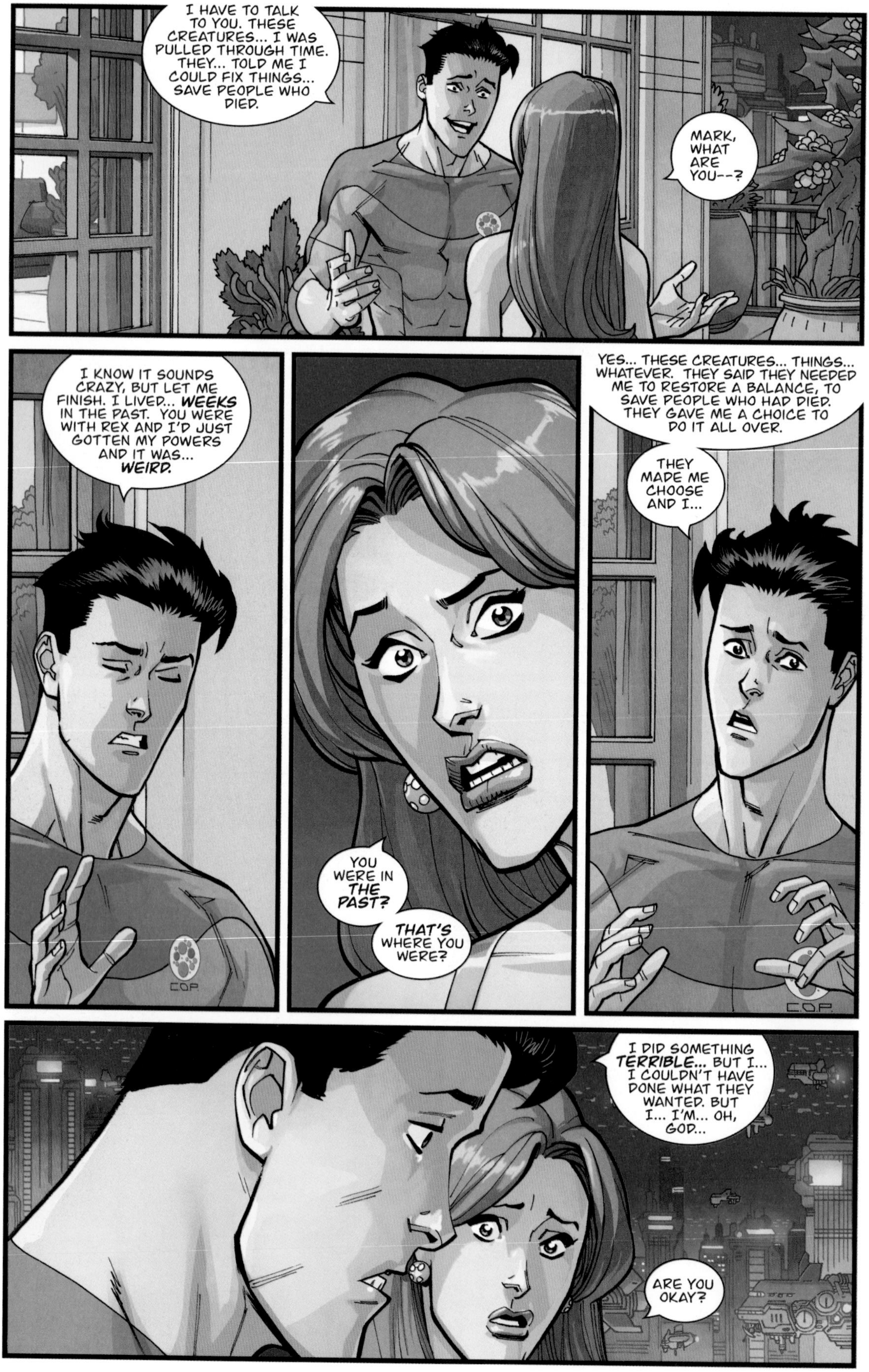
I HAVE TO TALK TO YOU. THESE CREATURES... I WAS PULLED THROUGH TIME. THEY... TOLD ME I COULD FIX THINGS... SAVE PEOPLE WHO DIED.
MARK, WHAT ARE YOU--?
I KNOW IT SOUNDS CRAZY, BUT LET ME FINISH. I LIVED... WEEKS IN THE PAST. YOU WERE WITH REX AND I'D JUST GOTTEN MY POWERS AND IT WAS... WEIRD.
YOU WERE IN THE PAST?
THAT'S WHERE YOU WERE?
YES... THESE CREATURES... THINGS... WHATEVER. THEY SAID THEY NEEDED ME TO RESTORE A BALANCE, TO SAVE PEOPLE WHO HAD DIED. THEY GAVE ME A CHOICE TO DO IT ALL OVER.
THEY MADE ME CHOOSE AND I...
I DID SOMETHING TERRIBLE... BUT I... I COULDN'T HAVE DONE WHAT THEY WANTED. BUT I... I'M... OH, GOD...
ARE YOU OKAY?

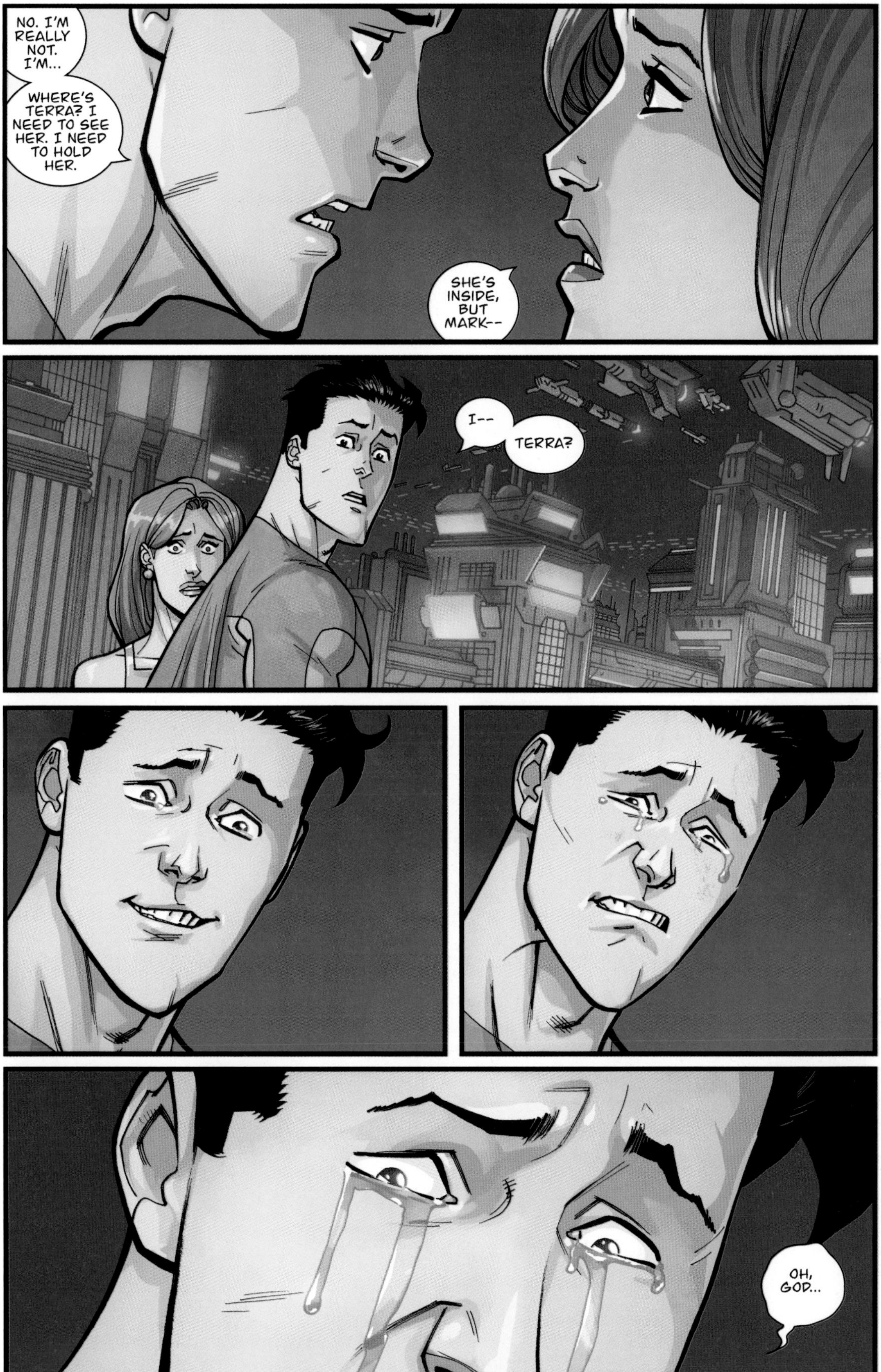
NO. I'M REALLY NOT. I'M...
WHERE'S TERRA? I NEED TO SEE HER. I NEED TO HOLD HER.
SHE'S INSIDE, BUT MARK--
I--
TERRA?
OH, GOD...

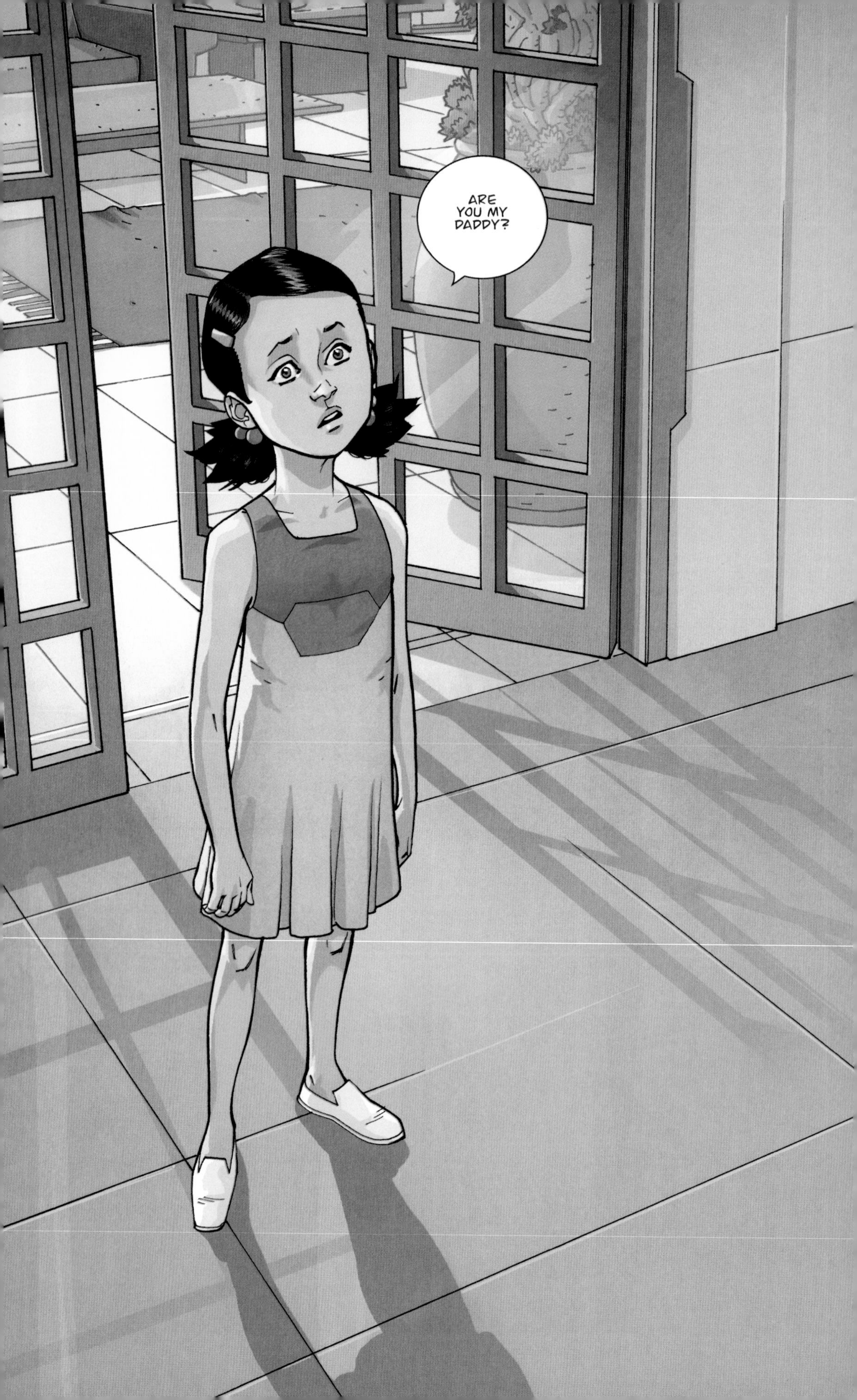
ARE YOU MY DADDY?

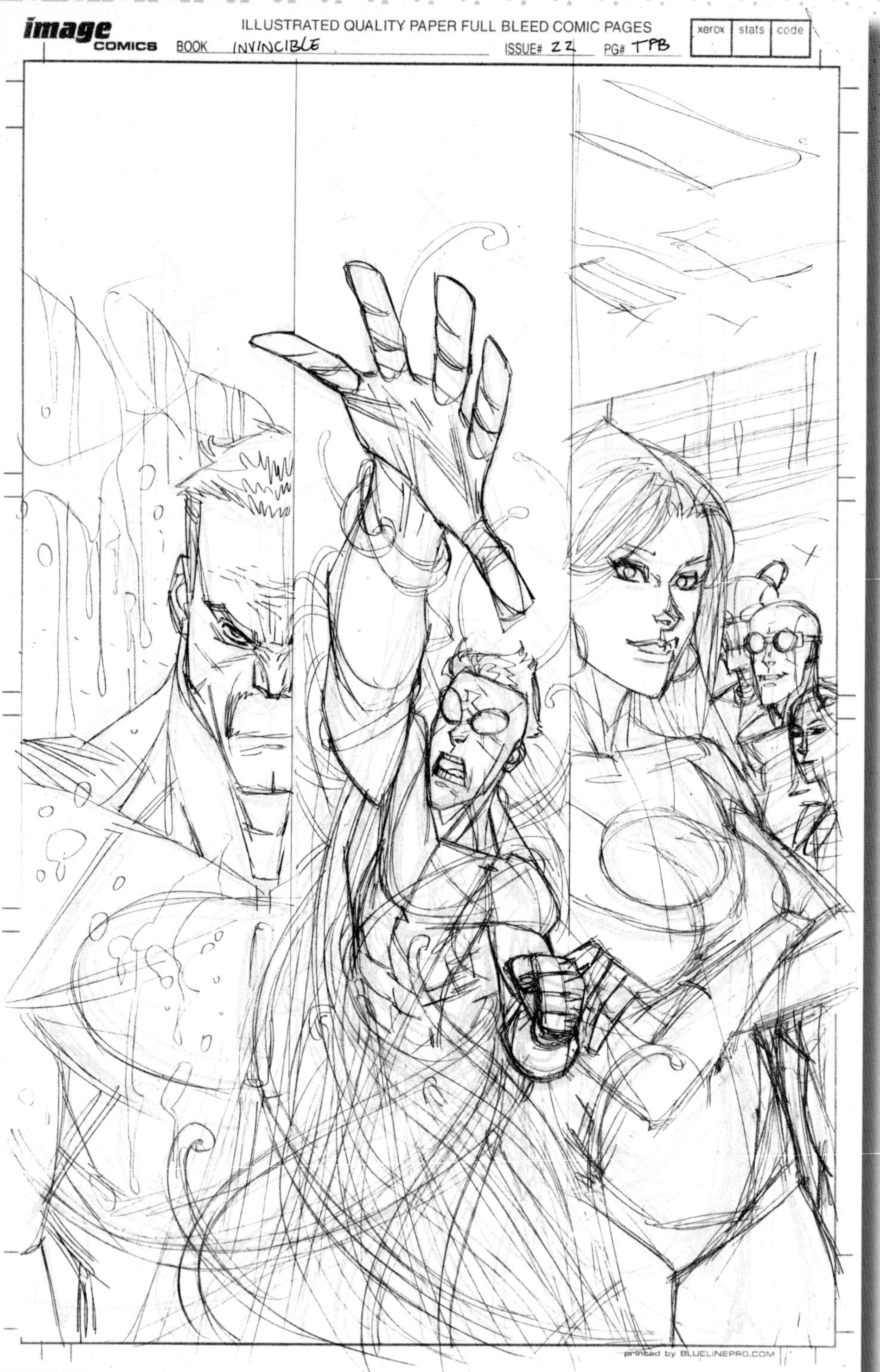
image COMICS
ILLUSTRATED QUALITY PAPER FULL BLEED COMIC PAGES
BOOK INVINCIBLE
ISSUE# 22
PG# TPB
xerox
stats
code
printed by BLUELINEPRO.COM

RYAN OTTLEY: Hello, world! Welcome to yet another sketchbook section where you can see the artist's scribblings and see how it all came to be, but mainly get to read the amazing banter between Robert and I. We are pretty unbelievably entertaining, am I right, Robert?

ROBERT KIRKMAN: Do we have to? I don't know if I can handle that pressure right now. This is volume 22... so there's a lot of built up expectations. I mean... how do we live up to that?

RYAN: We'll find out!

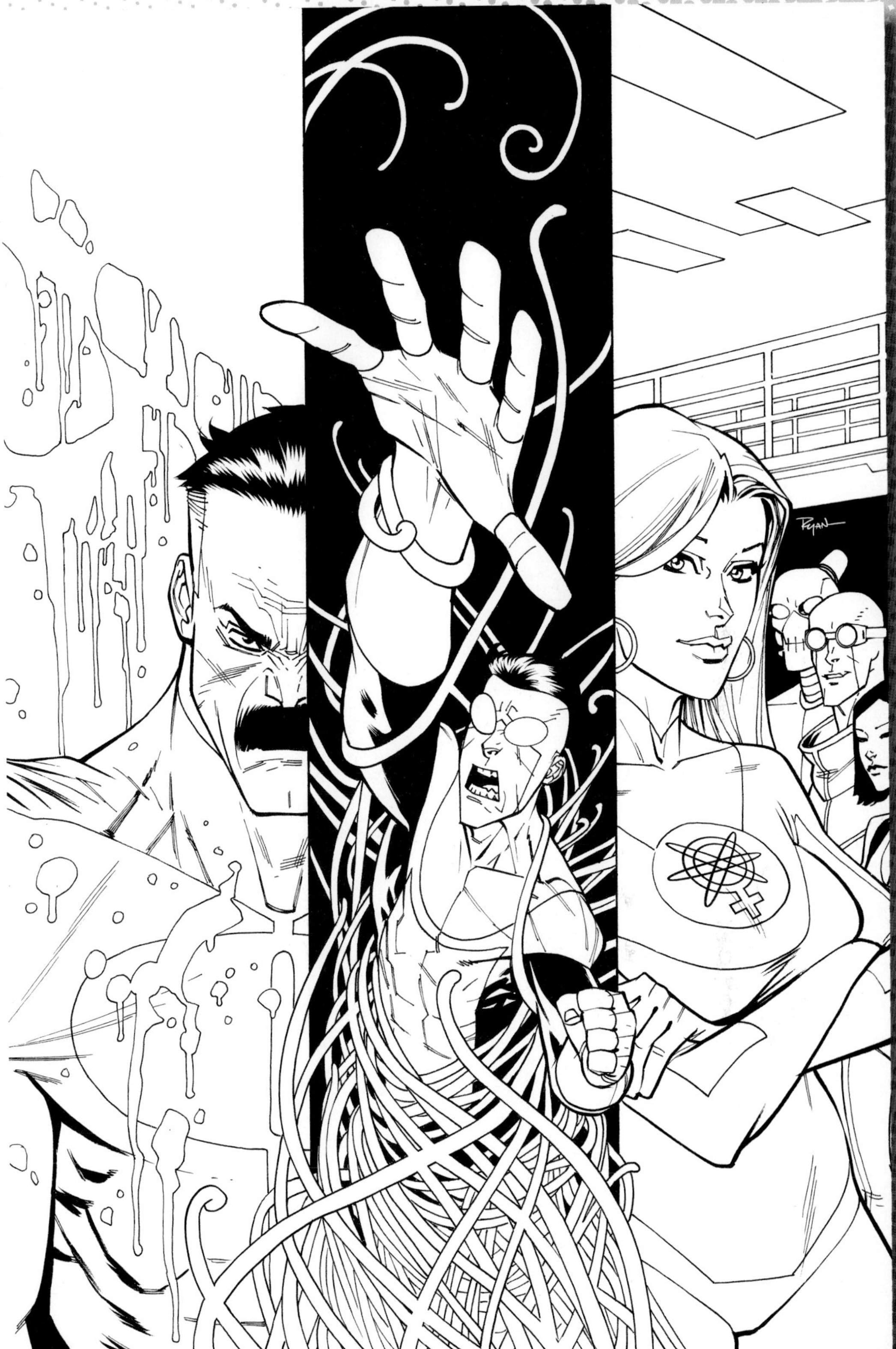
RYAN

RYAN: I love drawing the noodle alien. Robert asked for the alien to be a glowing thing. I could have just left it to the colorist to just make a glowing mass in Photoshop, but I wanted something more and food was on the brain and I wanted to draw some delicious noodles. So noodles you get. Hope you like noodles, everybody! If not, then why are you reading this book? We love pasta here at INVINCIBLE central.

ROBERT: Yeah... we're off to a GREAT start. Noodle talk? Wow. Volume 15 had MUCH better banter. I really liked this cover. There... comment with substance.

RYAN: Not sure what I can say about this cover. Robert told me to draw it or else. So I drew it. Then sent it to the colorist, who colored it or else.

ROBERT: That's not how I remember things at all. I remember you saying "That's a great idea! I'm going to love this! People will love this cover!" It's a cool cover. Very dramatic. I think Jean did an amazing job with it, too. Great stuff.

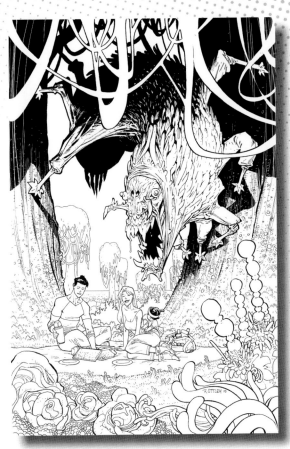

RYAN: Some of these I don't have the layouts for because I'll just draw them and not make any scan until I'm done. I'm pretty terrible at saving some stuff. I probably took a photo of the thumbnail sketch and then lost it. I think Robert needs to hire an artist more organized so these sketchbook sections are packed more with sketches!

ROBERT: How organized is Chris Samnee? Is he available?

RYAN: One of those misleading covers with some kind of symbolic meaning. I think.

ROBERT: Yeah... this one was more supposed to represent Mark having to go back into the field and not wanting to, more than actually showing something from the book. He doesn't even wear that costume in that issue!

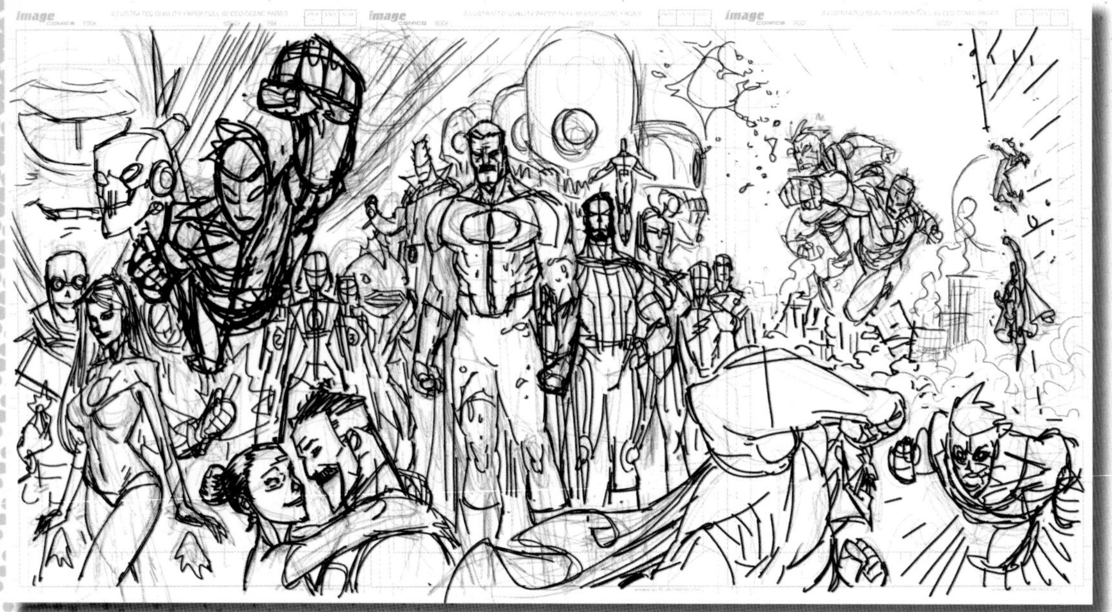

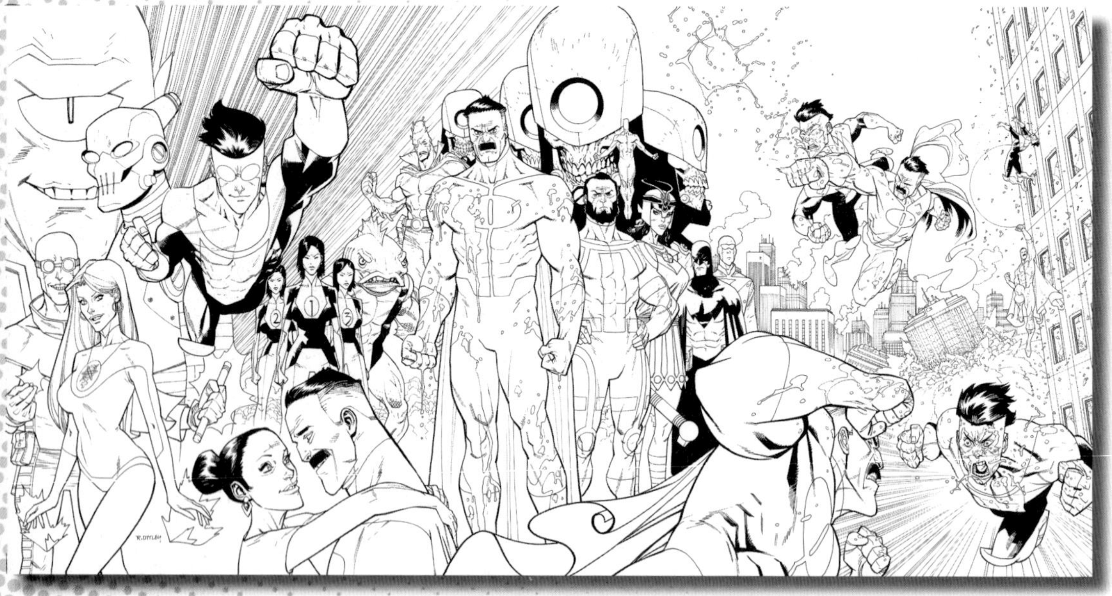

RYAN: This thing took me some time. It's the first time I've done a triptych cover and it's a different beast to tackle. Each cover has to work all alone and with each other. So it's a little more planning. Lots of fun though, going back to the past had me floored from the beginning. Lots of fans wish it was a little longer, to be honest so did I. So many places in the past to play with, but I understand why Robert didn't want to go on too long. It's because he hates when I'm having fun.

ROBERT: I do. That is for sure. But I think as much as it seems like it'd be fun and cool to dwell on the past... I think it would ultimately end up being boring. Also, in hindsight, seeing how the story ends, I think you can see that the point of the story was not to explore the past... but set up big changes for the future.

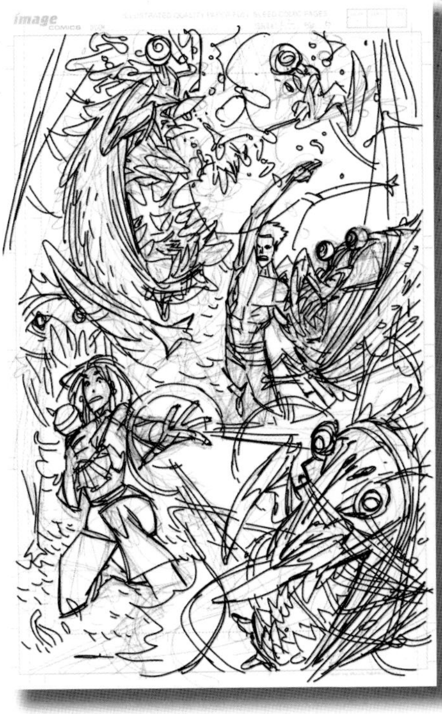

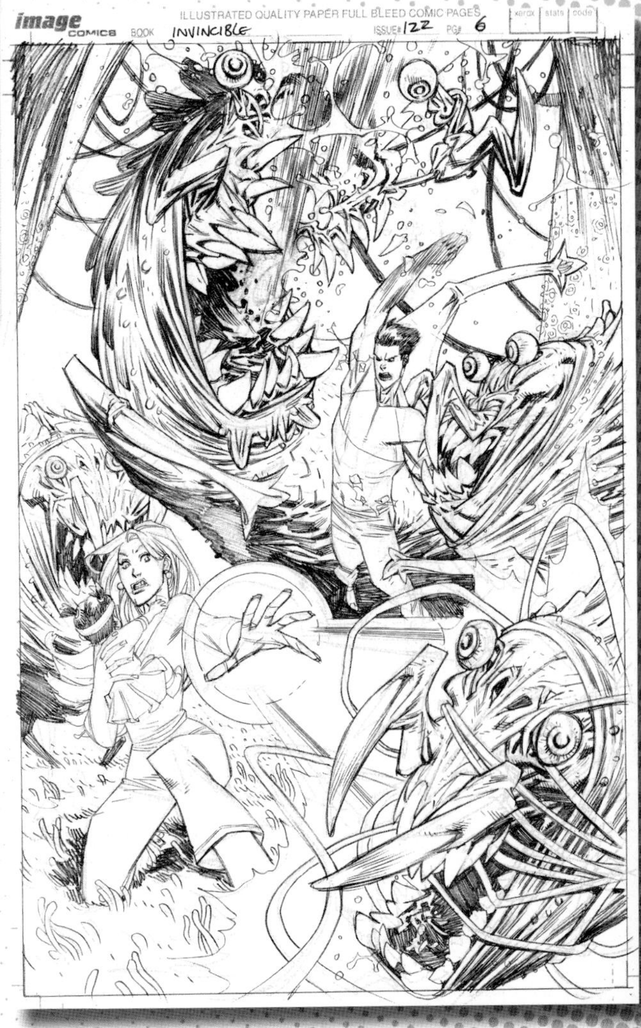
ILLUSTRATED QUALITY PAPER FULL BLEED COMIC PAGES
image COMICS
BOOK INVINCIBLE
ISSUE# 122 PG# 6
xerox stats code

RYAN: I like drawing people killing beasts and protecting babies. That's how I roll.

ROBERT: How do you feel about protecting beasts and killing babies? Because the next story arc...

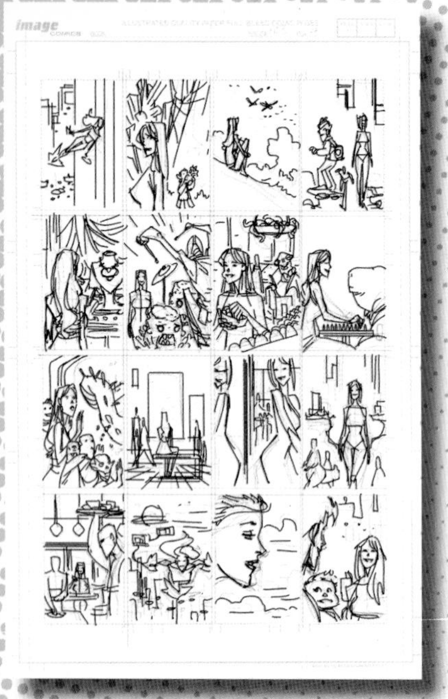

RYAN: This is the kind of page that makes an artist wanna cry and give up. Mainly because it's a few pages slammed into one page. Every panel is a new location, so each panel has to be established to look like a new place instead of sequentially. But I understand why Robert wanted to establish Eve having some alone time. It's mainly because he doesn't want the artist to get too lazy. Keeps us humble.

ROBERT: To be honest, these could have been two 9 panel pages instead of two 16 panel pages and MAYBE they would have had the same effect... but I wanted the scenes to be a little more involved than that. Regardless of how difficult it was... it turned out GREAT!

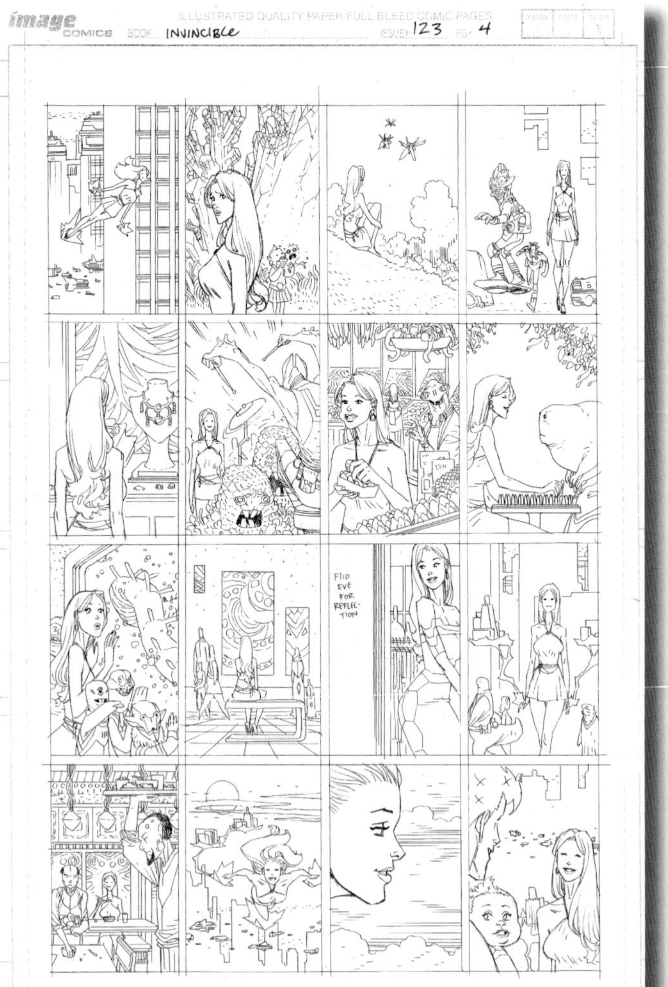
image COMICS
ILLUSTRATED QUALITY PAPER FULL BLEED COMIC PAGES
BOOK INVINCIBLE
ISSUE 123 PG 4
FLIP EVE FOR REFLECTION

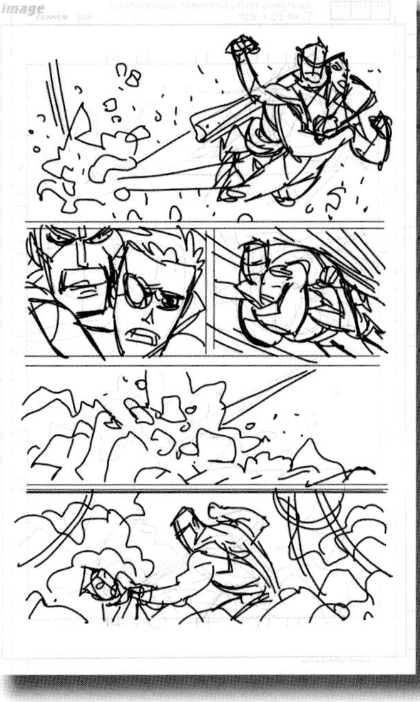

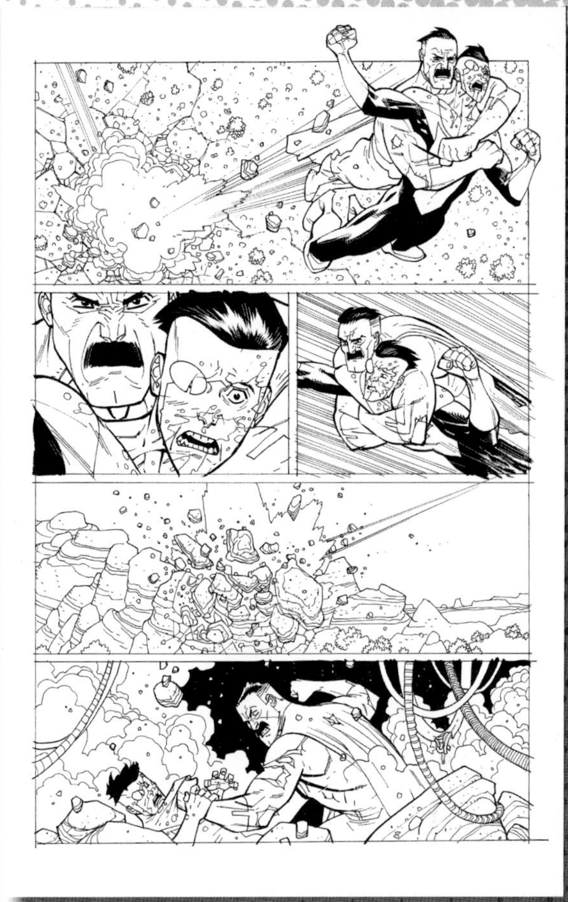

RYAN: Here's why I loved going back to the past. These pages are all stuff I've drawn before, but it went down a little differently, of course. But it was a huge déjà vu moment to revisit scenes from when I started with #8 about 12 years ago: fighting the Elephant, Doc Seismic, Lizard League, the big Omni-Man fight, the gutting of the Immortal. And I inked myself like I used to do for so many years. I always miss that. Anyway, enough reminiscing.

ROBERT: Thankfully... it looks a lot better than when you started on #8. The writing is better now, too... right? Is it better? Have I gotten better? Have I? I hope so. Ryan? RYAN?!

RYAN: ...

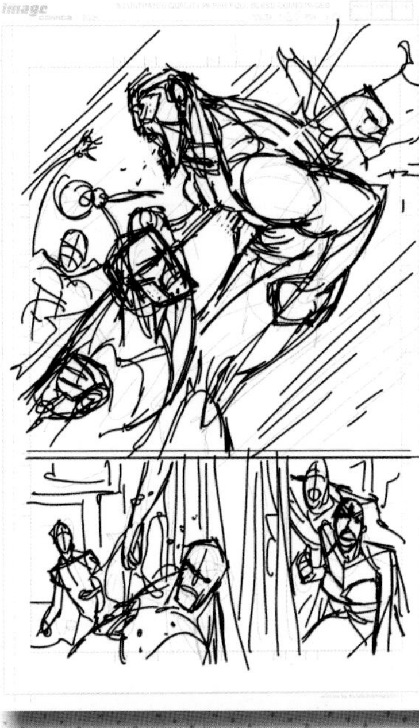

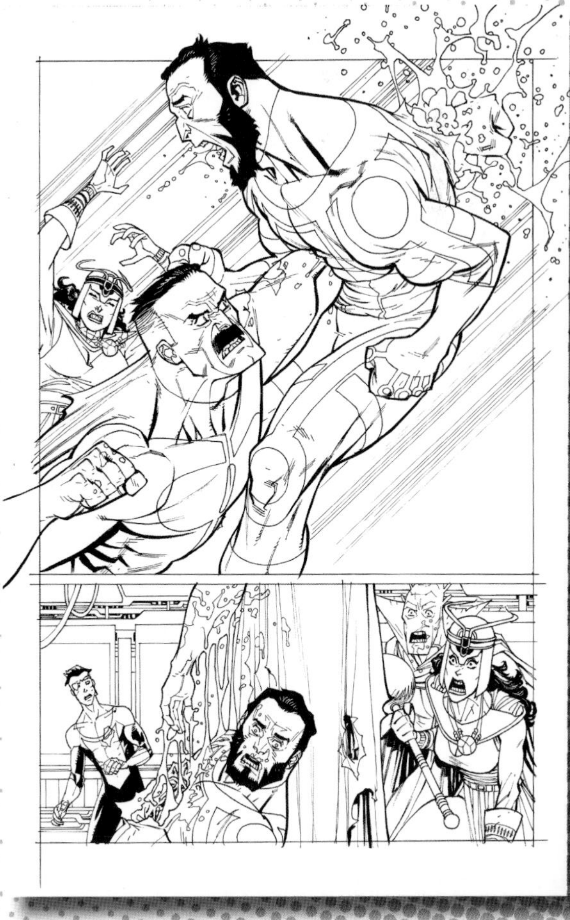

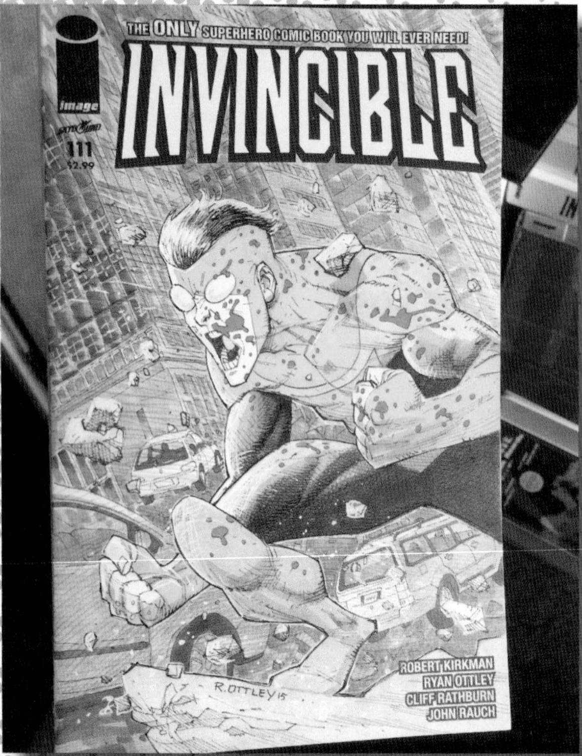
THE ONLY SUPERHERO COMIC BOOK YOU WILL EVER NEED!
INVINCIBLE
image
111
$2.99
R.OTTLEY15
ROBERT KIRKMAN
RYAN OTTLEY
CLIFF RATHBURN
JOHN RAUCH

RYAN: Here's a butt load of sketches I did at conventions around the country last year. You'll notice a bit of a theme: fans like beat-up Invincible. Luckily, so do I. I hope to beat him up again soon!

ROBERT: Boy, Invincible sure does eat a lot of ketchu--oh, nevermind. Thanks for reading, folks!

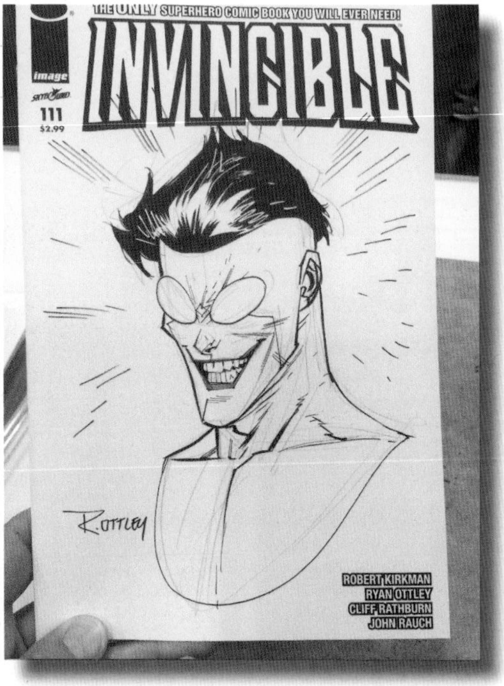
THE ONLY SUPERHERO COMIC BOOK YOU WILL EVER NEED!
INVINCIBLE
image
111
$2.99
R.OTTLEY
ROBERT KIRKMAN
RYAN OTTLEY
CLIFF RATHBURN
JOHN RAUCH

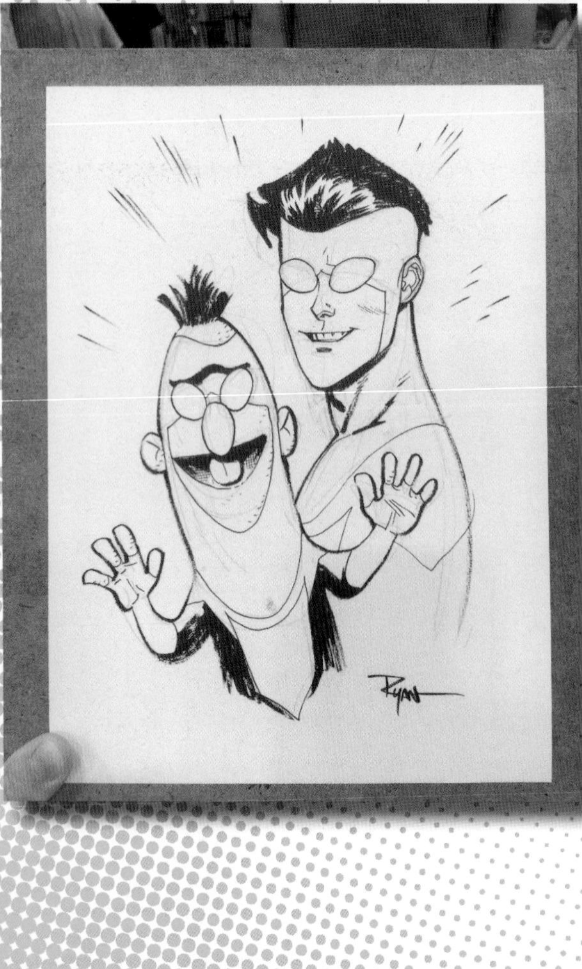
RYAN

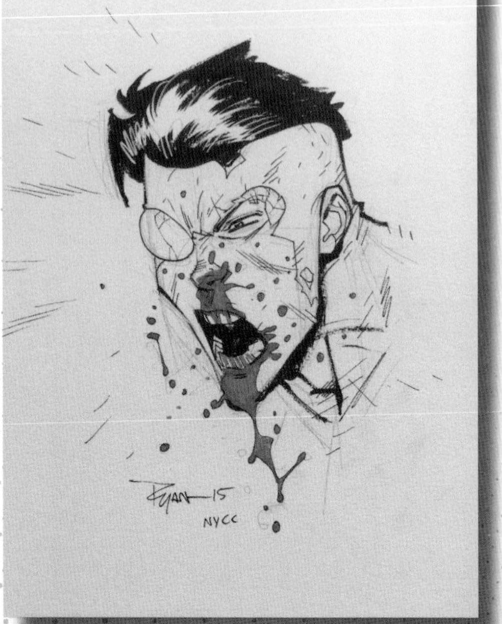
RYAN 15
NYCC

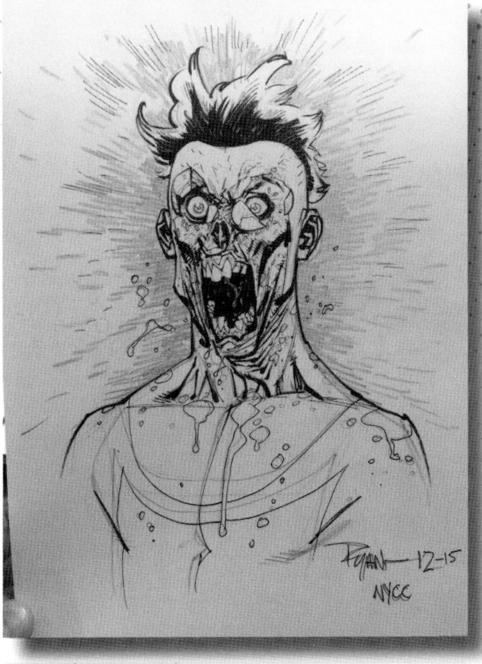
NYCC

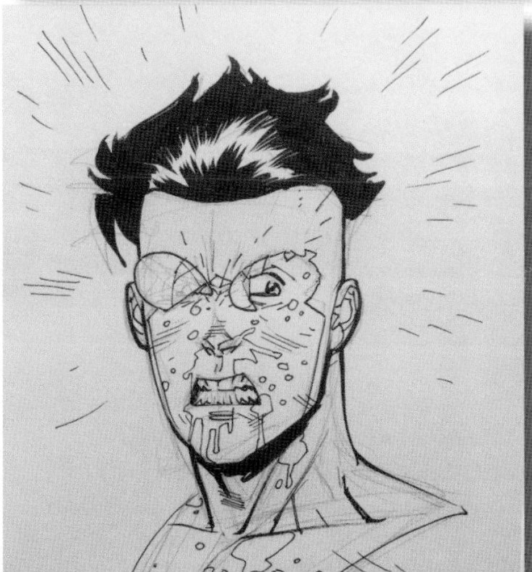
NYCC

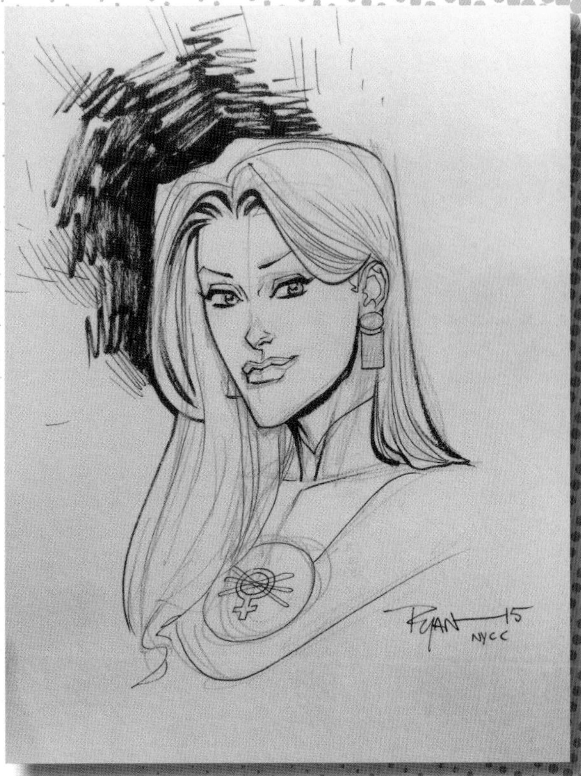
NYCC

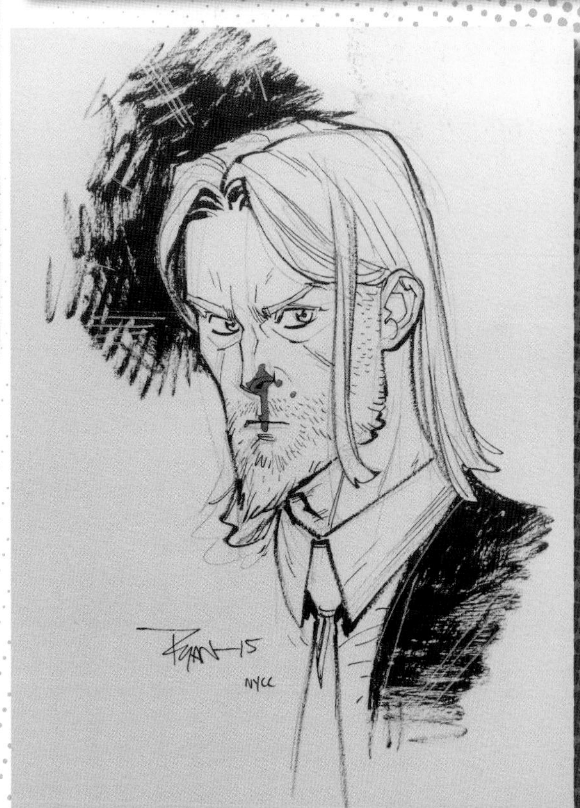
NYCC

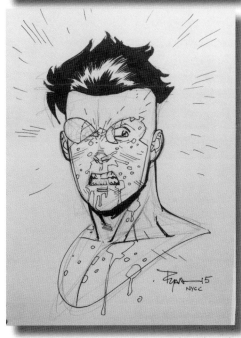

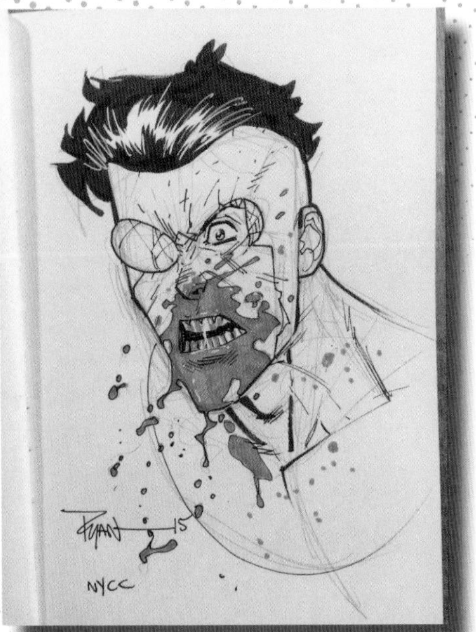
Ryan 15
NYCC

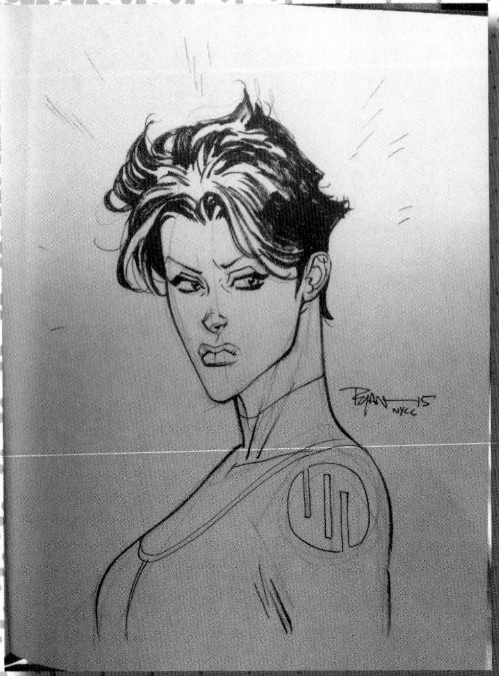
Ryan 15
NYCC

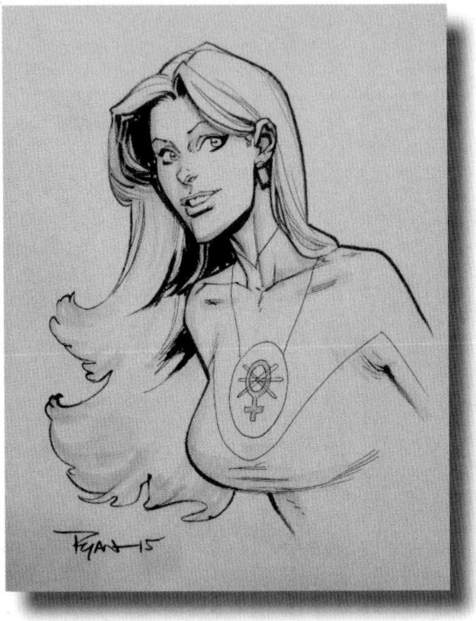
Ryan 15

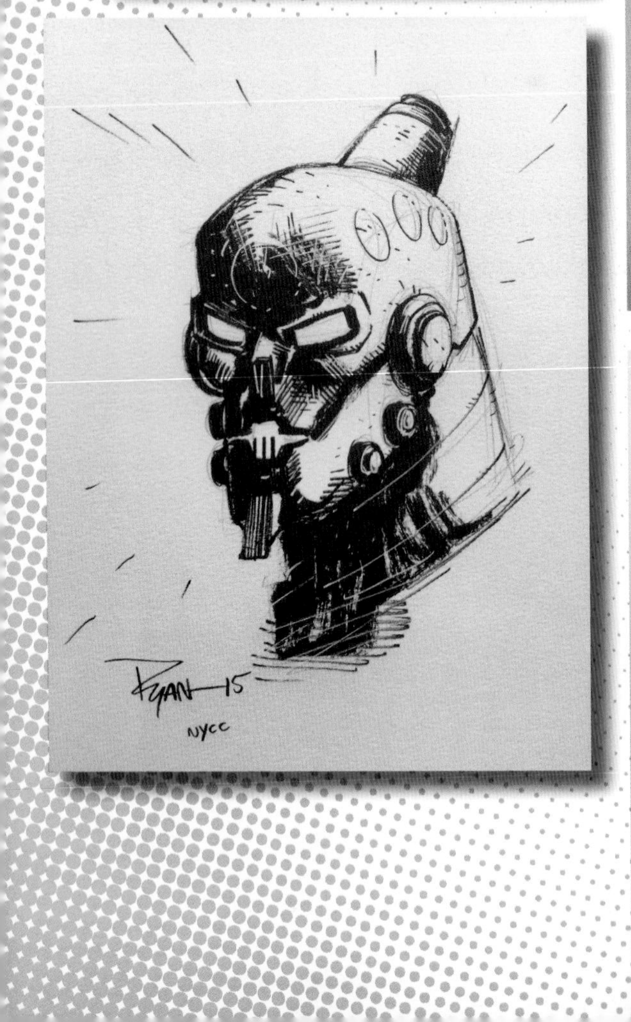
Ryan 15
NYCC

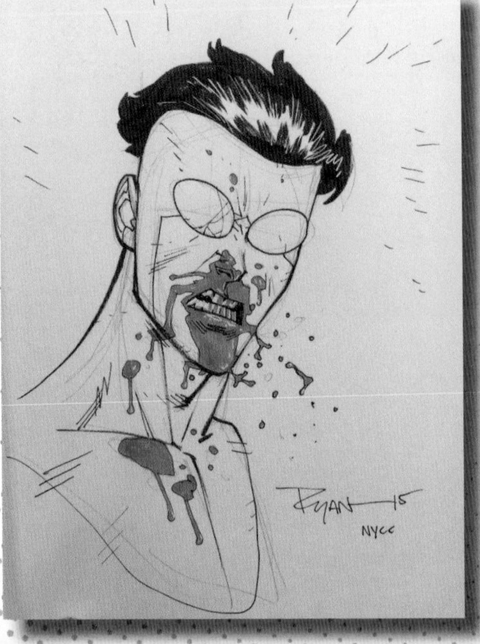
Ryan 15
NYCC

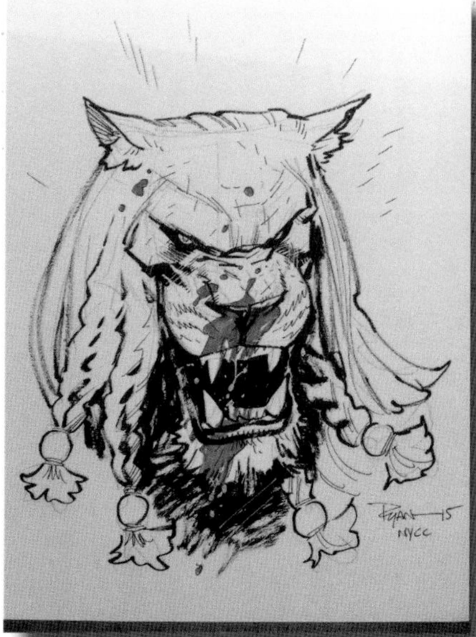

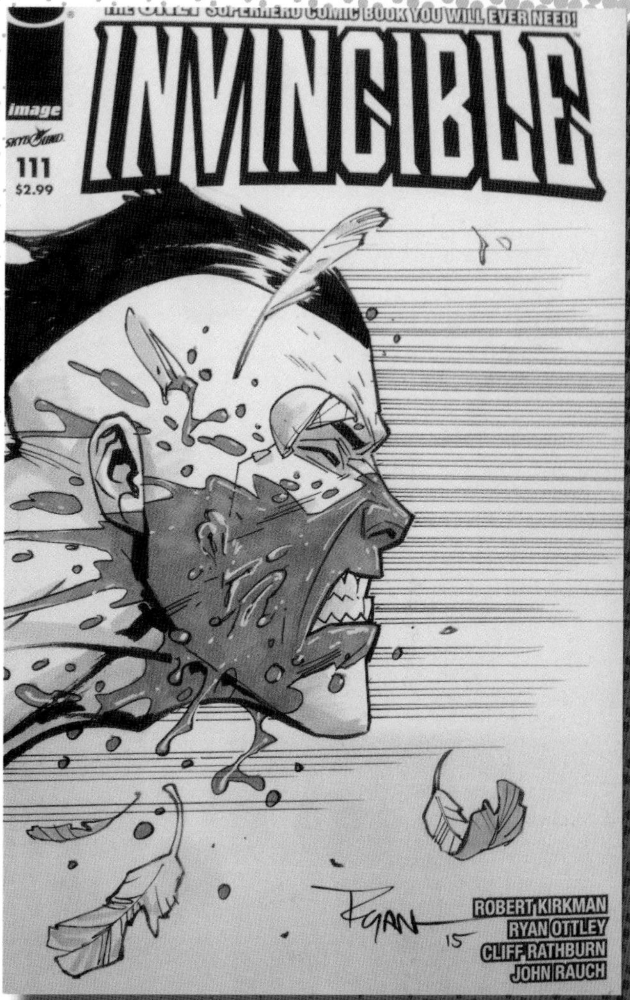
THE ONLY SUPERHERO COMIC BOOK YOU WILL EVER NEED!
INVINCIBLE
image
111
$2.99
ROBERT KIRKMAN
RYAN OTTLEY
CLIFF RATHBURN
JOHN RAUCH

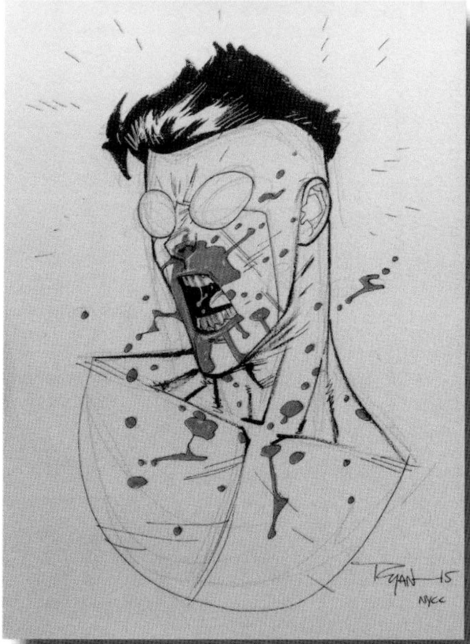

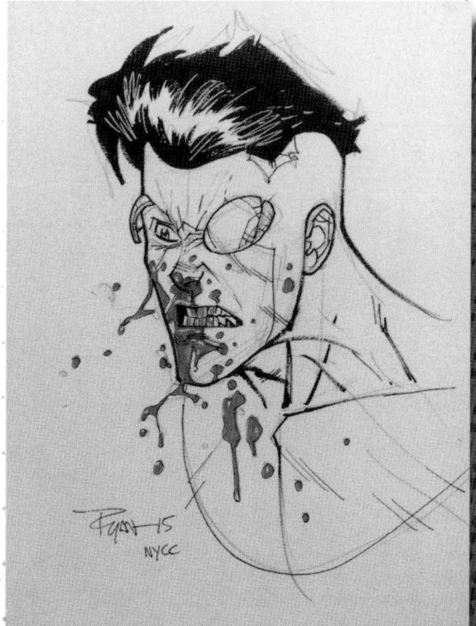

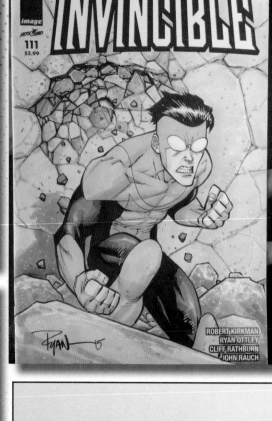

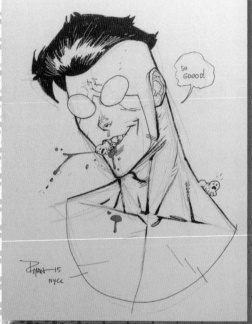

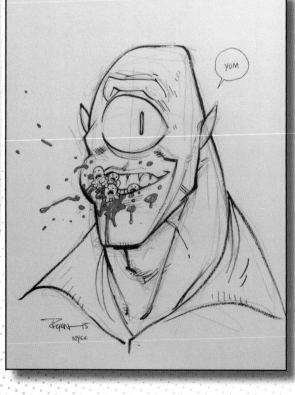

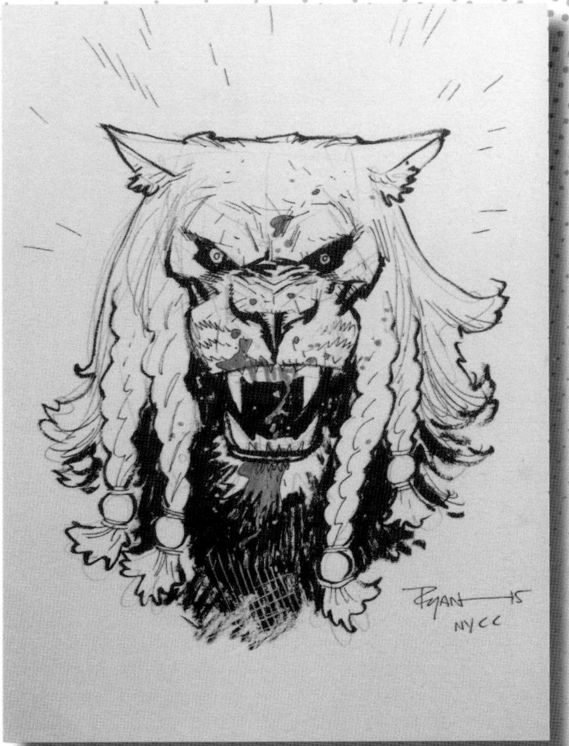
RYAN 15
NYCC

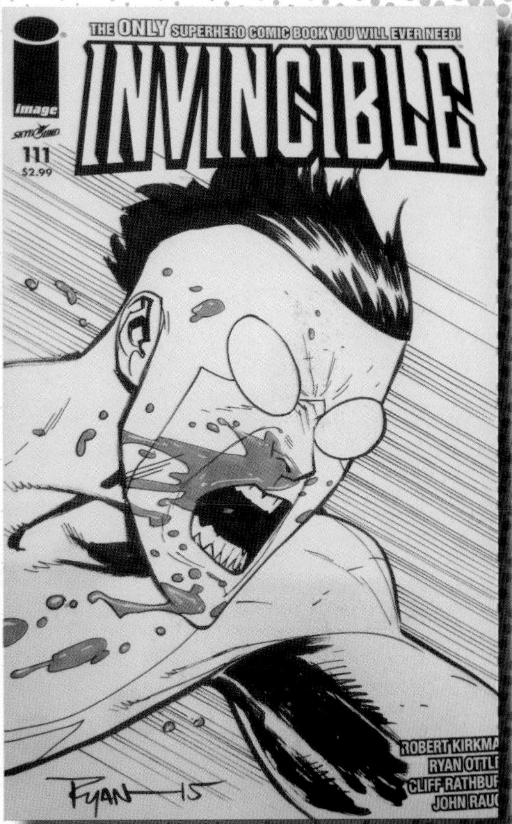
THE ONLY SUPERHERO COMIC BOOK YOU WILL EVER NEED!
INVINCIBLE
image
111
$2.99
ROBERT KIRKMA
RYAN OTTL
CLIFF RATHBU
JOHN RAU
RYAN 15

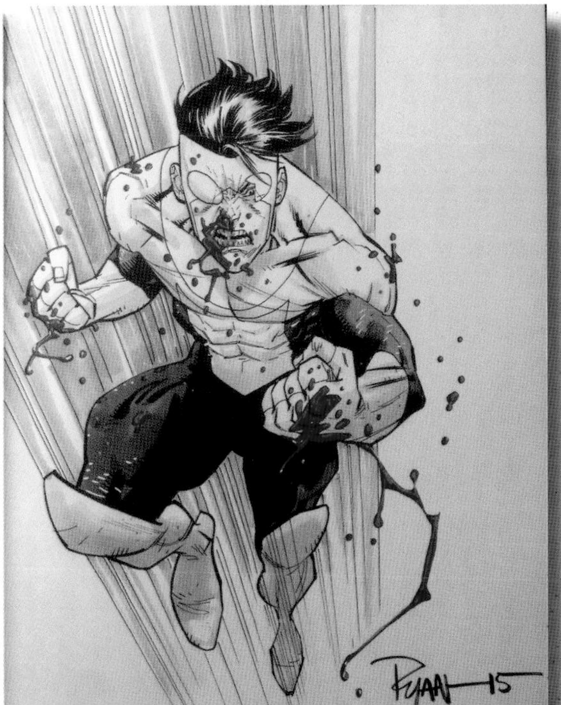
RYAN 15

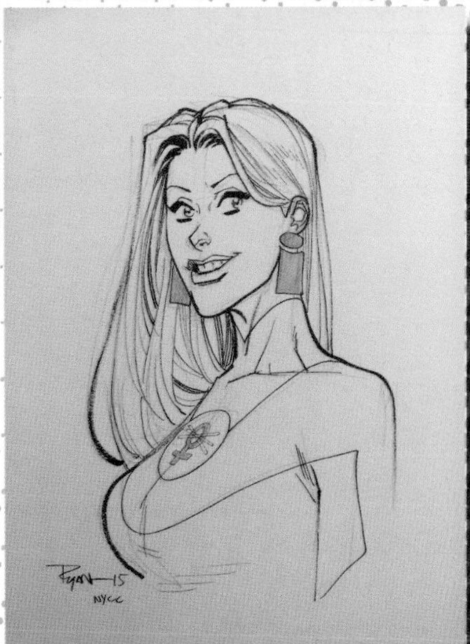
RYAN 15
NYCC

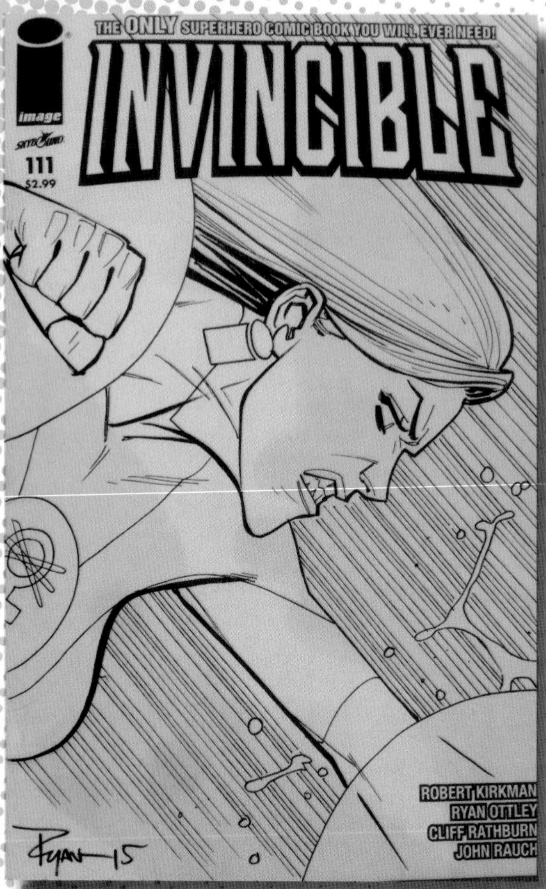
THE ONLY SUPERHERO COMIC BOOK YOU WILL EVER NEED!
INVINCIBLE
image
111
$2.99
ROBERT KIRKMAN
RYAN OTTLEY
CLIFF RATHBURN
JOHN RAUCH

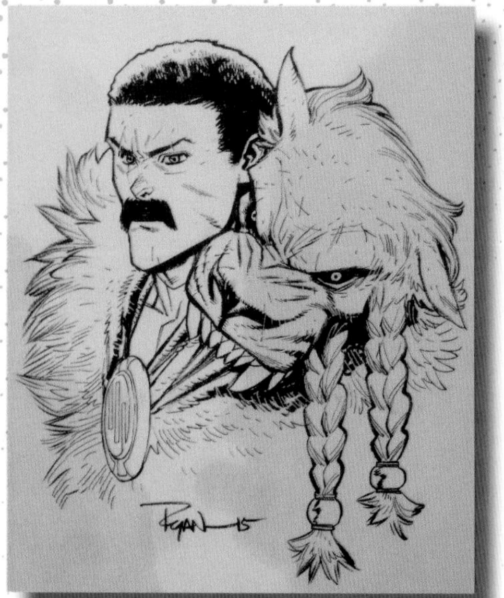

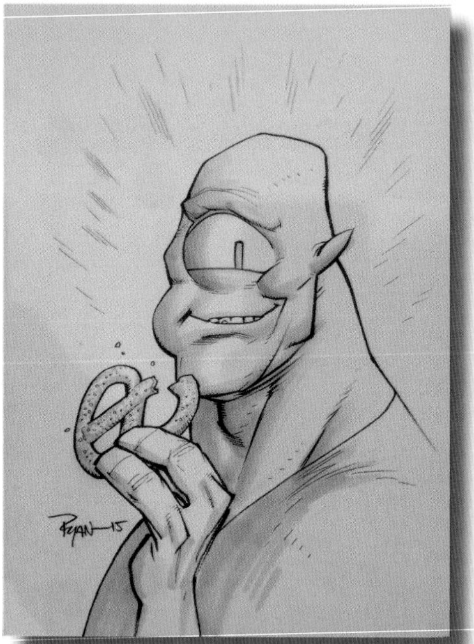

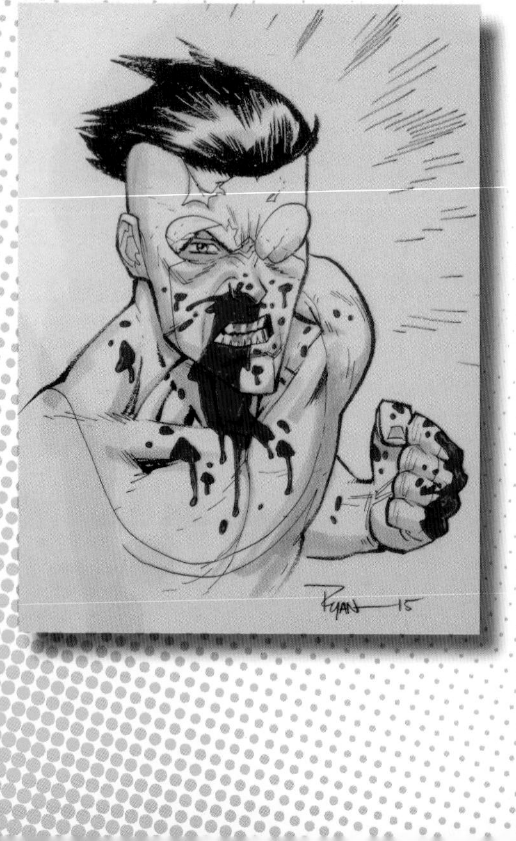

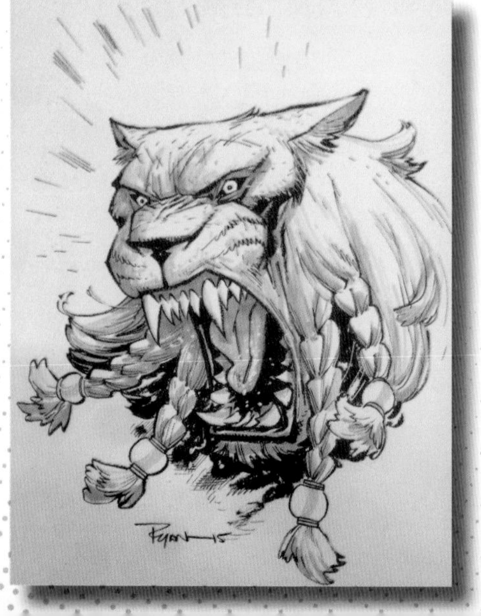

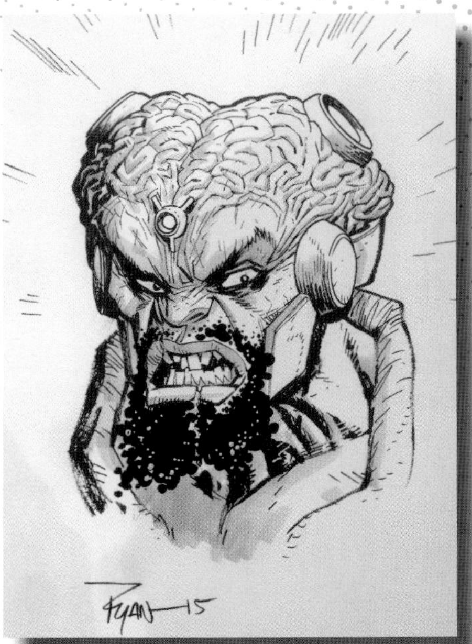

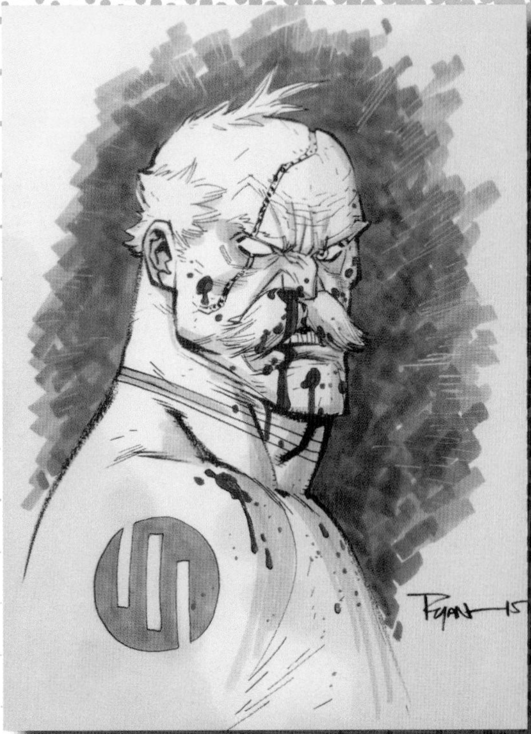

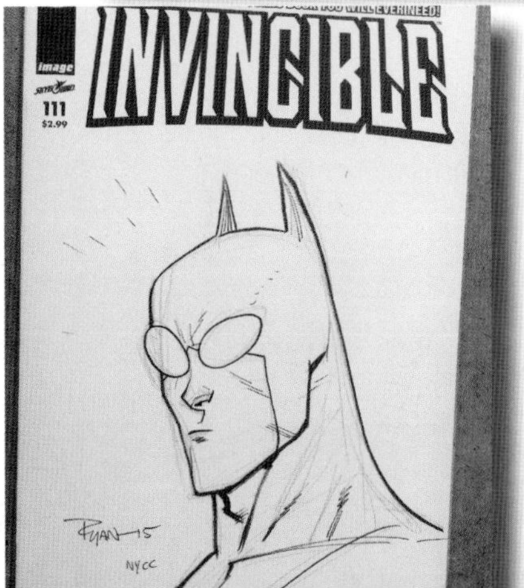
image
INVINCIBLE
111
$2.99
RYAN 15
NYCC
ROBERT KIRKMAN
RYAN OTTLEY
CLIFF RATHBURN
JOHN RAUCH

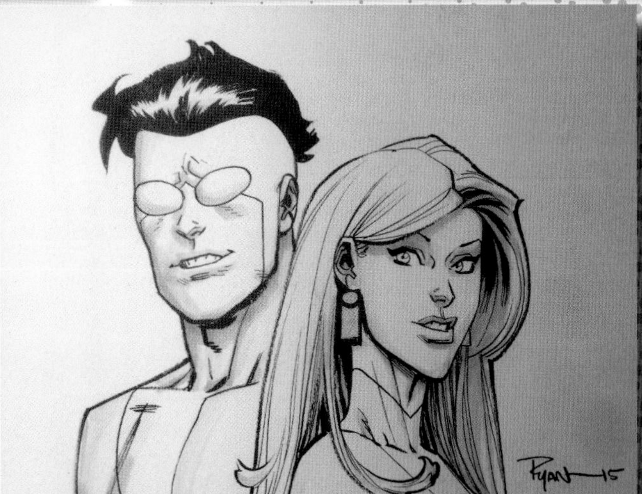

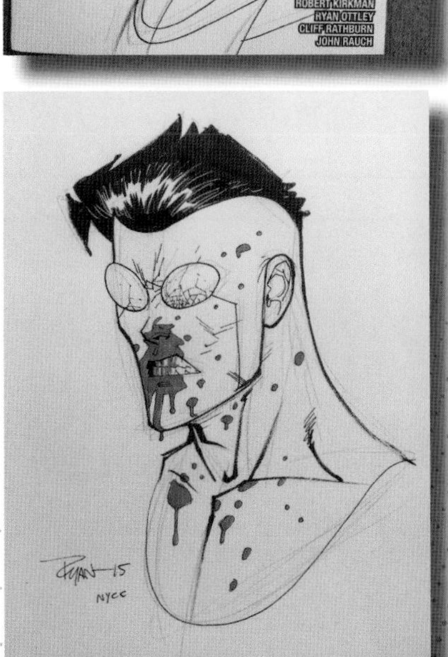
RYAN 15
NYCC

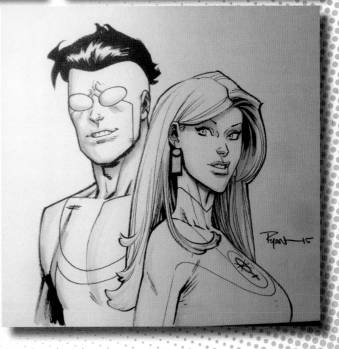

FOR MORE OF INVINCIBLE

TRADEPAPERBACKS

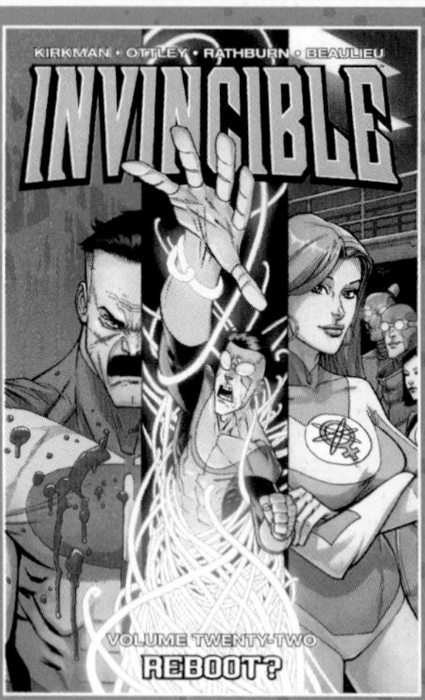
KIRKMAN • OTTLEY • RATHBURN • BEAULIEU
INVINCIBLE
VOLUME TWENTY-TWO
REBOOT?

VOL. 1: FAMILY MATTERS TP
ISBN: 978-1-58240-711-1
$12.99
VOL. 2: EIGHT IS ENOUGH TP
ISBN: 978-1-58240-347-2
$12.99
VOL. 3: PERFECT STRANGERS TP
ISBN: 978-1-58240-793-7
$12.99
VOL. 4: HEAD OF THE CLASS TP
ISBN: 978-1-58240-778-4
$14.99
VOL. 5: THE FACTS OF LIFE TP
ISBN: 978-1-58240-554-4
$14.99
VOL. 6: A DIFFERENT WORLD TP
ISBN: 978-1-58240-579-7
$14.99
VOL. 7: THREE'S COMPANY TP
ISBN: 978-1-58240-656-5
$14.99
VOL. 8: MY FAVORITE MARTIAN TP
ISBN: 978-1-58240-683-1
$16.99
VOL. 9: OUT OF THIS WORLD TP
ISBN: 978-1-58240-827-9
$14.99
VOL. 10: WHO'S THE BOSS TP
ISBN: 978-1-60706-013-0
$16.99
VOL. 11: HAPPY DAYS TP
ISBN: 978-1-60706-062-8
$16.99
VOL. 12: STILL STANDING TP
ISBN: 978-1-60706-166-3
$16.99
VOL. 13: GROWING PAINS TP
ISBN: 978-1-60706-251-6
$16.99
VOL. 14: THE VILTRUMITE WAR TP
ISBN: 978-1-60706-367-4
$19.99
VOL. 15: GET SMART TP
ISBN: 978-1-60706-498-5
$16.99
VOL. 16: FAMILY TIES TP
ISBN: 978-1-60706-579-1
$16.99
VOL. 17: WHAT'S HAPPENING TP
ISBN: 978-1-60706-662-0
$16.99
VOL. 18: DEATH OF EVERYONE TP
ISBN: 978-1-60706-762-7
$16.99
VOL. 19: THE WAR AT HOME TP
ISBN: 978-1-60706-856-3
$16.99
VOL. 20: FRIENDS TP
ISBN: 978-1-63215-043-1
$16.99
VOL. 21: MODERN FAMILY TP
ISBN: 978-1-63215-318-0
$16.99
VOL. 22: REBOOT? TP
ISBN: 978-1-63215-626-6
$16.99

THE OFFICIAL HANDBOOK OF
THE INVINCIBLE UNIVERSE TP
ISBN: 978-1-58240-831-6
$12.99
INVINCIBLE PRESENTS,
VOL. 1: ATOM EVE & REX SPLODE TP
ISBN: 978-1-60706-255-4
$14.99

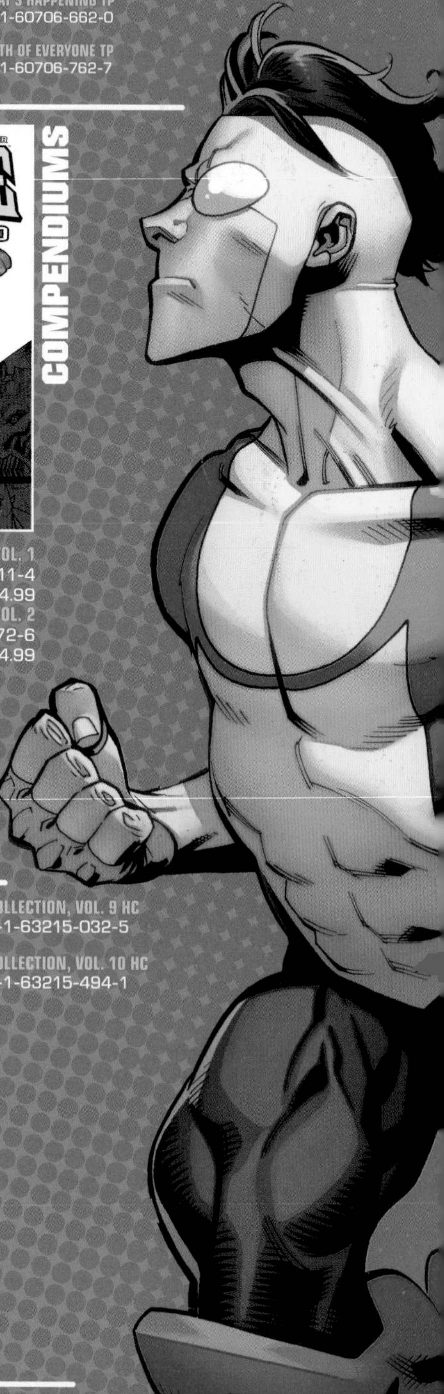

COMPLETE LIBRARY

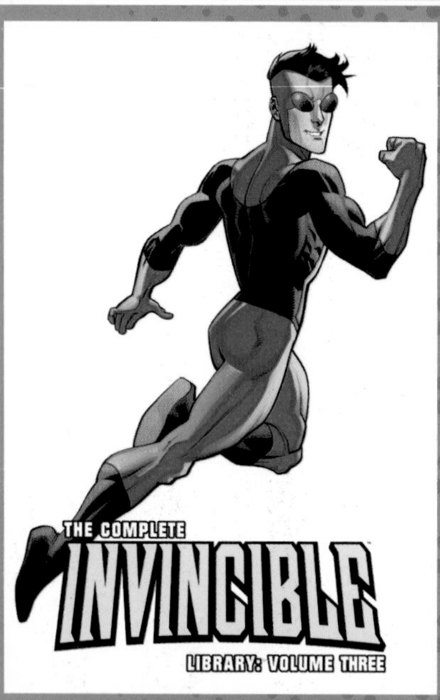
THE COMPLETE
INVINCIBLE
LIBRARY: VOLUME THREE

THE COMPLETE INVINCIBLE LIBRARY, VOL. 2 HC
ISBN: 978-1-60706-112-0
$125.00
THE COMPLETE INVINCIBLE LIBRARY, VOL. 3 HC
ISBN: 978-1-60706-421-3
$125.00

COMPENDIUMS

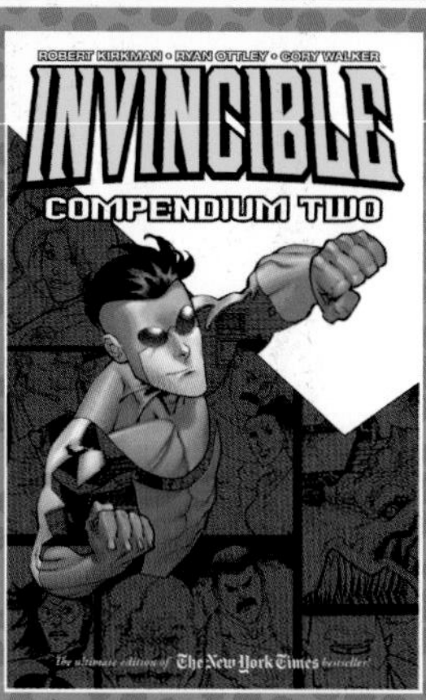
ROBERT KIRKMAN • RYAN OTTLEY • CORY WALKER
INVINCIBLE
COMPENDIUM TWO
The ultimate edition of The New York Times bestseller!

COMPENDIUM VOL. 1
ISBN: 978-1-60706-411-4
$64.99
COMPENDIUM VOL. 2
ISBN: 978-1-60706-772-6
$64.99

ULTIMATE COLLECTIONS

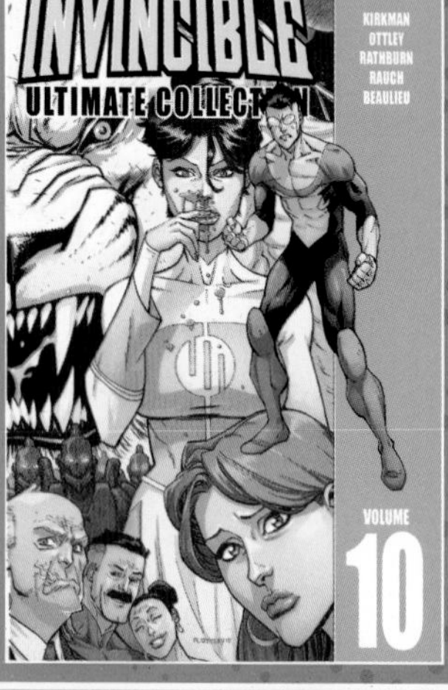
INVINCIBLE
KIRKMAN
OTTLEY
RATHBURN
RAUCH
BEAULIEU
VOLUME
10

ULTIMATE COLLECTION, VOL. 1 HC
ISBN 978-1-58240-500-1
$34.99
ULTIMATE COLLECTION, VOL. 2 HC
ISBN: 978-1-58240-594-0
$34.99
ULTIMATE COLLECTION, VOL. 3 HC
ISBN: 978-1-58240-763-0
$34.99
ULTIMATE COLLECTION, VOL. 4 HC
ISBN: 978-1-58240-989-4
$34.99
ULTIMATE COLLECTION, VOL. 5 HC
ISBN: 978-1-60706-116-8
$34.99
ULTIMATE COLLECTION, VOL. 6 HC
ISBN: 978-1-60706-360-5
$34.99
ULTIMATE COLLECTION, VOL. 7 HC
ISBN: 978-1-60706-509-8
$39.99
ULTIMATE COLLECTION, VOL. 8 HC
ISBN: 978-1-60706-680-4
$39.99
ULTIMATE COLLECTION, VOL. 9 HC
ISBN: 978-1-63215-032-5
$39.99
ULTIMATE COLLECTION, VOL. 10 HC
ISBN: 978-1-63215-494-1
$39.99